"*The Lame Will Leap* will make you want to leap for joy, not only because of the uplifting and positive message this story delivers, but your spirit will also leap at the truth you will hear—that God is still in the miracle business, and if He can deliver this family, He can also deliver me and you."

—Cheri Cowell
Author, *Direction: Discernment for the Decisions of Your Life*

"Very well-written and very moving."

—Stephen Naifeh
Founder Best Doctors, Inc.
Winner, 1991 Pulitzer Prize for Journalism

"You don't have to read a whole book in one sitting unless, of course, you can't put it down. Such is the case with *The Lame Will Leap*. This story of personal crisis and God's provision will grip and speak to your heart. If you think God is too busy to bother with your needs and you've forgotten that God has a plan for your life, then I suggest you block out a few hours to read *The Lame Will Leap* and be reminded of God's love and faithfulness."

—Richard Swift
Senior Pastor, retired
Cedar Creek Church, Aiken, South Carolina

"*The Lame Will Leap* transformed me!"

—Lorie Swift
Teacher & Pastor's wife
Aiken, South Carolina

"A wonderful book, superbly written and so filled with God's wonderful love! It is awesome! Each time I read it, I received a greater blessing! The dialogue is genuine. I felt that I was reading words that had been said, as they were said. Your wry humor...is outstanding. And your mixture of the tragic and the necessity for everyday, mundane life to continue, no matter what, is brilliant!

—Doris Baker
Editor & High School English Teacher, retired
Elberton, Georgia

The
Lame
will
Leap

Once you have found Him,
He never lets you go!
In His grip!

Michael Farrant

The
Lame
will
Leap

*The True Story
of Jesus'
Miraculous
Appearance in
the Midst of
Turmoil*

Michael Smith Tarrant

WinePressPublishing
Great Books, Defined.

WinePress Publishing (PO Box 428, Enumclaw, WA 98022) functions only as book publisher. As such, the ultimate design, content, editorial accuracy, and views expressed or implied in this work are those of the author.

Unless otherwise noted, all Scriptures are taken from the *Holy Bible, New International Version®, NIV®*. Copyright © 1973, 1978, 1984 by Biblica, Inc.™ Used by permission of Zondervan. All rights reserved worldwide. www.zondervan.com

Scripture references marked KJV are taken from the *King James Version* of the Bible.

Scripture references marked NASB are taken from the *New American Standard Bible*, © 1960, 1963, 1968, 1971, 1972, 1973, 1975, 1977 by The Lockman Foundation. Used by permission.

ISBN 13: 978-1-4141-2014-0
ISBN 10: 1-4141-2014-1
Library of Congress Catalog Card Number: 2010943388

"…when you *pray*, I will listen.
If you *look* for me wholeheartedly, you will *find* me.
I will be found by you," says the Lord.
—Jeremiah 29:12-14

To Karin.
We prayed, we looked, and we found.
Love,
Michael

Chapter One

*To everything there is a season, and a time to every purpose
under the heaven.*

—Ecclesiastes 3:1

AT 6:45 ON THE warm, misty evening of October 29,
2002, Lauren Tarrant walked out of the glass double doors of the
Hendrix Center on the Clemson University campus in upstate
South Carolina, near the foothills of the Blue Ridge Mountains.
The doors swung closed behind the pretty, petite co-ed as she left
the meeting of the Clemson University Guide Association. Her
boots clicked as she walked down the same sidewalk her father
had while a Clemson University student almost thirty years
earlier. She stopped at her purple-and-orange moped parked
near the building. The Greek letters, Kappa Kappa Gamma,
decorated the rear fender.

Before Lauren climbed on the moped, she gathered her
curly brown hair in her right hand, then deftly slipped it into a
hair band with her left. Her "Class of 2003" gold ring glistened
in the light of the street lamp overhead. She zipped her blue

Columbia jacket to her chin for protection from the spray of the automobiles she would encounter on the rain-slick boulevard leading to her off-campus apartment.

Throwing her right leg over the saddle, Lauren put the key into the ignition and turned it once. The tiny engine hummed to life. Its single headlight came on automatically, cutting like a torch through the gathering gloom. With her right hand, she twisted the handlebar throttle and slowly pulled onto the street that led away from the Hendrix Center and down the hill to the intersection. She turned left onto the perimeter road, then left again onto the boulevard and began to accelerate toward home.

At 6:45 on the same evening, Xiang Liu and his wife, Zi Chu, closed their office doors in Brackett Hall, the red-brick chemistry building on Clemson's rolling, tree-lined campus. They slipped into light rain parkas and stepped into the misty, nearly vacant parking lot.

Such dank weather was rare in Shanghai, and Zi Chu shivered even though the evening was warm. Xiang unlocked the driver's side door of his white Dodge van and hit the power lock button so Zi Chu could get in on the passenger side. They climbed in and fastened their seat belts. Xiang turned the key in the ignition, and the engine reluctantly obliged. He steered the vehicle out of the parking lot in the direction of the small campus apartment the two graduate students shared. Xiang turned on the windshield wipers to help clear a path through the damp darkness. He turned north onto the boulevard, absorbed in conversation with his wife in their native Chinese.

At 6:51, Xiang began a left turn off the boulevard onto the street where the couple's apartment waited. At that moment, a single beam of light illuminated Zi Chu's face. She twisted in her seat and saw the approaching moped, now only inches away.

The earth's rotation slowed.

Chapter One

The moped first struck the van at the passenger side door. Zi Chu's scream coincided with the metallic crash of the impact. The little machine began to crumble as it slid down the passenger side of the car, still carrying its precious cargo. The class ring on Lauren's right ring finger scraped along the sheet metal of the door as the delicate bones in her hand broke.

While pieces and parts of the rapidly disintegrating bike skittered across the highway, the door jam on the van sliced Lauren's right leg open and carved away her knee. Momentum lifted her body into the air and over the top of the van, catapulted her thirty-five feet closer to her apartment, and slammed her onto the wet asphalt with a sickening, lung-crushing thud. The van screeched to a halt against the opposite curb.

And then, for a moment, the earth stood still.

Standing in front of the largest furniture store in Augusta, Georgia, I glanced down at my watch. "Oh, man, Karin. It's ten 'til seven. We better get going if we're gonna meet Andrea and Chad for supper." But we kept our noses pressed against the plate-glass windows of the store for another twenty minutes and squinted to make out the colors and textures of the treasure trove of domestic adornment just beyond our reach. The store displayed its motto, "Yes, You Can!" on a banner inside the front doors. Peering ever harder to discern the price tags, the magnitude of the numbers we encountered finally quenched our desire to continue window shopping.

Karin and I looked at each other as we walked back to the car and simultaneously chanted, "No, We Can't!" Then we laughed. Not that it was unusual for us to say the same thing at the same time. After twenty-six years of marriage and raising two daughters, we often did that. It always made Karin laugh. I love the sound of my wife's laughter, and I especially love it when I'm the source of her merriment.

On this evening, Karin's beautiful, radiant green eyes danced with carefree happiness. With our older daughter, Andrea, almost on her own and our younger daughter, Lauren, set to graduate from college in a few months, we finally had enough time and a little money to begin a serious remodeling job on the house where we had raised our family. New paint, carpet, and wallpaper had already been installed throughout most of the house. The kitchen, downstairs bathroom, and laundry rooms were the only areas that still required work, although they represented the biggest part of the project.

Earlier that day, the contractor had completely gutted all three of those rooms, and I'd pulled our little camper into the driveway for use as a make-shift kitchen and dining room for the next few weeks. New appliances had been purchased and were waiting at Lowe's. Tile, countertops, cabinet designs, "the works," had been selected. Karin and I were as excited as two kids before Christmas. With a little luck and good weather, by Thanksgiving we'd be ready to celebrate the holidays in style.

"Hey," I said as we walked through an increasing mist to the car. "Did you get a chance to pay the bills today? It's almost the first of the month, you know. I'd hate to have the house foreclosed on before we get it fixed up."

"Why, yes, I did, sugah," Karin answered in an exaggerated Southern drawl. "I sat in yo' little ole campah and paid every one of yo' debts. Those Yankees won't be takin' anything from us, dahlin'."

Despite her British birth and heritage, my wife conversed without a trace of an accent, but she was fond of teasing me with her impressions of Scarlet O'Hara. "Anyway, they're all stamped and addressed and in the pocket of the car door. I can drop them off at the post office tomorrow," she finished in her own dialect.

Still laughing, I opened the car door. Our white Maltese bounded from the back seat. We'd decided to let Boo ride over to Augusta with us and wait in the car while we ate supper with Andrea and her new friend. We'd be home in a couple of hours. Plus, with the damp weather, Boo hadn't been out of the house all day; she'd enjoy the outing.

Boo's wagging tail dusted the car's dash, flinging to the floor the cell phone I had switched off before we left home to conserve the depleted battery. I powered it up and watched as the phone's display indicated the time: 7:15 PM, and two missed calls. *Andrea*, I thought, *calling to tell us it's time to eat.*

I punched in the message retrieval code and listened as the electronic voice announced the messages and then played the first message. I was standing in the drizzle outside the car with the driver's door open. Karin was already in the passenger seat, door closed and ready to go. In my mind, I anticipated Andrea's voice.

But the waiting voice was not my daughter's. It was Leslie, one of Lauren's roommates at Clemson. A happy-go-lucky girl from the mountains of southwestern Virginia, she generally spoke with just a hint of the lilt of the Southern highlands.

"Mr. Tarrant, this is Leslie. Lauren is all right, but she's been in an accident. Please call me on Lauren's cell phone as soon as you get this." The words were deliberately and distinctly enunciated, her voice over-controlled— struggling it seemed—to quell an underlying panic. As much as she had tried to hide it, the exigency in her voice overrode the relative innocuousness of her words.

I felt my hands turn cold, and the strength left my knees. My back jerked straight as if a rod had been inserted in my spinal column. With stiff, cold fingers, I pushed the number five to play the next message and slid onto the seat behind the steering wheel.

Karin watched me enter the car and mouthed, "What's wrong?"

The next message began, "Mr. Tarrant, this is Leslie again. I'm in the ambulance with Lauren. She's being taken to the Memorial Hospital in Greenville. I think ya'll better come up here right away. I have Lauren's cell phone. Please call me as soon as you get this."

I looked at Karin. The sound of my voice surprised me as I spoke. Every nerve in my body was firing, but my voice was firm: "It's Leslie. Lauren's all right, but she's been in an accident. Leslie says she's in an ambulance with Lauren on the way to a hospital in Greenville. We need to get there immediately. She has Lauren's cell phone. We have to call her right now."

In less than a second, the color left Karin's face, replaced by pure anguish. "Michael! No! No! Call her back!"

I sat rigid behind the steering wheel, Karin leaning toward me, searching my face as if she expected me to renounce what I'd just said. Stiffly, my fingers punched in Lauren's cell phone number.

Leslie answered on the first ring.

"Leslie, this is Mr. Tarrant. Is Lauren there? Can I speak to her? What's happening?"

"Oh! Mr. Tarrant. Thank goodness! I'm in the ambulance with Lauren. She can't talk. The attendants are working on her. She has a badly broken leg. Her life is not in danger, but you need to come up here right away."

"We're leaving Augusta right now. We'll be there as fast as we can. Tell Lauren we're on our way. Can you tell me what happened?"

"Lauren was on her way home on her moped and a car hit her. I don't really know more details. Lauren asked someone at the accident to call her roommates, and I answered the phone."

"Are you okay?" I asked, trying hard to control my breathing.

"Yes, sir. I'm fine. But I better go."

"Okay, Leslie. Thank you for being there for Lauren. We'll call you back in a few minutes. We're leaving now."

My mind was racing. The Greenville hospital. She's going to the Greenville hospital. Why Greenville? I knew the closest hospital was in Seneca. Why weren't they taking her there? Or Anderson, which had a much larger hospital and was twice as far away as Seneca, but still half the distance of Greenville.

Greenville was equipped for serious trauma cases.

I tried to shake off the deepening despair. The situation seemed far more serious than Leslie had conveyed.

Tears welled in Karin's eyes as I told her what Leslie had said.

"Oh, Michael," she replied. "She's hurt and in an ambulance and we're hours away! We've got to hurry. I'll call Andrea. What'll we do about Boo? We can't leave her in the car. We don't know how long we'll be up there."

The drizzle had become light rain—enough to make the asphalt surface of the parking lot shine like it had just been waxed. The streets and roads were slick. How to get there, at this hour of the night in the increasing dreariness? US Route 25 ran from Augusta to Greenville, but half a dozen little towns lined the mostly two-lane, 130-mile route. Halfway up, there was no avoiding Greenwood, a bigger town with plenty of traffic lights.

The other alternative was to take the interstates to Greenville, adding almost sixty miles to the trip, but the speed limit was seventy all the way, with no traffic lights. In this weather, that option might be faster and safer. I knew next to nothing about

Greenville, including the location of Memorial Hospital. Maybe there'd be a sign on the interstate coming in.

Karin grabbed the cell phone and reached Andrea right away. With amazing control, she filled Lauren's big sister in on what was happening then looked at me as she clicked off. "Andrea wants us to meet her at Wendy's on I-20. It's two minutes away. She's going with us. Chad is driving her there right now. We can grab a sandwich if you want one, but I can't eat. I'll call Mum and Dad and see if they can meet us at McDonald's at the Aiken exit. We can drop Boo off with them."

Within minutes we made the connection with Andrea and Chad. Chad insisted on following us. Andrea remained in his car; Karin and I led the way. Turning out of the parking lot, the car in front of me zigzagged across the exit lanes, apparently undecided whether to go left or right.

From somewhere inside me a voice exploded, "Get out of the way, you stupid moron!" The energy and fury of my own outburst shocked me. For the first time, I fully realized how desperately I needed to regain control of this out-of-my-control situation.

I merged onto the interstate and pushed the Buick to ninety as soon as we crossed the Savannah River into South Carolina. I couldn't discern Chad and Andrea in my rearview mirror in the dark and the drizzle. Karin sat stock-still beside me. Neither of us spoke.

A few minutes later, we were at the McDonald's parking lot, handing Boo off to Karin's parents. We grabbed their cell phone charger and started out of the parking lot just as Chad and Andrea pulled in. He screeched to a stop and Andrea hopped out of his car.

"Daddy, wait!" she yelled. "I'm riding with you and Mama. Chad can't keep up with you. He's afraid to go that fast. He's going back to Augusta."

The three of us rocketed back onto the interstate. As usual, there were more eighteen-wheelers than cars. The rain and the truck spray only added to the nightmarish aura of the drive. I turned on the four-way flashers and pressed the accelerator into the carpet. The car responded immediately. I felt the front end of the big Buick lift as the needle on the speedometer soared past one hundred.

Only the absence of wings prevented the vehicle from taking flight. The steering became tremendously light and loose, but I couldn't back off. As desperation and fear mounted by the mile, I realized this was the beginning of a situation I would have a difficult time handling on my own.

As had been my custom throughout life, I wondered if, at last, the time had come to pray. My philosophy had always been: don't bother God with my problems as long as I can handle them myself. Surely God was too busy handling the problems of those who either would not or could not take care of themselves. There were so many big messes in the world, like wars and famines and terrorist attacks…and all the hate. My petty problems couldn't stack up as any kind of a priority against that.

So I tried to restrict my "air time" with God to a nightly check-in at bedtime to let Him know I was still here and to humbly and sincerely thank Him for giving me the wife and children of my dreams. I hadn't wanted to cause Him any more problems. My hope was that He'd look upon me as one of His bright spots, His child who operated for the most part on auto-pilot. After all, my father had taught me a man was supposed to take care of his family and stand on his own two feet.

But now, traveling down this rain-slick highway at breakneck speed, imperiling the most precious cargo imaginable, with barely controlled panic, I decided it was time to call on Him, at least this once.

Lord, I am not capable of controlling this automobile at this speed under these conditions. Please take control of my hands on this steering wheel. Deliver us swiftly and safely to Lauren. I can't be in that ambulance with her now, but I know You are. I ask that You grant her Your comfort and the peace that surpasses all understanding, and that You provide Karin, Andrea, and me with the strength and wisdom we'll need to help her heal.

Incredibly, we sped through the Columbia interchanges without attracting the police.

Karin connected to the hospital on the cell phone. The operator patched her through to the emergency room.

Lauren had arrived a few minutes earlier. Karin's voice sounded amazingly calm as she spoke with the doctor, and her composure quelled my rising anxiety. But I didn't like the words I heard: collapsed lung…facial cuts…broken hand…open fracture of the right leg…exposed bone.

Then Karin said, "I understand. Time is of the essence. Of course you have our permission to take Lauren to surgery. We'll wait for you in the surgery waiting area. We should be there in another hour. Doctor, please, tell Lauren we're on our way and that we love her." At that, Karin's voice faltered.

She turned to me. "They're taking Lauren to surgery *now*," she said, regaining her composure. "They need to know how badly her leg is hurt, and they say time is critical. They needed our permission. We can't make it before she goes in, but we'll be there before she gets out, whether we're going a hundred or eighty. *Please* slow down. We don't need another tragedy tonight. We'll do Lauren no good if we're all three dead."

"Mama's right, Daddy."

It was the first time Andrea had uttered a word throughout this dreadful trip. I had almost forgotten my older daughter in the back seat, reminded of her presence only when I dared take my eyes off the shimmering highway to glance in the rearview mirror.

My two children are as different as two people can be, yet they remain each other's best friend. When they were little, Lauren used her innate obstinacy to her advantage in school and relationships, sometimes overpowering Andrea and her amiable tolerance of a little sister's whims.

I glanced at the sweet face in the rearview mirror for as long as I dared. Her jaw was set in determination, revealing an inner core of strength Karin and I had seen many times, but I suspected Andrea had not yet realized was within herself. My blue-eyed, blonde daughter had inherited her mother's natural coordination and poise, which, despite her introversion, had won Andrea consecutive positions on the cheerleading squad in high school and eventually a college scholarship.

Nevertheless, in her junior year at the University of South Carolina at Aiken, school had become a chore to which Andrea would no longer attend. Instead, she landed what she thought was her dream job, a flight attendant with United Airlines. But September 11th and too many nights in lonely motels proved too much to bear, so our first child had come home.

Now she said softly, "Slow down, Daddy, please. We all wish we were there, and you're doing the best you can. But we can't afford to hurt ourselves too."

I backed off the accelerator and let the speedometer fall back to ninety. Road construction was everywhere as we approached Greenville. Both the weather and the traffic closed in even more. Finally, blue lights flashed as we roared past a cop who was doing the speed limit in the left lane. I pulled onto the construction-mangled shoulder as quickly as I could and jumped out of the car into the driving mist. I ran back to the policeman before he could get his door open.

"My daughter's been injured in a car wreck!" I shouted over the traffic noise. Water dripped into my eyes. "I need to get to the emergency room at Memorial Hospital right away. I'm from out of town. Can you guide us in? Can we follow you?"

"You're endangering my life, yours, and everybody on this road…" he began, finger waving at me through his lowered window.

I cut him off. "Look, I don't have time for a lecture now. You can give me a ticket later. Right now I have an extreme emergency and need to get to the hospital. Will you help me?"

With more anger than empathy, he agreed to escort us to the hospital. "But I won't break the speed limit. You'll have to slow down."

"Okay, Okay. Let's just go!" I yelled and sprinted back to the car.

We followed the policeman's car as he slowly wound through downtown Greenville. He stopped for every traffic light, even if there was no cross-traffic to be seen. It seemed to take more time to poke along from the south side of the city to the hospital than the rest of the entire trip.

When we finally arrived in the emergency-room parking lot, I tossed my driver's license to Andrea. I shouted for her to talk to the cop as Karin and I began jogging to the emergency room doors.

"Hey, I need to talk to you!" the cop shouted across the parking lot.

"My daughter has my driver's license," I shouted back. "Talk to her. Give me a ticket if you want to. Right now, my child needs me."

As Karin and I raced toward the hospital, the glass doors of the emergency room slid open. We stepped across the threshold into the sterile, glaring whiteness. A large clock on the wall read 9:51.

I glanced backward into the murky outdoors, punctuated by the blue-and-red flashing strobes of the policeman's car. The automatic doors slid closed behind us.

And though I didn't realize it at the time, the doors were also closing on the universe as our family had always known it.

Chapter Two

The Lord is close to the brokenhearted and saves those who are crushed in spirit.

—Psalm 34:18

LIKE ANY GOOD mother with a lick of sense, Karin had opposed Lauren's purchase of a moped. Karin recited horror stories of victims of motorcycle accidents and the dangers of drivers who don't look where they're going, of treacherous terrain that lies imbedded in streets, and highways waiting to topple even the most experienced rider.

Lauren countered with recitations about the advantages of being able to move around town and campus without driving a car, the ease of parking, the boost to her busy schedule that the extra time she'd gain from scooting, instead of walking, would give her. The advantages seemed irrefutable. Besides, a moped wasn't a motorcycle. It was more like a speedy bicycle, and almost everybody at Clemson had one.

As for me, it just looked like a whole lot of fun.

Lauren had always saved her money for special purchases instead of blowing it on clothes or whims, so she had the cash. She was an excellent driver and very responsible with schoolwork, summer jobs, and taking care of herself. A moped seemed to suit her spirit of adventure, and it was certainly safer than mountain climbing, sky-diving, or whitewater rafting!

Speed limits were low on campus and around town. I reasoned that most drivers there were more accustomed to seeing kids on wheels than in most non-college towns. Between my reasoning and Lauren's cajoling, Karin caved. Lauren bought her moped her sophomore year, over Christmas break.

The little cycle was cute as a button. Most importantly, it seemed stable and safe. The headlight came on automatically when the motor started; it had rear-view mirrors, turn signals, and a top speed of about forty. I rode it every chance I got.

From the beginning, we insisted Lauren wear a helmet. She protested that nobody on campus wore a helmet. And what would a helmet do to her hair, anyway? I mean, get real!

Again, we caved to her wishes.

Unfortunately, the little contraption suffered from chronic flat tires. If there was a loose nail or a big thorn, the moped found it and remained out of commission for weeks. Earlier in the semester, a pyracantha thorn had found its target and deflated the rear tire, so at the end of a football weekend, I heaved the machine onto the back of the camper and brought it down to Aiken for repair.

I had just returned the moped to Lauren the Friday before the accident.

We had camped that weekend at Devil's Fork State Park, cradled in the foothills of the Appalachians. The park is a series of peninsulas jutting into Lake Jocassee, about thirty miles above Clemson. With autumn in the air and the hardwoods and pines in the foothills reflecting their splendor in the crystal clear lake, the campground provided a serene escape from the raucous party atmosphere that prevailed on campus after a home game.

That Sunday, Lauren brought Robbie up to the campground and we all rode up to Highlands, North Carolina, the highest incorporated town east of the Mississippi River. The four of us planned to cover a favorite hiking trail on Whiteside Mountain before heading back down to Clemson.

We reached the trail. Lauren and Robbie raced ahead of Karin and me, challenging each other to see who would make it to the top first. From behind, I watched my daughter's curly pony tail bounce from side to side, the color of the autumn leaves shining like the sunbeams peaking through the forest canopy. There went my little girl, the one who had ridden my shoulders almost continuously since she was old enough to balance herself by holding on to my forehead; the one Karin and I had watched cheer and dance with the cheerleading squad at almost every high school football and basketball game, kicking her legs straight up over the top of her head like a rocket, while the band played "The Horse."

This was the little girl I knew was equipped to make it on her own in the world.

Running alongside her was the boy Karin and I suspected was the one destined to become a member of our family. Good-natured and fun-loving, Robbie was our favorite among the boyfriends Lauren had brought home. We'd had several opportunities to get to know him; he'd been to Aiken quite a few times since they had begun dating only five months earlier. He was always ready for any game, from Monopoly to softball—and he played to win. Though fiercely competitive, he had a gentleness about him, especially with Lauren, that was reassuring.

Karin and I caught up with them near the top of the mountain. They stopped to pose for a picture on a narrow precipice, nothing behind them but the blue sky and the sprawling valley, awash in Southern sunshine and decked in brilliant autumn majesty stretching as far as could be seen. Two beautiful kids on the verge of beginning life's journeys, with everything they needed to carry them anywhere their dreams might take them.

Two days after that happy trek up the mountain, Karin, Andrea, and I stepped out of a hospital elevator into the harsh uncertainty of a surgery waiting area.

The doors opened to a mezzanine with a waist-high glass wall that allowed a view of an atrium lobby below. A kind-faced, elderly lady in pink sat at an information desk directly in front of us. Beyond her, the waiting area was filled to capacity—to our amazement—with dozens of Lauren's sorority sisters, fellow Young Life leaders, roommates, friends, even parents who lived nearby. We stepped first to the Pink Lady.

"Are you the parents of the young lady who was in the accident over at Clemson?" she asked.

There must have been something about the way we exited the elevator and the expressions on our faces that proclaimed our identity before we spoke. At our nod, she continued in a hushed tone. "Well, she's only been back there for about ten minutes. I'll call and let them know ya'll have arrived. In the meantime, I think those folks over there are anxious to look after you all."

We turned to the surreal gathering. Kids slouched on couches and on the floor, some studying, some clustered in circles talking. It was a typical scene from the Clemson campus, in a study area or in a dorm, lifted out of context and placed in a hospital waiting area. There was so much life, so much youth. I expected Lauren to run out of their midst and bound up to us.

Instead, the ones who knew us best rushed to us with welcoming embraces and words of encouragement. At some point, we found Katie, Emily, and Leslie—Lauren's roommates—and the events of the night spilled out.

Lauren had received a phone call from a fellow Clemson University Guide Association member, telling her that a special meeting of the guides had been called at the Hendrix Center. CUGAs, as they were called, were selected based on their love for

Clemson and their infectious enthusiasm. CUGAs knew every inch of the sprawling campus and every obscure but interesting fact about the school's history. They were often the first face a prospective student and parents saw when they arrived for campus tours. Lauren had joked that they had to know how to walk backward, real fast, while talking, without tripping.

Though the Hendrix Center was no more than a mile from the girls' house, Lauren had hopped on her moped to quickly cut through the misty evening. She had worn her beloved blue Columbia jacket, a Christmas present from Karin and me.

The meeting had not lasted long. Less than an hour later, Lauren was back on her moped and headed home. She had just turned west onto Highway 93, the busy boulevard in front of Bowman Field, the parade ground used by Clemson ROTC cadets and the most popular and conspicuous green area on campus. A white van approached from the east. The driver made a left turn directly in front of Lauren, seeing neither the ill-fated little vehicle nor its approaching, gleaming headlight.

Bowman Field is highly trafficked by pedestrians and cyclists. Quite a few students witnessed the accident. Someone was by Lauren's side almost immediately. Conscious but in tremendous pain, Lauren was able to give that Good Samaritan her name and address, the phone number at her house, and Robbie's name and phone number. The rest of the story was a blur with the arrival of ambulances, wreckers, Leslie, and Robbie. I stood listening—dazed and unaware of the lateness of the hour.

"What about the driver of the car?" Andrea asked. "Where was he? Who was he? Was he hurt? Where is he now? Does anyone know? There was a crowd of people. My gosh! It was right in front of Bowman Field. Surely somebody saw him."

The roommates turned and looked from face to face. Emily spoke for the group. "We haven't heard anything about him or her. That's a piece of the story that we just don't know."

"I'm sure the police will know," Leslie added. Tears were welling in her eyes. She had been brave not only for Lauren, but for us too. She looked away but continued speaking, as much to herself as to the little group. "Lauren talked to me the whole time we were waiting for the ambulance. I don't think her head is hurt at all. She'll be all right. She was so brave. I know she'll be all right. The Lord will take care of her."

Often I had heard it said that until you've had a child of your own, you can't possibly understand how connected you can be to another person. How could anything like this have happened to my child and I not know it was occurring? How could Karin and I have been in Augusta, frivolously window shopping, laughing at silly slogans, while one of our children was hurt and suffering in the middle of a highway? We had always been there for every major event in both our children's lives. Every fall from a bicycle, every broken arm from playing soccer or cheerleading, every hurt feeling, every injury—real or imagined—we had been there. We had known what to do. We had made it right.

Now this had happened, and we had felt nothing, had known nothing. How had we not known, and how could we ever make it right?

We thanked each girl and hugged them extra tight. I looked at Karin and Andrea and saw the tears pooling in their eyes, too. But we all kept a stiff upper lip as we waited for word from the operating room. We circulated throughout the waiting area. The kids were fantastic. One made a reservation for us for the night at a motel; another brought us coffee; some huddled in prayer. Parents offered their homes if we needed to stay another night. By their very presence, Lauren's friends made the wait less excruciating. We were with almost every person from Clemson who meant the most to Lauren, all except Robbie. He had not been seen, and so far, was not to be found.

The Pink Lady approached. "Dr. Moore is coming out of surgery now. He'd like to talk to all three of you. If you'll wait here, he'll be out in just a minute."

Momentarily, a tall, youthful, ex-football-player type— dressed in green scrubs—approached us. "Mr. and Mrs. Tarrant, I'm Dr. Moore, the orthopedic surgeon. I was on call when Lauren was brought in. I'm sorry to have to meet you under these circumstances. I'm sure this has been a rough night for you, but I'm glad you made the trip safely." With a blonde crew cut, I thought he looked hardly old enough to be an experienced orthopedic surgeon, but he had a confident, yet kind manner that was immediately apparent. I liked him.

After we introduced Andrea, we followed him to a quiet corner of the waiting area.

"Lauren's out of surgery and in recovery," he began. "In a few minutes, once they get her settled in, I'll let you see her. She'll be groggy, of course, but awake enough to know you're here. I think that's important for her right now, and for ya'll. She's been through a pretty rough time tonight, but we've got her stabilized, and we've been able to assess the extent of most of her injuries.

"I think you already know that your daughter has been seriously hurt. She has a few stitches under her chin; another surgeon worked on those, and I think he's done a beautiful job. I doubt she'll need plastic surgery. She has a collapsed right lung, so we've put a chest tube in for drainage and to allow the lung to reinflate. That'll need to stay in for a few days. She also has a broken right hand. We've set that, and it'll need to be in a cast for several weeks, but it was a simple closed fracture. I don't see any problem with it. I don't see signs of other internal injuries, but we'll run some more tests tomorrow to make sure.

"Most importantly, she doesn't appear to have any spinal cord injuries or head injuries. Given the nature of the accident and the fact that she wasn't wearing a helmet, it's nothing short of a miracle."

Jesus caught her, I thought, more in hope than conviction, but I began to feel some degree of relief.

Dr. Moore looked from face to face. His voice lowered and his expression became more intent. "But we're not without some problems. Lauren's right leg took the full force of the impact. Her right quadriceps has been crushed. It appears there's a lot of muscle damage. I don't exactly know how an injury like this happened, but Lauren lost a major section of bone, including most of the condyle in her knee, which allows you to bend your leg. It's an extremely unusual injury—a very *serious* leg injury—and about as bad as it gets.

"When I first saw the extent of the damage, I didn't think we could save her leg. But I wanted to talk with you all first, and I was under the impression you weren't here yet. On the positive side, the injury is all the more unusual in that although she's suffered massive bone loss, she appears to have all the nerves and major blood vessels intact. That's an incredible miracle. In fact, I have never seen or heard of anyone suffering bone loss of this magnitude, yet have no collateral damage to adjacent nerves and blood vessels."

He shook his head and continued, "Couple that with the fact that she's only twenty-one years old, I decided not to amputate tonight."

Karin, Andrea, and I exchanged anxious glances. The momentary relief I felt only seconds earlier was replaced by confusion and disbelief.

"I don't understand," Karin whispered. "You're telling me a large piece of my daughter's bone is…what? Lying out in the street somewhere over in Clemson?"

"I'll go get it!" I announced. "I'll leave right now. We'll all go—Karin, Andrea and I, and all Lauren's friends. We'll stay until we find it. You can clean it up and put it back in. We'll find it, drop it in milk just like a tooth that's been knocked out, and bring it back."

Under different circumstances, my simple but pathetic suggestion might have been funny. But at this late hour, the four of us huddled around an ottoman in a hospital waiting area, it was an idea born of desperation.

"I wish it were that simple, Mr. Tarrant," Dr. Moore answered. "But the chances of anyone finding that bone are practically nil. Even if you found it, the bone would be so contaminated that it would be impossible to put it back in Lauren's leg. But there are things that can be done.

"There's a procedure where we take a bone from a donor, usually a cadaver, and transplant that into Lauren's leg. It's called an allograft. Right now, I'd say that's our best option. I can do the procedure, but Lauren's much too injured to attempt it at this point. She's going to need some time to heal. Best-case scenario? I'd say we're looking at late December or early January before Lauren is well enough. The most immediate threat is infection. The wound looks good now, and I don't expect any infection. However, I want you to realize that if an infection does develop, all bets are off."

Dr. Moore sighed. "I know I'm not telling you what you want to hear, but there's still a chance, although not a very big one, that Lauren will lose her leg. I'm not trying to scare you, or paint a bleaker picture than what's reality, but you must understand that Lauren has been *very* seriously hurt. What you three need to focus on tonight is the fact that you still have your daughter and your sister. Take it one day at a time for now, and be thankful she's alive, she's not brain-damaged, and that we can concentrate our efforts on fixing her leg. You all must be very thankful for that."

Thankful? I glanced at Karin, whose eyes brimmed with tears as she nodded at the doctor.

"Now, all I was really able to do in surgery tonight was clean up the wounds. I'll need to take her back to surgery, probably on Friday, to see how things are going with her leg. At that time I plan to put a kind of cement block in place of the bone she's lost. It'll be impregnated with an antibiotic that will help prevent infection. I'll know better after that what the next steps should be and how soon we can take them."

"When can we see her?" Andrea asked.

"She should be in recovery and settled in by now. Why don't you follow me down the hall and wait outside the recovery room door? I'll go back there and send someone for you in a minute. They'll only allow two at a time, so I'd suggest that two of you go back while someone waits, then swap off."

As Karin, Andrea, and I silently followed him down the antiseptic corridor, Dr. Moore looked from face to face. "I know this is hard. Lauren's got a long road ahead of her—you all do—but I can't remind you enough…that no matter what, you've still got your daughter. In that, we have witnessed a miracle tonight. I'll see you all in the morning."

No matter what, you've still got your daughter.

His words gave us hope. We thanked him and shook hands. Dr. Moore was impressive. He had delivered difficult news, but he had done it in a way that inspired confidence.

The double doors swung open a few seconds later, and a nurse quietly asked us to come with her. Karin and I hugged Andrea again, left her slumped against the wall, and followed the nurse into the stark, cold, white cavern of modern medical technology.

Walking amid the quiet, punctuated with electronic beeps and mechanical clicks, the nurse led us to a bedside draped with cords, tubes, and wires. Beneath that web of equipment lay our precious, hurt little girl.

The instant I looked down at that fragile, familiar face, the independent, self-confident college coed who ran on auto-pilot vanished. She was my little girl again, who needed her mommy and daddy more than ever.

Lauren must have sensed our presence, for her eyes fluttered open. There was a flash of recognition, and then tears started to flow.

"I'm sorry!" she whispered in anguish. "I'm *so* sorry. I couldn't stop. The car cut right in front of me. I don't know where my moped is. I never should have gotten it. I ruined my Columbia jacket. They had to cut it off. I don't think it can be fixed."

Carefully avoiding the tangle of tubes and wires, Karin and I found a way to hold our child.

"Shhh," Karin whispered. "Mama and Daddy are here, Larnie Jane. You're going to be all right. You have nothing to be sorry for. Don't you worry about your moped or your jacket. You just rest. Andrea is here too. None of us are going anywhere. You just go to sleep. You're going to be all right. I promise."

I knew Karin well enough to know that she was fighting to maintain a brave front. Under no circumstances would she let Lauren see the despair and fear that she struggled to keep hidden.

Lauren closed her eyes and slipped back into a doze. Peace replaced her expression of anguish, possibly as much from our presence as from the drugs.

A recovery room nurse perched on a stool at the foot of Lauren's bed. Older than Karin or I, she looked like a mother herself. "What's this button in Lauren's left hand?" I asked in a whisper.

"It's the control for the morphine pump," she whispered back. "Lauren's getting a constant dose of morphine, a basal level. But if she feels any discomfort, she can push that button for an extra boost. Don't worry; I'll make sure she's comfortable. I'll be right here all night, and I'm going to take good care of her."

There were only a couple of other patients in this critical care unit, though it was obviously equipped to handle dozens.

It was a large room, divided into two sections, with machinery and electronic equipment parked haphazardly throughout. In places, nurses were talking among themselves. Every now and then, there was quiet laughter. Normalcy in such a place only added to its other-worldliness.

Lauren might weigh one hundred pounds soaking wet. She looked so tiny lying in that hospital bed. Her right arm was in a cast that bent at a ninety degree angle at the elbow, and was propped up high. The injured right leg was bundled in massive bandages and similarly propped. Her chin was stitched and stained with Betadine. Flowing brown locks framed her face, as pale as the white hospital sheets and blankets covering the rest of her.

Karin sat on a stool at Lauren's left, resting her head on the raised bed railing. She held just three dainty fingers so Lauren could grip the morphine pump button with her thumb and index finger. Those fingers and Lauren's forehead were about the only places that could be touched.

Every few minutes, though she looked asleep, Lauren's thumb pushed the red button. A nearby black box clicked, and clear liquid flowed through a tube connected to the IV. Each time it happened, Karin lifted her head from the bed rail and looked at me. No words were spoken, but I knew her thoughts: *Our child is hurting, Michael. Is there nothing we can do?*

With Karin still holding Lauren's fingers, I slipped out to let Andrea in, then waited in the hallway, slumped against the wall as Andrea had been. Several minutes later she reemerged, fell into my arms, and buried her face in my shoulder, shaking with sobs.

We continued taking turns in and out of the critical care unit. Finally, at about 1:30 in the morning, the nurse turned to me. "It's very late. She's going to be okay for the rest of the night, but you three need some rest. I promise I'll be right here.

of the three of us stroked her cheek or held the free fingers of her left hand.

I stood beside her bed, looking down at my broken little girl. There was no hint of the ever-present smile that had been a permanent resident on her face from the time she was a baby. This daughter had been a perpetual motion machine, the family jokester and entertainer. She proudly accepted the title of Class Clown, bestowed upon her by her classmates during her final year of high school.

I stroked her cheek and let my mind wander back to a trip to Fripp Island. It must have been early April. We had taken a day trip to the beach—something we did a lot with the girls. The water was still chilly, but that didn't stop Andrea from plunging right in. Lauren could not yet walk, so we set her on the sand, intending to let her crawl around on the beach. She took one look at her sister splashing in the shallow waves and made a beeline for the water, grinning so widely she couldn't close her mouth. With Karin and me beside her, she hit the water, and took wave after wave right in the face, still smiling with her mouth wide open.

She must have swallowed a gallon of salt water, but nothing could dampen that smile. And in the twenty years that had passed, she was rarely without that happy face, making her current, pained expression even more foreign.

My reverie ended abruptly when two orderlies in green scrubs approached to roll Lauren down for the first set of tests.

The day progressed at a snail's pace. Lauren was wheeled from one lab and x-ray room to another. But as the nurse had promised, the three of us were allowed to follow her gurney on its odyssey through the inner corridors of the hospital.

Lauren was given a room of her own about mid-afternoon. A big picture window overlooked the hospital atrium. It was good for people-watching in the main lobby, but not good for letting in the sunlight. But it was the only room available, and Lauren was exhausted and obviously glad to be parked in one spot.

The room was small. The hospital bed, a recliner, and a couple of straight chairs filled it to capacity. There was a ledge in front of the atrium window; a television was mounted to the wall. One corner held a bathroom. Another sink was located on the opposite side of the room. The tile floors gleamed.

No test results were due until after five. While Lauren slept, Andrea kept watch over her. Karin and I left to find a Kmart, Walmart, or someplace where we could pick up some toiletries and a change of clothes for each of us, since it was apparent we weren't going home anytime soon.

Though we were connected via cell phone, being away from our injured offspring, even for a few brief moments, was disconcerting. We found a Walmart and grabbed a few essentials. Earlier in the day, someone at the orthopedics desk at the hospital told Karin the Hilton had the lowest rate in town for folks who had a family member in the hospital. We found it, checked in, and rushed back.

We walked in the room to find Andrea, along with roommates Leslie, Emily, and Katie, surrounding Lauren. The black morphine button was, for the first time, free of Lauren's grasp. But the most illuminating presence shone from Lauren's face. There, shining above that stitched and stained chin, that beloved smile had returned.

The girls chatted and laughed and talked about school, providing a sense of normalcy that visibly comforted Lauren. She intermittently dozed off, then woke and rejoined the conversation without missing a beat. Robbie came in, bringing more smiles.

The happy presence of all this youth and energy and the corresponding rally it produced in Lauren buoyed everyone's spirits. I began to feel that maybe this tragedy was nothing more than a bump in the road, requiring only a brief convalescence.

Maybe this whole thing would be just a memory in a month or so.

Shortly after six, one short rap on the door heralded the entry of a mini-squad of white-robed professionals. Dr. Moore was first through the door, followed by a grim-faced Dr. Ellis. On his heels came stocky, middle-aged Dr. Frederick. Robbie and the rest of the kids retreated to the lobby waiting room with a promise they'd be back as soon as the business at hand was completed. Karin, Andrea, and I lined up on one side of Lauren's bed, facing the three doctors lined up on the other.

Dr. Moore spoke first. "I have some good news," he began. "Lauren, your test results indicate no internal injuries, confirming what I suspected when you came in last night. We see no sign of any head or spinal cord injuries. I'll be honest with you; that's nothing short of a miracle. Accidents like the one you've been through, especially without a helmet, don't leave people without a head or spinal column injury. You're one in a million."

He paused and flashed a comforting smile. "What I want to do is take you back into surgery day after tomorrow and take a look at that leg. My plan is to give it a thorough cleaning, then we'll put a spacer in, made of a type of cement and impregnated with an antibiotic. Early next week, we'll get you fitted with a brace, and we'll start thinking about letting you go home, maybe the middle of next week."

"But what about school?" Lauren asked. "I've got a shot at a 4.0 this semester. When do you think I'll be able to go back to Clemson?"

"Let's just take it one day at a time. We'll try to get you back as soon as possible. It's going to be at least a couple of weeks, though."

Worry crossed Lauren's face. She turned to the three of us. "It's my senior year. I've never made a 4.0 before. I've gotta get back."

"We'll call Clemson," Karin said. "We'll let them know what's going on. I'm sure they'll work with you, Larnie Jane."

Lauren's eyes wilted, signaling she was quickly fading back into her intermittent, drug induced slumber. "I don't mean to be rude," she said softly, "but I think I'm going to have to close my eyes and take a little nap." And with that, she was out.

Dr. Moore smiled. "Well, she's out of here, and I have to be also. I'll see you all tomorrow morning. I think my two colleagues want to spend a few minutes with you now. Good night."

Next, Dr. Frederick turned to us. "Lauren's collapsed lung is sounding better, so we'll probably pull her chest tube tomorrow or Friday. I wanted to stop by and let you know she's coming along well. From our perspective, all the tests have come back negative."

He promised to see us again tomorrow then left us alone with Dr. Ellis. He stood on the opposite side of Lauren's bed, between the three of us and the door. He was young. I guessed not long out of med school and residency. Tall and thin with a dark complexion, he was the reverse of Dr. Moore in appearance as well as demeanor.

"I want to talk to you and Lauren about amputation," he began.

If he had leaned across the bed and slapped each of us in succession like we were the Three Stooges, we could not have been more shocked. I glanced down at Lauren to ensure she was still sleeping.

I recovered enough to respond. "I'm not sure why you want to bring that topic up, but if you must, then we'll continue this conversation in the hall."

"Your daughter has a severe injury," Dr. Ellis persisted. "She's twenty-one years old. She has a right to understand what she's facing."

"That may be true," Karin interrupted. "But at the moment, she's hurt and in no position to be saddled with additional concerns that may not be pertinent, especially at this point in time. As her mother, I am as concerned about her emotional well-being as I am about her physical health. So any discussion with Lauren regarding amputation will be held only with my permission or that of her father. Otherwise, the subject will not be raised in her presence. I don't care if she's twenty-one or *fifty-one!*"

Karin moved swiftly past him, opened the door, and stepped into the hall. I followed. With his audience reduced to a sleeping Lauren, guarded by Andrea, who had taken up a position in the chair beside her sister's bed and very defiantly opened a magazine, Dr. Ellis followed us. The three of us walked to a quiet corner.

"Look," he started again, "I work with Dr. Moore. He's an intelligent, compassionate man. He's trying to offer you encouragement that there's a chance Lauren's leg will not have to be removed. But there's also a chance she *will* lose it, and you have to face that reality. It's a reality Lauren may have to face herself. She has a difficult road ahead of her, even if she keeps her leg."

Tell me something I don't know, I thought. The solemn faced doctor continued.

"There are some distinct advantages to prosthesis. Prosthetics have come a long way in the past several years. Lauren could walk, run, swim, ride a bicycle, and play sports with almost no restrictions. The recuperation period would be much, much shorter. She could be back at Clemson in a few weeks. But with her current injuries, and with no complications, and barring an infection, we might be able to do reconstruction surgery in January. There will be multiple surgeries. Then she has months—maybe years—of physical therapy. That's the very best case."

Any vestiges of my earlier up-beat mood had now been thoroughly wrung out of me. I glanced at Karin. I could tell she'd had her fill of the young doctor's speech, as well.

But he wasn't finished with us yet.

"If complications should occur and especially if she gets infected, she could be in for a very serious situation. You must be aware of the circumstances, and you need to know the alternatives. Even though you don't want to hear it, amputation is a very real alternative that may provide her with the most satisfactory life in the long run."

Neither Karin nor I were moved.

"I appreciate what you're telling us," Karin said. "But no matter what anyone tells me, I know an above-the-knee amputation is a formidable handicap. No prosthetic leg in the world is going to come close to a natural leg. Lauren has lost her knee and much of the nearby bone, but she still has every nerve and blood vessel intact. That's a miracle. She will overcome this, and in the process she'll be able to show others what God's power can do."

At that, Karin's voice cracked. "She's twenty-one years old; she has her whole life ahead of her." Her composure returned. "If you feel it necessary to discuss amputation again in the future, please remember that no mention of it will be made in Lauren's presence."

Obviously unaccustomed to being issued orders, Dr. Ellis left us without directly agreeing to Karin's request, but she and I were both confident the message had been received.

Karin walked back to Lauren's room, while I went out to the waiting area and issued the "all clear" to Robbie, Emily, Katie, and Leslie.

Lauren continued to talk and doze. As the evening progressed, other kids filed in, bringing flowers and stuffed animals, cards and candy, baskets and balloons. The dim little room grew crowded with young well-wishers. It began to look quite festive. In that better environment, it wasn't too hard for me to relegate Dr. Ellis's grave warnings to an out-of-the-way corner of my mind.

Karin, too, visibly relaxed. Still, she maintained a constant vigilance. The grim warnings we had all received about the possibility of infection had been duly noted, and in her characteristic determination, Karin was not about to allow unwelcome bacteria anywhere near Lauren. She reminded every visitor, no matter who they were and what position they held, to wash their hands.

About mid-evening, a nurse bustled into the room and walked directly to Lauren's IV tree. She had both hands thrust in front of her, just about to make an adjustment, when Karin spoke up:

"Did you wash your hands?"

"Who, me?" The nurse looked at Karin with widened eyes.

"Yes. I didn't see you wash your hands. We want to do everything we can to make sure Lauren doesn't get an infection, so please be sure you wash your hands when you come in here."

Without a word, the nurse huffed over to the sink and washed her hands. She returned to the IV tree and made her adjustments in stony silence.

"That didn't sit too well with her," I said when she'd left.

"Guess not," Karin answered.

But we didn't have to remind that nurse again—or any other hospital employee—to wash their hands when they entered Lauren's room. Apparently, word gets around fast in hospitals.

As the evening progressed, the number of kids in the room dwindled. Even Robbie had left with a promise to return tomorrow.

For the first time since the accident, Lauren, Andrea, Karin, and I were alone. Lauren had assumed the role of hostess for the evening, and had clearly enjoyed it. Now she looked drained. And she was pushing the morphine button a lot more often.

I looked at my little girl, lying pale and uncomfortable in that hospital bed. Her broken right hand was propped on a pillow; a tube ran from under the covers to a receptacle on the floor, draining her collapsed lung. Her right leg was propped on several pillows; an IV was in her left hand. Other lines and tubes ran in and out from under the covers at various points. As wired and tubed and propped as she was, Lauren had no choice but to lie flat on her back. Yet she had not complained all day, except when she had been forced to drink the liquid for the x-ray early that morning.

Karin sat in a chair, pulled herself up to the bed, and laid her head on Lauren's pillow. A tear rolled down her cheek and dampened the pillow case.

Lauren looked at her mother. "Don't cry, Mama."

"I know I shouldn't cry," Karin whispered. "But I can't help thinking: why you, Lauren? You've always been so happy and funny. All your life you've made everyone around you laugh. Now you're a senior at the college you always dreamed of attending. You've met the love of your life. You've worked so hard to inspire other people to have faith in God. You've tried to help others any way you can. So why you?"

"It's all right to ask why, Mama," Lauren replied. "But, why *not* me? Jesus said we'd have troubles in this world, but He'd bring us His peace. So I'll just rely on Jesus."

Karin looked at Lauren with wonder. If Lauren could handle this with such grace, surely the rest of us would have no choice but to follow her lead.

We knew now we'd be in Greenville for several days, probably until the middle of the following week. We needed more stuff than the few things we'd picked up at Walmart, so Andrea and I would drive down to Aiken the next day, Halloween. We'd pick up some clothes and personal items, and I'd make arrangements so the remodeling at the house could continue while we were away. Karin would spend Halloween day with Lauren while Andrea and I were in Aiken. We would be back in Greenville in time for supper.

It made the most sense for me to take the night shifts at the hospital with Lauren, while Karin and Andrea went back to the hotel. Then when they arrived in the mornings, I'd go to the hotel to get cleaned up. The only proper chair in the cramped little hospital room expanded into a make-shift bed, so I would be pretty comfortable.

I was glad to stay nights. I drew comfort from Lauren's acceptance and peace and faith. I knew Karin and Andrea did as well.

On those occasions when I was out of her room, whether a run for food or to make phone calls back home or to work, I felt compelled to return as quickly as possible. Away from Lauren, my mind wandered to the circumstances that led us to this hospital, to the interruptions, fears, and uncertainty that had suddenly been injected into our lives.

But in Lauren's presence, those feelings were pushed aside. Instead, I felt that no more harm could come to her if I were near. I hadn't protected my child that day, but I could make certain that she would not be hurt again.

Not on *my* watch.

We set about getting Lauren settled in for the night. Gingerly, we adjusted the position of her leg and made her as comfortable as possible. Karin tucked her in as tight as she dared, making sure all necessary buttons were within easy reach.

Reluctantly, she and Andrea kissed Lauren and me good-night. Before they walked out the door, I gave each of them an extra-long hug. Karin whispered so that no one else could hear, "Please don't let anything happen to her, Michael."

"I won't. I promise," I whispered back.

Alone with my daughter, I sat down in the straight chair by Lauren's bed and stroked her cheek.

"Daddy," she said as she drifted off to sleep, "I'm really glad you're here."

"Me, too, Chicken Little. Me, too."

A half hour later I got up and went over to the convertible chair. I lay back on the narrow bed, but I wasn't brave enough to close my eyes. The darkened room still flickered with unfamiliar lights; strange sounds clicked and whirred. Just beyond the door, I was aware of an undercurrent of constant activity in the halls—nurses walking briskly, their voices sometimes carrying into the room, ubiquitous visitors talking and laughing too loudly. Did this hospital have visiting hours, or was it just a popular nightspot for folks in the upstate?

Whatever. Rather than feeling annoyed, I was thankful for the distraction. Closing my eyes would mean being alone with my imagination.

I still had no clear conception of what had happened on that street in Clemson the night before. Throughout the last twenty-four hours, fleeting thoughts of what Lauren must have endured ran through my mind, but I willed those images out of my head.

Unable to keep my eyes open any longer, a scene began playing in my head like a movie. I saw Lauren on her moped, coming down that busy, rain-slick street, the car turning in front of her. I felt her panic when she realized there was no way to avoid a collision. I saw her fragile frame hitting the cold, rigid steel of the car, the moped spinning and grinding into the pavement...

Enough! The imagery was too excruciating.

Prayer offered the only possible escape. *Lord,* I prayed, *I'm not ready to deal with what happened to my child. I don't want my mind to take me there. There will come a time when I'll have to find a way to deal with this, but I can't let this sap my strength now. I need to be 100 percent in every way so that I can best help her. Please take this image out of my mind. My child has such strength through her faith in You. Please grant me that same strength. Please grant me Your peace that surpasses all understanding.*

I opened my eyes. The vivid, torturous imaginings ceased. Instead, my thoughts carried me back in time to my own childhood. I was six years old, standing barefoot and shirtless in shimmering heat in the backyard of the house I grew up in.

We lived on Reynolds Pond Road, about eight miles out of Aiken, in the country right near the forty-acre Reynolds Pond. An immense swamp flowed east from the pond, cloaking both sides of Shaw's Creek until the swamp and the creek merged into the Spanish-moss-canopied Edisto River, the longest black-water river in the world. Our house stood on sandy earth, amidst pine trees, cedars, and Carolina cherries, the first high ground beyond the tupelos rooted in the muck of the swamp. Many a wayward rattlesnake, cottonmouth, or copperhead slithered off course into our yard on summer afternoons.

In our young years, my older brother, Bobby, and I had already been the consistent victors in countless battles with snakes. Bobby was deadly with a BB gun, known to pump as many as two hundred BBs into a single snake. He was also handy with a hoe. But he was savvy enough to know when it was safe to take on a snake by himself and when to call in reinforcements.

Our reinforcement was Becky. I guess in today's vernacular Becky would be a housekeeper or a nanny, but back then we didn't know that. Becky was black, but we didn't know that either. All we knew was that Becky was almost always at our house, especially when Mama was sick, which was a lot because Mama had cancer. We knew Becky took care of us, and we knew she loved us and we loved her.

On this particular afternoon, Bobby and I were out in the sand pile between the house and the well house, which was a shed with a brick foundation. It housed the pump. It was also where we parked our bicycles and kept other outdoor toys.

A rustle in the pine straw caused us to look up from our dump trucks. A big water moccasin was holding its shovel-shaped head above its thick body, surveying the surroundings by flicking its forked tongue in and out. Recognizing that this snake was not to be fought by two little boys, we ran to the house for Becky.

"Becky, there's a big ol' snake in the backyard!" Bobby yelled as we slammed through the back porch door. "I think it's a cottonmouth!"

Becky stood no more than four feet tall, her hair always pulled tightly back into a knot. She wore a white apron over skirts that almost touched the floor, and sturdy, white leather shoes like the kind nurses wore in those days. Despite her diminutive size and cumbersome clothes, she could move with lightning speed to rescue little boys when she had to. She was out the back porch door in a split second, with Bobby and me right behind.

Apparently sensing the commotion and its impending doom, the snake made a beeline for the well house and any potential sanctuary it might offer. In hot pursuit, Becky grabbed the hoe, which was always kept at the ready beside the back door during the months when snakes were active. But the water moccasin had too much of a lead. Finding a broken brick in the foundation, it slithered out of sight under the well house. Undaunted, Becky quickly set up surveillance.

"Bobby, you stay right here on this side of the well house. Michael, you go round to the back where you can see the well house, but don't you get too close. You chirren watch underneath, and if that snake comes crawlin' out, you holler.

I'm goin' to boil some water. We're go'ne boil that snake out from under that well house."

I ran to my designated spot, keeping a healthy distance from the well house, with one eye on the back foundation, the other eye on my brother, who had retrieved his BB gun and stood stock still, staring at the front of the little white shed. No sign of the snake.

Before long, Becky came out of the back door at a trot, carrying the kettle from the stove. Steam spewed from the spout, even in the withering afternoon heat. She ran to the hole in the foundation where the snake had crawled down and emptied the boiling kettle into the crevice. To my horror, within seconds the water moccasin shot out of a previously unnoticed crack on my side of the well house. At lightening speed, it sped right at me, its huge mouth wide open and whiter inside than the freshly laundered sheets hanging motionlessly on the clothesline.

"Here it comes!" I shrieked. Before I could break into a run in the opposite direction, Becky's hoe swung down like a guillotine, decapitating the monster with one swift, deadly stroke.

The severed body of the serpent lay writhing at our feet while Becky walked out into the field and dug a hole with the hoe. She came back with the hoe and picked up the remains, which coiled around the hoe like a kudzu vine. Then she placed the carcass in the hole and covered it with the sandy soil.

"Ya'll boys stay away from that snake now, 'cause you know a snake don't die 'til sundown," she called. Then she placed the hoe against the house and disappeared onto the back porch to resume the daily chores.

Becky was not only our protector, but a one-of-a-kind teacher as well. We learned some of life's most important lessons from her. She was brave, fast, and knew how to handle herself amidst the challenges of life in rural South Carolina. She was a champion of small boys' causes.

But her most awe-inspiring ability was a simple part of her daily routine. Late in the afternoons, when the heat of the day was just beginning to abate, she set up her ironing board at one end of the kitchen, where the breeze from the front of the house flowed through to the back. There, while she ironed, she talked.

"Yes, Jesus," she'd say. Then a few sentences that couldn't quite be heard, then, "No, Jesus." This apparently one-sided conversation would continue for as long as there was ironing to be done. I'd sometimes play on the floor and try to listen in, but I could never make out the topic of the conversations.

Finally, one day, curiosity overwhelmed me. "Becky, who you talkin' to?"

"I'm talkin' to Jesus, chile."

"Does He hear you?"

"He sho do."

"But how do you know? Does He answer you back?"

"He do. Sometimes He answers me right back. And sometimes He don't answer for a while. But He always answers."

I hadn't understood her at the time. I thought that for all her outstanding virtues, Becky was a little delirious by late afternoon, after chasing two boys and keeping up the house and helping Mama all day. Sane people knew the only time you talked to Jesus was right before you went to bed, or had a big meal, or if you were in Sunday school or church.

But this night, lying on a cot in that hospital room, with my child lying helpless and hurt a few feet away, I thought of Becky.

I talked to Jesus too.

And at last I began to understand.

Chapter Four

Do not be anxious about anything, but in everything, by prayer and petition, with thanksgiving, present your request to God.
—Philippians 4:6

A HOSPITAL IS no place to be if you need rest. Shift changes occur around midnight, ushering in a fresh crop of nurses shackled to clanging, old-fashioned blood pressure monitors like a ball and chain. They drag their restraints through the halls, waking patient after hapless patient for the next few hours.

The medical students begin making their morning rounds about five. Jacked on caffeine and adrenaline, their primary function seems to be snapping on overhead lights in patients' rooms and engaging sick or injured folks in pre-dawn, redundant conversations about topics that were previously discussed in depth a day earlier with their primary physicians.

Nonetheless, Lauren's second night in the hospital passed quietly. Every couple of hours, I was awakened by a quiet voice calling, "Daddy, can you get me a glass of water?" or "Daddy, can you move my leg a little?"

I took comfort in those wake-up calls. They gave me something concrete to do. They made me feel less powerless. No matter how small the task, I felt I was helping in some way. And my child was right there, speaking to me. I knew how close I had come to losing her, and I realized what a blessing it was to still be with her now. I felt I had failed to protect her; I had let my child get hurt. Taking care of Lauren now, I could make certain she would not get hurt again!

Karin and Andrea arrived early in the morning with coffee and a bag of Egg McMuffins. As planned, Andrea and I left Karin with Lauren and headed south towards home to pick up enough clothes and essentials to get us through several more days. As we walked through the hospital parking lot to the car, the Carolina sun began to shine through the relentless gloom of the past two days, promising a warm and cheerful Halloween.

We had just buckled in the car when my cell phone rang. *Karin*, I figured. *She's thought of something else we should bring up from home.*

Andrea answered, then, "Hold on just a minute, please." With a puzzled look, she handed the phone to me.

"Hello?" I said.

The voice on the phone had a pronounced, practically incomprehensible, Asian accent.

"This Xiang Liu," the caller said. "I call to see how is Lauren?"

"I'm sorry," I replied. "I didn't understand your name. Who are you?"

"I Xiang Liu," he repeated. "I am calling to see how is Lauren?"

I gave up trying to decipher the mysterious caller's name.

"Are you a friend of Lauren's?" I asked. "Do you know her from Clemson?"

"No, I work at Clemson. I teach there." He struggled to get the words out. "I am one driving car. I am one who ran car into your daughter. I so worried about Lauren. Please, can you tell me…she is okay?"

As the man's identity burst into my mind, the cheerfulness of the sunshine flared into a blinding, painful glare. Andrea and I were suddenly caught in another ambush. Everywhere, life had abruptly changed over the last few days. It was no longer safe to answer a phone or open a door. The brief moments we had just passed, walking through the sunshine to the car, had seemed like the first time in days I had allowed myself to take a deep breath. No sooner had I begun to let my guard down, than we were assaulted again.

So this is the idiot who ran his car into my child, I thought. *My gosh, he can't even speak English. How can he possibly follow American road signs?*

I felt my face turning red. From somewhere deep in my gut, a boiling anger began seething its way to my hands holding the steering wheel. My grip tightened. We had now exited the parking lot onto the busy, unfamiliar street. There was no place to pull over so I could focus on the conversation suddenly thrust upon me. Forced to grapple with traffic, I strained to understand this unwelcome intruder, this man—this *foreigner*—who had crippled one of my children.

I'm sure there were things that I should have said, questions that I should have asked. But this assault, just like the others of the past few days, had taken me by surprise. Our whole family, it seemed, was being sucked into a tornado. Lifted off the ground and suspended in mid-air, we swirled helplessly in the evil whirlwind, taking intermittent hits from debris that we couldn't see coming and had no way of anticipating.

"No, Lauren's not okay," I finally replied, my voice rising. "How did you get my cell phone number?"

"Clemson police gave me this number. You Lauren's father?"

"Yes, I'm Lauren's father," I answered with no attempt to conceal my anger.

"I so sorry. So sorry. I never see her. My wife and I very worried." Even his thick accent couldn't disguise his genuine anguish.

I didn't want my fury to ebb. I wanted to yell back into the phone: *What are you, blind? How could you not see her? How'd you ever get into this country? And how in the name of all that's good did you ever get a driver's license? Do you have the slightest idea what you've done? My daughter will never be the same! Our whole family will never be the same! Do you know how many dreams you shattered because you have no business being behind the wheel?*

I wanted to say all that and more. Here was my chance to vent a small part of my pent-up frustration. Here was a golden opportunity to inflict a portion of the pain this man had caused, back onto him. He deserved it. He had it coming.

But I couldn't sustain my wrath. Maybe the emotional trauma of the last several days had left me weak. Maybe I was just too tired to tell the guy where he ought to go. Maybe it was because his contrition was evident even through his broken English.

And maybe he was like us—just another helpless, pathetic soul caught up in an evil whirlwind.

The blinding rage subsided. I asked if he was all right; he replied that he was. He appeared nervous, and his voice cracked as if he were on the verge of tears. The phone conversation lasted about ten minutes, but all I could understand was the depth of his remorse. In response to his repeated questioning, I tried to better explain Lauren's condition. The call ended with my feeling that he had understood as little of what I had told him as I had been able to understand of what he had told me.

So, this devastation that had beset my innocent child had been sent from the other side of the world. I shook the conversation off and consciously decided to revel in the brilliant sunshine. I decided not to mention the phone call to Lauren, at least not until she was much, much better.

The day remained bright and sunny as we drove down US 25. The South Carolina piedmont in the fall doesn't get the recognition it deserves. Our state is much better known for its Low Country, green and lush all year, draped with Spanish moss and bordered by broad, sandy, palm-crowned beaches with warm gray-green water. But as Andrea and I drove south across the upstate that late October morning, the golden shafts of sunlight turned the red, purple, orange and yellow of the dogwoods, sweet gums, and hickories into a fiery tapestry laid over a tri-colored background of blue sky, green pine forests, and red-clay earth.

In marked contrast to the breakneck speeds of the frantic trip up to Greenville that we'd made two nights earlier, I stayed within the speed limit on the way back down. Andrea and I chatted about everything and about nothing. We practiced Vincent Price's evil laugh at the end of Michael Jackson's "Thriller," played countless times on the radio in honor of Halloween. During the hours we spent together in the isolated, protective environment of the car, we could pretend things were normal and that our family was just the way it had always been.

We could pretend, but we couldn't forget.

At home, workmen were busy laying tile in the kitchen. Strewn across what used to be the laundry room, construction debris spilled from there all the way into the backyard. But the remodeling that had been the focal point of our lives just a few days before was now nothing more than an inconvenience. Andrea and I tiptoed over loose tiles, arms loaded with the stuff that was the purpose of our trip. We gathered what we needed, returned a few phone messages that had been left on the answering machine, then headed back up the road.

Night had fallen by the time we found our way back to Lauren's room, where about a dozen college kids had gathered, most in full costume. Freckled-faced farm girls, a Martian, a cow, and a big, goofy dog mingled, while a movie played on a portable TV/VCR one of the co-eds had brought in. Lauren lay in her bed in the middle of the fray, playing the perfect hostess. With her ever-present smile in residence on her face, her unbroken hand still clutched the small, black button that released the morphine at regular intervals.

The room reverberated with the laughter and chatter typical of a sorority house, making it easy to forget the second surgery scheduled for the morning. Eventually, though, the make-shift Halloween party wound down. When at last Karin and Andrea had kissed Lauren and me goodnight and left for the hotel, I resumed my role as private-duty-nurse daddy. Sitting beside Lauren's bed holding her free hand, the two of us watched Chevy Chase in *Christmas Vacation*, until my little college girl fell asleep.

If God has created kinder, gentler, more compassionate creatures than older, Southern ladies, I have yet to discover them. Two such ladies arrived early the next morning to wheel Lauren to surgery. While Karin, Andrea, and I watched, the two ladies, dressed in crisp, green scrubs, swooped in and readied Lauren, like a couple of angels swaddling a new baby to hand her over to the stork for delivery.

"Oh, just look at this sweet baby. Child, you look like a livin' doll. Ella, is she not the prettiest little thing you ever saw? Just look at those big green eyes and that pretty curly hair! Just like a little angel," cooed one of them as she leaned over Lauren's bed.

"Now, baby, don't you worry about nothin'. Me and Ella are gonna stay right with you. Then just as soon as you wake up, we're gonna bring you right back here to your mama and daddy, and we ain't gonna let nothin' happen to this sweet baby."

The two women chattered on while they deftly moved Lauren's wheeled bed down the hospital corridors, barely giving Lauren time to think about what was really happening. We walked alongside as far as we could, then each of us leaned down and kissed her when we could go no further. When it was my turn, I leaned down and whispered, "You know you're not going in there by yourself, Chicken Little. Remember whose child you are."

Tears puddled in her green eyes as she nodded bravely. Then she was rolled through double doors and out of sight. I could no longer see her, but I heard both ladies still rattling on—"Precious baby, you gonna be just fine"—more like hairdressers taking a bride-to-be back for a hair-do than orderlies rolling a scared young girl into surgery.

Unlike the waiting area that had been crowded with friends and supporters three nights earlier, just the three of us gathered in Lauren's hospital room during the operation. Without the large hospital bed, the room seemed to burst forth with flowers, house plants, stuffed animals, cards, baskets of fruit, candy, and snacks stacked in every space.

We paced around the room, picking up the cards and reading them out loud to each other. Some were funny, many were touching, but almost all of them mentioned something about how Lauren had been such a good friend, a good listener and advisor, had helped in times of need, and had been inspirational with her always cheerful outlook. Almost without exception, each one said something about her faith and the example she set in living for the Lord. Now that she needed them, her friends were lifting her up in prayer.

What has this kid learned in the three years she's been away at school? I thought. Thirty years earlier, myself a Clemson student, I learned a little about my major courses and maybe a little more about football weekends and water-skiing on Lake Hartwell. I definitely learned a lot about how to party! But I had learned nothing about how to touch other people's lives, or how to be an example of God's love, or how to be a blessing to those who knew me. Evidently Lauren was not only learning all that, but teaching it too. Surely God wanted her ministry to continue. Surely He'd make her walk again. She'd need to be able to go and tell her story.

The morning wore on. I remembered Becky's talks with Jesus, and uncharacteristically, I initiated several conversations with Him myself. We pulled three small, straight-backed chairs into the middle of the room and sat huddled in a semi-circle, staring up at the television, anchored high on the wall, where Bob Barker was helping a frail old lady spin the big wheel on *The Price Is Right.*

"What's taking so long?" Andrea verbalized what we'd all been thinking. "Shouldn't we have heard from Dr. Moore by now?"

Just then, one quick knock on the hospital door signaled the entrance of a tall figure silhouetted against the brightness of the hospital corridor behind him.

Robbie stepped forward out of the shadow. "Lauren's not out of surgery yet?"

"No, we haven't heard anything," Andrea answered. "We thought you were Dr. Moore."

Robbie stepped back out of the room, returned momentarily with another straight-backed chair, and joined our semi-circle beneath the television. I looked over at the dark-haired young man who had become so important to our daughter in the last several months. His stone-faced expression mirrored the tension that hung in the room like a cold, damp fog.

Unable to focus on Bob Barker and the Showcase Showdown that blared on the television just above our heads, I thought back to the first time I met young Mr. McKenzie. Early last spring, Lauren invited him down to Aiken for a weekend trip, ostensibly to attend an Aaron Tippin concert in Augusta.

"You know Robbie was voted 'Best Eyes' his senior year at Fort Mill High School," she told us on the phone one day before they came down.

"Well, good eyesight is important," I quipped.

"Hey, that's my line," Lauren fired back. "Don't forget, you're talking to the Class Clown!"

"I know you took him to the Kappa dance in February," Karin chimed in on the extension. "But how'd you meet him?"

"You remember I went to Young Life Camp at Sharp Top in North Georgia right after Christmas break?" Lauren asked. "Well, one of the kids in my group wanted to go down the zip line. It was freezing cold, and the zip line runs from a tree on the side of a mountain all the way down into a lake. They told us the lake had ice on it a couple of weeks earlier, and the air temperature was in the 40s. But this kid really wanted to try it and wanted me to do it with her. So naturally, I said, 'Sure.'"

"Naturally," Karin replied into the phone. "Go on."

"So, we come flying down the mountain, screaming at the top of our lungs, and hit the water like a ton of bricks. It's so cold that it sucks the breath right out of you. As I'm emerging from the icy lake, teeth chattering so that I can't even speak, all my clothes and hair totally drenched, here's this good-looking guy playing football with some other guys beside the lake. He takes one look at me and yells, 'Hey, is the water cold?' Then he starts laughing like crazy."

"And the good-looking guy was Robbie?" I asked.

"No, Daddy. That was another guy. Robbie was just some dweeb out there playing football...Of *course* it was Robbie! But I'm not through with the story."

"Okay, *continuez s'il vous plait*," I replied with one of our family colloquialisms.

As requested, Lauren continued. "I'm shivering my way back to my cabin to change into dry clothes, and I run into Emily Jackson. And she yells, 'Oh my gosh, you've been down the zip line! Will you please go with me?' Well, I felt sorry for her because she was absolutely dying to ride it and nobody would go with her, so like a complete moron I agreed. Hardly another soul has been down the zip line even once, but twenty minutes later here I am coming up out of the water for a second time. And who is still playing football right by the lake but Robbie. This time he looks at me and yells something like, 'I guess the longer you stay in a frozen lake the warmer it gets.' And he had the biggest smile!

"I saw him again the next week at Young Life Club on campus, and we started talking about Sharp Top and the lake and stuff. When I got back to the house I was telling my roomies about him, and they all dared me to call Robbie up and ask him to the Kappa formal, so I did! And he accepted."

"But that's not the funny part." Lauren was on a roll now. This was a story she obviously enjoyed telling. "The funny thing is, one night after I asked Robbie to the formal, I was sitting at a computer kiosk over in Brackett Hall with Katie. This guy in a baseball cap comes up and starts talking to me. He had his cap pulled way down, almost covering his eyes. I was really into what I was working on at the computer, so I hardly looked at him. Well, this guy keeps talking and talking, and I figured it was just some guy trying to put the moves on me, you know. So I pretty much ignored him, and finally he went away."

"Don't tell me...!" Karin gasped into the phone.

"Yep," Lauren replied. "It was Robbie. When we were at the formal, he finally asked me what was up with that night at the computer lab. I was like, 'You're kidding! That was *you*?' Then we both laughed so hard...I thought I'd split my side. That formal was a blast! The sorority made T-shirts—'Dancin' in the Moonlight' was the theme—and that's exactly what we did."

Karin and I thought there was something unique in the way Lauren talked about Robbie during that phone call. We hadn't heard that level of interest in any other boy before. So it was with great anticipation that we awaited the weekend when Lauren was to bring Robbie home.

I was ready with my mental checklist when they arrived. At dinner before the concert, I did my fatherly duty and sized Lauren's new suitor up. He passed all the prerequisites with no problem: no apparent tattoos or piercings, good teeth, adequate personal hygiene, appropriate attire and conversation, proper diction, acceptable table manners, pleasant personality. But the young man had one trait I hadn't expected—he seemed a little shy. At least he appeared to be around Karin and me. Not that there's anything wrong with being quiet, but every father knows that sometimes you've got to watch out for the quiet ones. So I decided I'd better keep a keen eye out for PDAs—Public Displays of Affection.

Later that evening, we sat with jackets on at Lake Olmstead stadium in Augusta, home of the Green Jackets. But that night was not about baseball; it was about southern country rock. Wrapped up in jackets of red Georgia Bulldogs, garnet-and-black Gamecocks, and purple-and-orange Tigers, the crowd went wild when Aaron crooned "Blue Angel," then roared when he jumped into "The Call of the Wild." Too inhibited to really rock out at a concert, I stood and clapped while Karin and Lauren hooted and hollered along with our fellow Georgialinians. Robbie mirrored my restraint. During the break, Karin and Lauren headed off to the powder room, leaving Robbie and me alone to get better acquainted.

We sat there on the cold metal bench, just the two of us, staring out at the diamond painted on the brilliantly illuminated green field below us and the stage that had been set up over the pitcher's mound. With my lower back aching from the assault of the damp night air and my fanny fairly frozen to the icy bleacher, I could think of nothing entertaining to say. Robbie's lips were likewise sealed.

A really quiet guy, I thought. I crossed my arms in front of me and rubbed my upper arms in a vain attempt to warm up. *Too quiet. I'm gonna watch him like a hawk.*

Walking to the car after the concert, Karin and I trailed behind Robbie and Lauren. I had my PDA detection radar turned up to maximum sensitivity. But Robbie walked alongside Lauren with both hands thrust in his pockets, keeping plenty of personal space between himself and our daughter.

"Maybe he knows I'm on to him," I whispered to Karin as we walked hand-in-hand.

"What are you talking about?" Karin replied in a normal tone.

"Shhhh. Just watch," I said, nodding towards the two walking ahead of us. "I'll fill you in later." Out of the corner of my eye, I saw Karin look at me like I had lost my mind.

Robbie had never been to Augusta, Georgia, so we drove him down Washington Road, past the entrance to the Augusta National Golf Club. Set in the midst of nondescript urban sprawl, there's nothing to suggest that just on the other side of a row of tall lagustrum hedges, one is passing perhaps the most famous and beautiful golf course in the world. I kept one eye on the road and the other discreetly focused on the rearview mirror as we motored around the city and eventually back home. My PDA radar registered a flat zero all the way, as it did for the entire weekend.

A few weeks later, Lauren was home on summer break. One afternoon, we sat in the backyard with our feet dangling in the swimming pool. The conversation turned, as it often did in those days, to Robbie.

"So, what's the deal with you two?" I asked. "Are you going together?"

"We're talking." Lauren replied. "We're still talking."

"Talking is what you do when you're standing in the parking lot with a car salesman, trying to see whether or not you can trade cars. I don't get this 'talking' stuff," I said. "So, has he kissed you?"

My ears couldn't believe what had just come out of my mouth. I had never asked such a question of either of my daughters. I never needed to, because Karin always secured information of that nature for me.

"Daddy! What kind of a question is that?" Lauren looked shocked.

I was shocked too. But I decided not to back down. "Well, has he? I mean, it seems to me that you guys have been seeing an awful lot of each other in the past several weeks. I'm just trying to figure out if this is a friend-type relationship or something more."

Lauren gazed at her feet making little circles in the water. "Well, actually no. I mean, not yet. I can tell you this, it's not a 'friend-type relationship.' He's just sort of shy, I guess. There's been plenty of times when I thought he was gonna, but..."

"You know what, Chicken Little," I interrupted. "Sometimes you gotta take the bull by the horns yourself. You gotta break the ice. One of these days, just grab him by the ears and plant a big old smack right on him!"

"Daddy!" Lauren bent down and threw a huge splash into my face. "I can't believe you're saying that!"

"Neither can I, Chicken Little," I replied, soaked. "Neither can I."

A few weeks later Robbie came down for Lauren's twenty-first birthday party. We had a Low Country boil in the backyard, and along with the smell of boiling shrimp, there was the unmistakable essence of romance in the air.

They would come to call it their Perfect Summer. Robbie and Lauren both went back to Clemson for the second summer session. We'd get phone calls with descriptions of sunny days on the lake spent water skiing and wake boarding, and nighttime games of hide-and-seek played outside with dozens of their friends. Before fall semester, Robbie asked Lauren to travel to Michigan to meet his grandparents and the rest of the McKenzie clan. By the time school started again, there was no denying that the two were a couple. And Robbie's shyness around us was a thing of the past.

At half past one, Dr. Moore finally appeared in the doorway, looking tired.

"Lauren's in recovery now," he said. "You all can just wait right here for her; she'll be back up in an hour or so. Everything went pretty much like I thought it would. We cleaned out the wound again—still no sign of infection, and that's good. We put the spacer in with the antibiotic. Like I said, she's lost a lot of bone; that's not going to change.

"She lost quite a bit of blood during the operation, but that's to be expected too. We'll just play it by ear over the next several days. I'm still hoping she can go home by the middle or late next week. I'm going to have her fitted for a brace, probably Monday, and we'll start getting her up and around some then. Physical therapy will come by, and we'll teach you all and Lauren how to move with her leg injury."

Dr. Moore continued. "Like I've said before, she's got a long row to hoe. To tell you the truth, with it being November already, I don't see how she's going to be able to get back to Clemson this semester. But we'll just see what next week brings. I'll be back later on today, and I'm on call this weekend. Lauren's just going to need some rest for now. This is the second surgery in three days' time, so she's going to be tired. All of you just hang in there."

The same two ladies who had taken Lauren to surgery earlier in the day brought her back. While their tone had been upbeat and encouraging earlier, now they were soothing and hushed. "Here's your sweet baby back. Now ya'll take care of her and just let her rest. She's gonna be all right. We're gonna come by and see her next week. In the meantime, you folks take care of yourselves too."

Where following the accident and the first surgery Lauren looked injured, after this second operation she looked as sick as she did hurt. The dark black circles around her eyes contrasted sharply with her sallow complexion. The chest tube was gone, but in its place were a couple of new devices—one a plastic boot connected to an air pump that inflated and deflated periodically, the other a trapeze that had been rigged above the bed to allow her to reach up, with her good hand, and pull herself up. Not that she was remotely able to sit up in bed yet. Her leg, even more heavily bandaged than before, was an anchor that kept her pinned flat on her back.

Flocks of kids came again, and Lauren continued to do her best to entertain them. As usual, she never complained, but she did ask for something to subdue the itching caused by the morphine. As afternoon progressed into evening, she seemed too uncomfortable to even doze. We asked the nurse's station to limit the number of visitors with the exception of Robbie. Even then, Lauren's friends hung out in the lobby of the orthopedic wing, waiting for a chance to see her. I was amazed at their dedication and devotion to one of their own. It was the first day of Clemson's fall break; they could have been heading home or doing anything other than hanging out in a hospital.

Robbie remained Lauren's most stalwart devotee, sometimes quietly sitting with Lauren and studying when she dozed off, other times telling stories and jokes and making her laugh. If Lauren woke from a nap and found him not there, she asked where he'd gone. Now, with only a couple of friends at a time allowed in her room, Robbie, with his unfettered access, shuttled back and forth between Lauren and the friends waiting in the lobby, filling the role of information emissary and in-house entertainer.

He and I came to spend a lot of time together. Whenever there were "personal issues" to attend to in Lauren's room, all males were sent out. I had assumed the position of guardian of the door, making sure there were no disturbances until the all-clear was issued. I had my own chair that remained in the hall beside the door for just such purposes. If I happened to be the only male in the room, then I was banished to the hallway alone. On those occasions, I generally sat staring at my shoes, in an effort to avoid any knowledge of what was taking place in other nearby patient rooms. Having Robbie in exile with me provided a welcome diversion. On that Friday night, he told me of a plan that he and Lauren had developed before the accident.

"You know, tonight begins Clemson's fall break," he started. "We're out of school until next Wednesday, so we've got four whole days off. Lauren and I had planned to spend all four days together. We were going up to my parent's in Tega Cay. We were really looking forward to it. We were going to be away from school and all the people there, and we were just excited that we'd be together all four days, just the two of us—but with my parents at home at night, of course—and...well...none of that's gonna happen now."

The disappointment in his face was evident. Karin, Andrea, and I had wondered how Robbie was handling all this. So far, he'd been true blue, stick-like-glue. But this whole thing was a lot for any boyfriend to handle. He and Lauren had not been officially dating for very long. It was obvious that one of the things that had brought them together was a mutual enthusiasm for sports and all things outdoors. Robbie had to be contemplating what would happen to all that now. After all, his girlfriend was suddenly missing a bone in her leg. Would she ever be able to run, hike, play ball, or even walk again? Did he see a future with someone who might not be able to share all that with him? Could I blame him if he cut and ran? If he did, what would that do to Lauren? I braced myself for what he was going to say next.

Robbie went on. "Anyhow, I still want us to spend as much time together over fall break as possible. I don't want our plans to be ruined. After all, we promised each other, and I don't want to break that promise. So, I've been thinking. What would you and Mrs. Tarrant think if I spent the night with Lauren? No, wait a minute. I didn't mean that the way it sounded. I mean... what if I came up to the hospital on Sunday night and slept in a chair beside Lauren's bed? I could take care of her that night. You could still sleep on the cot in her room. I'd just take over the night-time duties. It could be like a slumber party." At that he broke into a grin from ear to ear.

"I think Karin and I would say that would be just fine," I replied. Then I quickly looked away, down the hallway, so he wouldn't see the tears shining in my eyes.

Chapter Five

What a friend we have in Jesus, All our sins and griefs to bear!
What a privilege to carry everything to God in prayer!
Oh, what peace we often forfeit, Oh, what needless pain we bear,
All because we do not carry everything to God in prayer.

"What a Friend We Have in Jesus"
Charles C. Converse
1832-1918

DROP...BY DROP...by drop...

Slowly and steadily, the strength, vitality, and love of a
stranger trickled into our daughter's veins. The weekend had
not brought the rally that we had hoped for following Lauren's
second surgery. To the contrary, we were told that without an
immediate transfusion, her organs would begin shutting down.

I watched the red liquid make its way through the tubes and
prayed that whoever had donated this precious part of themselves
had recently feasted on a T-bone steak. Bench pressed 400 lbs.
Led an immaculate life.

Gradually, the precious elixir wrought its changes. Color tinted the ashen face, sunken eyes brightened, and finally, pallid lips colored and curved into that familiar, glorious smile.

Truly, we are all one family. We are all brothers and sisters, children of God. Though we are different colors, sizes, and shapes, our parts are miraculously interchangeable, and are shared in love.

By Sunday night, Lauren had regained enough strength to be propped up, just in time to greet Robbie as he arrived for the much-anticipated slumber party.

"To start the festivities, I present you with this small token of our esteem, from the entire McKenzie clan." Robbie placed a coat-sized box carefully in Lauren's lap and stood back.

"What's this?" The smile on Lauren's face lit up with anticipation.

"Open it and see."

Still too weak to pull the paper away, Karin and Andrea stepped over and helped Lauren rip the package open.

Tossing the lid aside, all three girls peered into the box, then looked up simultaneously, grinning from ear to ear.

"It's my Columbia jacket! It's the one that was ruined the night of the accident!" Lauren beamed at Robbie. "Only it's brand new!"

Karin wrapped the bright-blue coat around Lauren's shoulders.

Lauren smoothed the garment with her good hand, "And you know what? *I'm* going to be good as new, too. Thanks, Robbie. It's my best get-well present ever!"

For the rest of the evening, we left Lauren's care in Robbie's capable hands. After Andrea and Karin headed back to the hotel, I retired to my corner cot and fell asleep amidst the quiet, happy chatter of my daughter and her most-devoted admirer.

Monday morning arrived, marking the beginning of Lauren's second week in the hospital. Though bright with the promise of going home, there was still much to overcome in only a few days. The challenge was shifting from stabilizing to strengthening—and that meant movement. Lauren was stronger, but she had been flat on her back for almost a week. If she was going to go home, she must find the strength to not only sit up, but to move.

First, she was fitted with a black, metal leg brace hinged at the knee so it could be locked out straight or adjusted to bend to a preset angle. Some of the bulky bandaging was removed, and then, ever so carefully, the brace was strapped onto Lauren's leg, starting at the top of her thigh all the way down to her ankle. That process was the most movement Lauren had attempted, without being totally under anesthesia, since the accident. As the recognized experts in moving Lauren's leg, Karin, Andrea, and I were pressed into service, helping reposition Lauren's leg as the fitting adjustments were made. When the nerve-wracking process was complete, we shared a feeling of significant accomplishment. At least it was conceivable that sometime soon, Lauren would be able to move.

Movement meant learning new techniques and using equipment often associated with the elderly. Since Lauren had a large gap caused by missing bone, putting any weight on her right leg was out of the question, even with the superstructure of the leg brace. A regular walker wouldn't do either, because her right hand was broken and she couldn't grip. Crutches would be a luxury that would have to wait until her hand healed. A wheelchair was certainly the best option for getting from point A to point B quickly, but because Lauren would be negotiating her way through a house, and hopefully soon thereafter, a college apartment, the focus of physical therapy was to learn to move in places where no wheelchair has ever gone.

So physical therapy began. Every move people take for granted was an ordeal of wrenching pain for Lauren and emotional torment for us. Getting out of bed for the first time and standing for a few seconds beside the walker was a two-hour ordeal that left us all sweating and exhausted.

Since the IV tree was well-adorned with multiple bags and gadgets, all lines and cords had to be untangled, repositioned, and dragged to accommodate standing. From there, it was still a long way to moving forward. While two people held onto her by a thick, cotton belt tied around her waist, Lauren had to pick her walker up with her left hand and scoot it forward as her right arm and hand rested on the other side of the walker frame on an elevated pad. By the end of the second day, this exhausting march had stretched not quite to the hospital room door.

It was hard to believe that only a few days earlier, I had watched my pony-tailed daughter race her boyfriend up a mountain!

I began to have serious doubts about our ability to take care of Lauren at home. When Dr. Moore left Lauren's room that night, I followed him into the hallway.

"I thought I'd be so happy to see Lauren get out of that bed today," I said. "And I *was* happy. But…I never imagined how painful it would be for her to move, or how difficult, and even how dangerous. Do you really think she'll be able to go home by the end of the week?"

"The first day or so is the hardest." he answered. "But Lauren's a fighter. She's young and strong and determined. She's got places to go and she intends to get herself there. That's obvious.

"I think you'll be amazed at how far she'll progress over the next couple of days. But if you're not comfortable with taking care of her at home initially"—he paused and looked me in the eye—"I can see about getting her into a nursing home for a couple of weeks. I'm sure there's a facility down in Aiken."

I took a step backward and looked away from his intent gaze. My mind raced back to years earlier. The girls were little. One evening, the family had gone to visit my nursing-home-bound grandmother. As we made our way down the white-tiled corridors, the typical pungent odor of disinfectant—laced with the consequences of elderly incontinence—was strong. Lined up outside of their rooms, residents were tied into their wheelchairs, waiting for lights out. My pig-tailed girls timidly walked that gauntlet, while aged, frail arms reached out with open hands, begging for a chance to cuddle and hold and be held in return.

The girls were so little. I wondered if they thought these sad, lonely people wanted to take them away from Karin and me, back into the dark recesses from which they had been rolled. Karin and I had been struck by their desperation and despair. Placing Lauren into such an environment was unthinkable.

Dr. Moore waited for a response, knowing full well that his suggestion had been more of a challenge for me to "step up to it" than a serious suggestion.

"Out of the question," I replied. "We'll make it work. After all, we're not in this alone."

Lauren's physical therapist was a bright, chipper young woman named Amy. Her can-do attitude and optimism infected the whole family. By mid-week we were surprising ourselves at how well we had learned the techniques required to help a disabled person get around.

Lauren amazed everyone. With rock-solid determination, she fought through the pain of moving her leg and heaved her way down the hospital corridors, pushing and pulling her walker and the IV tree like a prisoner struggling to break free of chains.

Amy set distance goals for each outing: first ten feet, then twenty, then thirty. Lauren tripled then quadrupled each objective. Next, Amy established an obstacle course in the hospital stairwell to teach Lauren how to ascend and descend stairwells by sliding her fanny up or down one step at a time, while someone supported her leg. Each new accomplishment brought us closer to going home.

By Thursday, Lauren was ready to be unhooked from the IV tree. We felt confident we could handle any barriers away from the hospital, and even capable of teaching Lauren's roommates how to help her get around at school.

Thursday afternoon, I measured the Buick to make sure the back seat would accommodate Lauren's leg, held out absolutely straight by the brace. Clemson's dean of students stopped by to personally assure Lauren that she was registered for the spring semester and would be able to make up what she had missed in the current semester, even if she didn't make it back until after Christmas.

Everything was falling into place. Although we still didn't know how or when Lauren would walk again, it was the eve of our homecoming. Excitement and optimism prevailed.

Andrea left early on Thursday afternoon, headed for Aiken, to get things ready at home. I'd been too busy to touch base with the remodeling crew since a week earlier. The condition of the house was unknown, but we knew for sure there'd be a mess to face. Andrea would at least clear a pathway from the front door to Lauren's room.

Karin stayed with Lauren in the hospital Thursday night. She'd get everything packed up and ready for an early departure on Friday morning. By the time I left the hospital for the hotel, all systems were go: T minus twelve hours and counting. We were on our way to final clearance from Mission Control, that is, Dr. Moore. At last, we'd have our daughter back home where she could rest and recuperate. God had graciously gotten her, and us, through the worst of this ordeal.

I woke early Friday morning and opened the draperies to get a final look at the foothills that cradle the city of Greenville. The landscape was alive with color as the first rays of sunlight began to burn through the morning mist. *Greenville's a beautiful city,* I thought, *but there's no place like home. I can't wait!*

I showered, shaved, and packed up. With suitcases ready and waiting by the door, I made a final check around the room for stray items. The cell phone in my pocket rang just as I was picking up the first suitcase and heading out the door. *That'll be Karin and Lauren,* I thought, *telling me to hurry up 'cause they're ready to hit the road home!* I glanced at the phone's display before I answered. Sure enough, Karin's cell phone calling.

Full of good cheer, I sang my impersonation of Robin Williams' "Good Morning, Vietnam," into the receiver: "Good morning, Homeward Bound!"

Lauren was crying. "Daddy, I can't go home. They're taking me back to surgery."

Blindsided by the same evil vortex that had attacked a week ago when Andrea and I were innocently leaving the hospital for a whirlwind trip back to Aiken, I stumbled back into the room and sat down hard on the bed.

"Oh, *no!*" I moaned. "No, no, *no,* Chicken Little. What do you mean? That can't be. What happened? I don't understand." A wave of nausea broke in my throat.

"Dr. Moore came in to sign me out," Lauren cried, heartbroken. The depth of her obvious devastation, and now my own, was frightening.

"He checked my leg and he says it's become infected. They're going to operate on me again, in just a few minutes. I just want to go home, Daddy. Please come over here quick!"

"I will, Lauren. I'll leave right now. I'll be there in a minute. Can you put Mama on the phone."

"Hurry, Daddy, hurry." Then she passed the receiver to Karin.

"What's going on, Karin?" I asked, surprised to hear my own voice begin to crack and my vision blur with tears.

"Dr. Moore came in for a final check. Oh, Michael! Lauren and I were so happy and excited. Then he unwrapped Lauren's leg and found signs of infection. He showed me; it's unmistakable."

As usual, Karin was maintaining control for Lauren's sake. She amazed me even then. Civilization as we know it might be falling down around her, but if her children needed her strength, Karin could be titanium.

"Just hurry, okay?" she said. "They're getting Lauren ready right now, and I really need you."

I burst out of the hotel room and took the emergency stairs two at a time down to the parking lot. Unlike Karin, I was alone and had no one for whom I must feign courage. Sucked into the wicked whirlwind that now seemed to swirl either directly around me or always somewhere nearby, I reeled through the parking lot to the car as if just bricked in the head by airborne wreckage from a shattering life.

The silence of the closed environment of the car seemed to increase the ferocity of the turmoil that swirled within me. I needed help—of what immediate sort I didn't know, but I needed something.

I pulled out my cell phone and dialed my brother. It was Friday, his day off. He should be home. The caller ID must have disclosed my identity, because he answered the phone with, "Hey, Bro! So, are ya'll on your way home with Lauren?"

At the sound of his voice, I lost it. I had shed more tears in the past ten days than in the previous forty-five years of my life. But I didn't care; the swirling whirlwind had sucked away personal pride.

"Bobby, Lauren's not coming home," I sobbed. "Her leg's become infected. It's the worst that could happen, Man. I'm scared to death. She's going back to surgery. I'm on the way to the hospital."

"Okay, Bro. What do you want me to do? Do you want me to come up there? Pat and I can leave right now if you need us. Just tell me what you want me to do."

"Yeah, I do. I want ya'll to come up here. I don't know what we need or what you can do, but I just want you to come up."

"Okay, Mike. You hang in there, Bro. We'll be praying for Lauren, and we'll see you in a couple of hours."

As I sped through the city streets, Dr. Ellis's dire predictions of a week earlier joined the rubble spinning in my mind. I felt as scared and helpless as the little brother who watched that water moccasin shoot out from under the well-house so many years ago. I needed my brother, and I needed Becky. I needed someone who could stop this whirlwind. I needed a savior for myself and my family.

I already have a Savior, I thought. But where is He right now when things are spinning out of control? Didn't He and I have a deal, of sorts, even if it was…well…unspoken? But in my mind, there was an agreement, nonetheless. Lauren had already begun a mission of helping others to know Christ. That was obvious, if only from the sentiments expressed in all the cards that we'd been reading in her hospital room and the endless parade of friends and high school kids that she had touched through Young Life.

Clearly, she had devoted her life to the Lord and was destined for a career in ministry. Hadn't we struck a bargain, He and I, over the last several days? I would entrust the care of my child to Him, He would protect her and make her whole again, and she would devote her life to spreading the gospel of Jesus Christ. I was upholding my end of the bargain, I reasoned. Surely He'd not double cross me and allow any additional harm to come to Lauren *now*.

Maybe I've been bothering Him too much the past week or so, my thoughts continued. *After all, haven't I always tried to handle everything myself as much as possible? Nothing's changed in the rest of the world—the same afflictions are out there as before Lauren got hurt. God's still got to handle all that. As devastating as Lauren's situation is, there are even greater problems out there. Maybe I've become too reliant. Maybe I better begin handling things a little better on my own; stop being blindsided by every circumstance that comes along.*

Recalling my conversation a few days earlier with Dr. Moore, I renewed my resolve to step up my game as I wheeled into the hospital parking lot. Racing to Lauren's room, I pulled myself together and arrived in time to meet the same kind ladies who had rolled Lauren to surgery a week earlier.

"Oh, look, dahlin'," the first lady said to Lauren as I entered the room. "Here's yo' daddy."

Lauren had already been sedated.

"Hey, Daddy," she whispered, "I'm glad you got here. I'm gonna be okay though, right?"

"You bet you are, Chicken." I smiled down at my little girl and stroked the hair from her forehead. "I'm just so sorry you've got to go through this. But you'll be fine. I know it."

The orderlies began the all-too-familiar trip down the hall. Karin walked on one side holding Lauren's unbroken hand. I was in my place on Lauren's other side. Then we returned to

Lauren's room, just Karin and I. At last, Karin could let down her brave façade, and she fell into my arms and wept.

"This is what they've been warning us about, Michael. Ever since Lauren was hurt, they've warned us and warned us. Now it's coming true. She can't lose her leg, she just can't! God won't let that happen, will He?"

I had no answers.

We stood for a long while by the window of that little hospital room, looking down at the atrium below. Andrea had packed up the flowers that were still fresh, along with the plants, stuffed animals, and candy and hauled them down to Aiken the day before. There was little left to disguise the stark reality of our circumstances.

Neither of us were aware of my brother's approach until I felt a hand on my shoulder.

There was little visually to suggest that the man in front of me was a relative. Bobby has the dark hair and fair complexion of my mother. I, according to my family, had been found in a turnip patch, since I bore no resemblance to any known family members. The age difference between us was enough to keep us at different stages growing up, but Bobby's advanced years and the worldliness that came with age, often gave me an advantage over my peers.

Once, when I was twelve and in junior high, a thug from the hood's corner of the playground cut the lunch line directly in front of me. Reeking of smoke, a pack of cigarettes rolled into the sleeve of his T-shirt, black hair slicked down with Vitalis, and wearing blue jeans and high-top sneakers, the ninth-grade hoodlum was more than a match for a pipsqueak of a seventh grader like me. But incensed at the injustice of the crime, I lipped off to the line-cutter, who promptly invited me to meet him after school behind the cafeteria, where we'd settle our differences properly.

High school was dismissed ten minutes before junior high. On this day, like every school day, Bobby waited to pick me up in front of Aiken Junior High. Supremely confident of his response, I explained the situation to my brother, who, true to my expectations, agreed to handle the situation for me. We rounded the corner of the cafeteria, where the hood waited, taking a drag on his cigarette.

"You got a problem with my little brother?" Bobby boomed. "'Cause if you do, then I got a problem with you, punk!"

"Uh, no…sir. Everything's cool." The hood snuffed out his cigarette under his sneaker. "Your little brother's got a lot of spunk. I was just gonna tell him that too. Hey, look, I gotta go. It was nice meetin' ya." At that, he took off toward the school bus parking lot.

Sometimes you need somebody to watch your back. Today, standing in that hospital room, was one of those days.

Karin and I packed up dirty clothes for Bobby and Pat to take to a laundromat. As they were leaving, I touched Bobby on the sleeve.

"Bobby, take our car, okay? Look in the door pocket; I can't remember whether the driver's side or the passenger side. In one of those side pockets there's a whole stack of mail. It's the bills for this month. We've been so distracted that we keep forgetting to mail them. While you're out, drop them in a mailbox somewhere, okay?"

"Sure, Bro. We'll take care of it. See you after a while."

Another hour passed before Dr. Moore came in.

"I cleaned the wound again." His face was serious, almost stern. "We've got Infectious Diseases working on what's causing the problem, but it may be a day or two before they can make a determination. Until we know the exact bacteria, I'm putting her on vancomycin.

"We're going to have to take her back to surgery day after tomorrow and do another clean out. I'm not on call this weekend, but I'm coming in on Sunday just to do this surgery. I want to see for myself how things are looking."

"Another surgery the day after tomorrow? So soon?" Karin's face grew white.

"This is what we were afraid of all along," Dr. Moore looked from Karin to me, then back to Karin. "It's not the end of the world, but it *is* a serious situation. We want to do everything we can to keep the infection out of the bone, or catch it as quickly as possible if it does spread to the bone. Right now, it seems to be localized. If it goes to the bone, then we've got an even bigger set of problems. I don't want that to happen."

"Will Sunday be the last operation?" I asked.

"Probably not," Dr. Moore replied.

"But how much can Lauren take? How many times can you do this?"

"We'll do it as many times as it takes." And then, with determination, Dr. Moore said, "We will do whatever it takes to get this infection under control. Whatever it takes."

Later, Lauren came back, reattached to the tubes and wires from which she had struggled all week to break free. Despite the return of the morphine, she was more uncomfortable than she'd been since the accident.

Bobby and Pat returned with clean clothes and confirmation that the bills had been mailed. Robbie came in and stayed late, vowing to return early the next day.

The weekend was a pit of pain, transfusions, frustration, anxiety, and fallen hope. Saturday night I sat in my chair in the hallway outside Lauren's room. Robbie had already returned to Clemson. The hallway was quiet. As usual, I stared down at my shoes, head in hands. Twelve days of sitting in the hall had made me as familiar a sight to the nurses as each of them had become to me. During those days, I watched the occupants of the nearby rooms change, then change again, then change again.

I marveled at how the steady stream of patients never let up. Only the faces were different.

From behind, someone gently massaged my stooped shoulders. It was one of the RNs who routinely worked the weekend night shift.

"Don't worry, Dad," she said. "She'll be all right. The Lord will take care of her. You'll see. Just trust Him."

"Yeah, I know," I replied.

But I was no longer convinced.

True to his pledge, Dr. Moore took Lauren back to surgery early Sunday morning. He was back in Lauren's room to speak to us before eleven o'clock.

"We don't have control of the infection yet. That wound is really angry. Infectious Diseases hasn't been able to determine what we're up against, either. All we know right now is that it's a gram-negative bacteria.

"It's making Lauren a very sick young lady. We're going to have to do whatever's necessary to get that infection under control. I'm afraid she'll have to go back for another surgery. We'll give her tomorrow to rest, but Tuesday morning we'll have another look. This is not a good situation."

"Oh, no," Karin groaned. "She's getting sicker and sicker. You can just look at her and see how she's suffering. How many more operations can she stand?"

"We'll come to a point where we have to stop," Dr. Moore replied. His face was evidence of his deep concern. "But, we're not there yet."

"Are we at the point where"—I hesitated in mid-question—"where removing her leg may be the only option?" The question had been sitting on my tongue, but I hadn't had the guts to put it into words. And I could not bring myself to use the A word. However, I had to know what Dr. Moore was thinking.

He paused for a long while before finally answering, "I don't know. Possibly."

I pressed on. "Do you feel there's a chance she'll come out of this next surgery without her leg?" I looked at him and felt my hands turning to ice.

Dr. Moore was past the point of being able to provide hope where there was none. Time was no longer on our side. The doctor was obviously struggling with what to say, but he seemed determined to give it to us as straight as possible.

Again, he paused before saying, "There's definitely that chance."

I needed more information. I needed to know exactly what he was thinking. I pressed again. "Do you think there's a better chance that she will *not* have her leg when she comes out of surgery on Tuesday, or a better chance that she *will* have her leg?"

I knew I was asking him to play God. No doctor wants to be forced to give odds. But I needed his honest opinion.

This time, Dr. Moore didn't hesitate. "I'd say there's a better chance that she will *not* have her leg after Tuesday's surgery."

Karin cupped her hands over her mouth and nose, as if she had just heard the unspeakable.

As much as I hated to hear his answer, this time no evil tornado swirled in around me. I wasn't unprepared for this. I glanced at my wife, still standing in the same astonished position. She returned my glance, but instead of fear in her eyes, I saw raw strength.

She dropped her hands and turned back to Dr. Moore. "What about a second opinion?" Karin searched his face for a sign that she had offended him. "Please don't misunderstand. Michael and I both believe you've been fantastic. You've done so much for Lauren and for all of us. I know you don't want this to happen, and you're doing everything you can to save Lauren's leg. But is there anyone else, or anyplace else that might have more experience with this type injury or infection?"

"Mrs. Tarrant, if I were in your position, I'd be asking the same questions. So don't worry that you're offending me. I admire your determination. The fact is, though, I don't know off the top of my head who or where you might turn. We already know the nature of Lauren's injuries is extremely rare. At this point we're more concerned about preventing amputation than we are reconstruction.

"I studied at Shands at the University of Florida," Dr. Moore said. "But the only doctor there who might have been remotely qualified in a case like this has long since retired. Frankly, you're already in one of the few places in the Southeast that's qualified to care for Lauren."

He paused and examined the floor for a moment, then looked up. "I don't want to discourage you, but let me share another recent case with you. I had a little boy who got his leg caught under a lawnmower. He got infected, and we reached the point where amputation was our only option. His parents airlifted him to Duke. But there was nothing they could do up there, either. He lost his leg. His parents spent thousands of dollars and endured untold anguish, but in the end there was no difference in the outcome.

"There is no magic cure out there that you'll find if you just look hard enough. I say that because I don't want either of you to feel like you've let Lauren down, that you could have secured a better outcome for her if you'd just tried harder."

He looked from Karin to me and back to Karin before he continued. "However, all that being said, I'll do anything I can to help you. But there's very little time. We can't afford to postpone Tuesday's surgery, or we'll be risking much more than Lauren's leg."

"If you could write down the exact, technical description of Lauren's injury," I said. "That would help us."

Dr. Moore pulled out a pen and pad, then printed a lengthy diagnosis.

He ripped the paper from the pad and handed it to me. Karin read it over my shoulder. After we asked a few more questions, Dr. Moore started toward the hallway. Then he turned back to us, scribbled something else on another piece of paper, and handed it to Karin.

"Let me know what you decide. I'll do whatever you want. Here's my pager number. If you need to get in touch with me, or if you contact another surgeon, have him give me a call." He smiled. "Good luck. If there's anybody out there who can help Lauren, I really hope you find them."

There was no doubting Dr. Moore's sincerity. Because of his kindness and personal concern, our family had formed a bond with this man during the past several days. I knew he would do everything possible to help Lauren, even if it meant transferring her somewhere else.

When the door closed behind him, Karin looked at me. Her eyes were tired but beautiful. They seemed to burn with intensity. The enemy about which we had been so amply warned, the one that filled us with dread, had finally raised its ugly head.

"Call Donna Hudson," she commanded.

There was no time for hand-wringing or woe-is-us pity parties. There was no need for discussion about what we should do. I was in complete agreement and ready to comply with Karin's directive.

"Andrea and I will stay here and wait for Lauren to come back from surgery," Karin continued. "You take the phone outside where you can get a better signal."

"It's almost eleven," I answered. "Do you think she'll be in church?"

"I think she might be Catholic." Karin rolled her eyes toward the ceiling, thinking. "Maybe she goes to Mass on Saturday. I don't know, maybe she's Methodist. It doesn't matter, call her anyway. You can leave a message if you have to. We're running out of time."

There was no time to wait for an elevator. I tore down the stairs and through the construction zone into an open courtyard, dialing 411 before the door slammed shut behind me.

"Alltel directory assistance. How can I help you?"

"Operator, I need the number for Donna Hudson, H-U-D-S-O-N, in Aiken, South Carolina.

"Thank you, hold for that number, please."

I memorized the number the computerized voice parroted back to me, dialed it, and prayed someone would pick up.

"Hello?" came the female voice on the other end of the line.

"Donna, this is Mike Tarrant, Karin Tarrant's husband. You used to work with Karin, remember?"

"Why yes, Mike, of course I remember Karin. And you too. How are you?"

"Well, right now I'm not so good, to tell you the truth. I've got an extreme emergency, and I need your help." *This lady must think I'm a mad man,* I thought. *She's not seen or heard from Karin or me in two years. And here I am frantically calling her, telling her I need her help.*

"Our younger daughter, Lauren, was hit by a car while riding a moped a couple of weeks ago. She's been in a hospital in Greenville ever since. I'm calling you from there. She has a badly injured leg, and it's become infected. She's had four surgeries already, the latest just this morning. Her doctor just met with Karin and me and told us that she'll have to go back to surgery again day after tomorrow. He'll probably have to amputate her leg then."

"Oh, My God, Mike. No!" she interjected.

"Yes, ma'am. But her doctor here is willing to do anything that might save Lauren's leg, including transferring her to another doctor. Karin and I will airlift Lauren anywhere. I hate to bother you, especially on a Sunday morning, but we have no time. The infection has to be brought under control. Would it be possible for you to search the databases for us, maybe even this morning?"

"Yes, of course. I'll go into the office right now. It's just around the corner from my house. I can be there in ten minutes. Read me the diagnosis and give me your cell phone number. I'll call you back within an hour."

I read the diagnosis and thanked Donna profusely before hanging up.

I sat down on a bench in the red-brick courtyard for a moment, just to wind down. Looking up at the overcast November sky, I remembered something Becky told me years ago: *The Lawd don't let nothin' happen that He cain't make good come of it.*

Several years ago, when the family was at one of those times when finances could use a boost, Karin contemplated going back to work. She used her degree in dental hygiene by working part time for various dentists when the girls were small, then for a couple of years as a part-time instructor in the dental department at Aiken Technical College. Though we got along fine for the most part on my salary, occasionally Karin's supplemental income came in mighty handy. One Sunday night, I sat in the den watching *60 Minutes* while Karin and the girls were elsewhere in the house. A segment came on about a company called "Best Doctors," founded by two men who lived in, of all places, Aiken, South Carolina.

Greg Smith and Stephen Naifeh are two New York attorneys who started a company that published a list of the best lawyers in America. They developed a method to research and identify, by specialty, the most competent attorneys in the United States. In their spare time they co-authored a Pulitzer prize winning biography of Jackson Pollack.

Apparently they grew tired of the big-city rat race and the northern ice and snow. Looking to the Deep South to defrag and defrost, they moved down and renovated an old, ramshackle mansion in Aiken, set amidst the evergreen enchantment of century-old magnolias and live oak trees.

But when Greg was suddenly stricken with an illness that doctors said would be fatal, the two partners used the research methodology they developed to identify America's best attorneys, this time to find a doctor who could cure Greg. Sure enough, it worked. They found a doctor who made Greg well again, and in the process a new company, Best Doctors, was launched.

The *60 Minutes* segment traced the history of the company and featured some of the miraculous recoveries that had been brought about by this remarkable organization. Best Doctors became the world's leading resource for patients, families, and physicians seeking expert medical information and guidance to treat illnesses and injuries of all kinds.

I was too fascinated to leave the TV set. When the show was over, I found Karin upstairs, taking a bath. I sat down on the floor in our bedroom and shouted through the bathroom door, excited about what I had just seen. Between splashes, she answered that she had seen an ad in the Aiken paper for a research assistant at the company.

Within a few days, she had the job.

Karin remained at Best Doctors for a couple of years. After she left, we understood that Greg and Steve had sold the company. The new owners had moved most of the operations up north somewhere, but there was still an office in Aiken where Donna Hudson, Karin's former colleague, worked.

As promised, in less than an hour, Donna called.

"Mike, I've got five names for you, all of them world-class specialists in limb salvage."

I wrote furiously while Donna read each name, the hospital with which they were associated, and their contact numbers. When she'd finished, I had a list of physicians associated with some of the most prestigious hospitals in America.

"Donna, how do I choose?" I asked. "How do I know which of these five guys to call first?"

"I don't think you can go wrong with any of them," Donna replied. "But if she were my daughter, I'd start at Johns Hopkins in Baltimore. That would be Dr. Baxter."

"Then that's where I'll start," I replied. "Donna, I can't tell you how much this means to Karin and me. How can I ever thank you?"

"You just get Lauren fixed, Michael. Call me and let me know what happens, okay? I want to know where you go. And if you need anything else, you call me immediately!"

"Yes, ma'am. I will. God bless you, Donna. I'll be in touch."

I dialed the after-hours number listed for Dr. Baxter as soon as Donna left the line. To my surprise, instead of an answering machine, a receptionist answered the phone. I explained Lauren's situation as succinctly as I could, then waited for her response, braced for a put-off. *These people don't know me. They probably couldn't care less.* The best I allowed myself to hope for was a recommendation that I call back tomorrow.

Instead, she gave me the telephone number of the physician on call and suggested that if I dialed him immediately, I had a good chance of catching him at the hospital. Steadying my fingers, I punched in the numbers she had just dictated.

"Bay Orthopedics, Dr. McCall." I couldn't believe my luck had held. Another human.

I introduced myself and explained the situation to the total stranger on the other end of the line. I finished the monologue by reading Dr. Moore's diagnosis.

"Can you help my daughter?" I asked, holding my breath as I waited for his answer.

"I have no doubt Dr. Baxter can help your daughter. How quickly can you get her up here?"

I thought for a second. I hadn't an inkling how to arrange a transfer, much less any clue as to how long it might take to work out the details.

"We'll be there tomorrow."

It had been just over an hour since we talked to Dr. Moore.

Late Monday afternoon, two paramedics from the ambulance company rolled a gurney to Lauren's hospital room door. The folks at Memorial Hospital, especially Lauren's patient coordinator, had worked tirelessly for a day and a half to complete arrangements for the transfer.

Lauren had been feverish and sick throughout the day—too sick to be aware of the transfer or the preparations of the past twenty-four hours. But now, the activity of nurses disconnecting tubes and reconnecting others roused her.

"What's going on?" She raised her head slightly, taking in the goings-on around her, managing only a whisper to Karin, as if mustering every ounce of strength left in her body.

Then her eyes opened wide. She looked from me standing at the foot of her bed, then back to Karin, sitting beside her.

Trembling with weakness and fear, Lauren propped herself up with her one good arm. Huge tears rolled from the corners of her eyes, down her cheeks and dripped onto the bed linens. "Am I going to die?"

"Oh, no, Lauren. No, no, no." Karin cradled Lauren's curly head in her arms and rocked her back and forth. "We're just transferring you to another hospital that has more experience dealing with injuries like yours. We think we can get you home faster that way. That's all, Lauren. I promise. You must believe me, Chicken. That's all."

Now tears streamed down Karin's face as well.

Too weak and too sick to do anything but accept Karin's explanation and reassurance, Lauren allowed the attendants to shift her onto the stretcher waiting beside the bed.

With Robbie holding Lauren's free hand, and Karin, Andrea, and I following, the attendants rolled the stretcher swiftly down the hallway of the orthopedic wing that had become so familiar to us.

We were forced to wait when staff members stopped what they were doing to tell Lauren goodbye. I knew most of them by their first names. They stopped for Angie, the one who called Lauren "Little Bit" and made us all laugh with stories of her kids. Farther down the hall Amy, Lauren's physical therapist, halted the entourage to whisper something in Lauren's ear. Nurses sprinted from behind the orthopedic desk to touch our sick child on the cheek one last time, or brush back her hair, or just smile.

What are we doing? I thought, watching our retinue progress toward the elevators. *These people love Lauren. They've been doing everything humanly possible to get her well—to save her leg. And we're taking her away from this to . . . who knows what? Are we doing the right thing, or are we making a mistake that Lauren will have to pay for, for the rest of her life?*

Dear Father in Heaven, I prayed as we walked, *I know I've called on You a lot lately. Two weeks ago, I couldn't drive up here without Your help. Or even fall asleep once I got here. Maybe it was selfish and wrong of me to ask so much of You, Father. Maybe Becky was wrong to talk to You every afternoon. I don't know. Maybe I was right to try to take care of my own problems before all this happened. Maybe now I need to start taking care of things myself again, without bothering You so much. I'll try not to be blindsided anymore and I'll try to handle the rest of this by myself. I won't ask You for so much hands-on now, Lord. Just please don't let any more roadblocks get thrown our way.*

We reached the elevator just as Dr. Moore approached. He flashed Lauren a huge, confident smile, then leaned down and said something I couldn't make out. He smiled again, straightened, and walked back to Karin and me.

"Infectious Disease just called." He handed Karin a note. *Serratia marcescens* had been carefully printed across the paper. "That's the gram-negative bacteria that's infected Lauren's leg. I'll get this info to the folks up in Maryland. They'll have it before you get there."

"Well, then should we—?" I started.

Dr. Moore interrupted. "Don't keep the ambulance waiting any longer. You know I'll be praying for Lauren. She's a wonderful girl. You're lucky to have each other. Let me know how things are going, and if you need me, you have my number."

The elevator slid open. The attendants pushed the stretcher in, Robbie still clinging to Lauren's hand. We rode in silence down to the ground level, where the ambulance waited. The attendants raised the framework under the stretcher, and Lauren began to slide into the back of the vehicle. Robbie stood on the ground, stretching his arm to keep hold of her hand as the bed rolled forward. He broke his grip only when his fingers could no longer reach.

Karin and Andrea climbed in beside Lauren, along with an attendant. I had the passenger door open and one foot on the running board when I saw two figures, dressed in immaculate green scrubs, appear at the back of the vehicle. In a flash of recognition, I realized they were the two ladies who had taken Lauren to each of her surgeries.

"Godspeed, child," one called gently as the rear doors slammed shut. "Godspeed."

Chapter Six

And Jesus said unto them…If ye have faith as a grain of a mustard seed, ye shall say unto this mountain, Remove hence to yonder place; and it shall remove; and nothing shall be impossible unto you.

—Matthew 17:20

THE LEAR JET stood poised on its landing gear on the runway at Greenville's downtown airport. With no hesitation, the ambulance driver drove directly onto the tarmac alongside the white jet, gleaming in the glow of the street lights that had just come on in the deepening twilight.

I was struck by the sheer beauty of the aircraft. The aerodynamic nose, the swept-back wings, the thin, almost delicate fuselage that ended in the graceful tail section, all thrust through the stratosphere by two small, twin jet engines attached to the rear of the fuselage just above the wings. The machine was the quintessence of man's successful attempts to defeat the pull of gravity, to approach the speed of sound, to control his own environment, and even defy the laws of nature. It was exactly what we needed.

As soon as we stopped, I hopped out of the front seat, ran to the back of the ambulance, and watched Karin and Andrea climb out. The attendants rolled Lauren's stretcher backward into the night air.

"We'll get her into the plane right away and out of this dampness," one of the attendants called as they rushed Lauren, wrapped in white blankets, to the jet's door. "The pilot's up there, just outside of the cockpit, waiting for you."

Karin and Andrea trotted alongside as the two men rushed to maneuver the stretcher into position by the doorway, then lifted the stretcher and Lauren off the framework. With one man halfway up the stairway, the other lifted the stretcher over his head while walking up, maintaining a level position front-to-back, as well as side-to-side, so Lauren's propped leg and arm remained stable.

Satisfied that she was safely inside, I approached the pilot.

"How ya' doin? I'm Mike Tarrant." I thrust my hand out to shake hands with the tall, graying man. "I think you'll be needing this."

I held out a check that represented a substantial chunk of Karin's and my rainy-day savings. But we had agreed this wasn't a rainy day, this was a monsoon. We'd have sold the house if we'd had to.

"Good to meet you, Mike. Thanks very much." He folded the check and placed it in his shirt pocket. "I'm Jeff Stevens; I'll be flying this thing. The guy down there by the tail, loading your luggage, that's Greg Williams, my co-pilot. Jim Flint is the EMT on this flight. You'll meet him when you board. He's inside getting your daughter ready for take off."

"So, Jeff, how long is the flight to Baltimore?" I asked.

"This," Jeff looked behind him at the jet, "is a hot rod! It's a Lear 25, and it cruises at about 525 miles per hour at 40,000 feet. We'll be at BWI in an hour. We just came over from Atlanta, been here about twenty minutes, and I guess we left there about forty minutes ago. With any luck, we'll have your daughter in Baltimore safe and sound, and I'll be back home in time to catch the end of Monday night football, so long as the traffic from the Atlanta airport's not too bad."

He put his hand on my shoulder as we walked toward the open door of the jet. "Looks like Greg's finished up. What say we go get that little girl of yours well?"

If the aircraft had looked small from the outside, it looked even smaller on the inside. The ceiling in the passenger compartment was low, too low to allow an average-sized adult to stand up straight. Two seats lined up against the port side, each with a window. The stretcher on which Lauren lay took up the entire starboard side. Karin and Andrea, already on board, were buckled in, side by side, on the bench seat that traversed the rear of the plane.

Jim, the EMT, directed me to a seat on the port side, then took the seat in front of me, just behind the open cockpit. In that position he was able to lean across the constricted aisle and easily tend to his patient. With the pilot and co-pilot in their positions, the craft was at full capacity.

The jets hummed with restrained power as Jeff maneuvered the plane forward into take-off position. We swung a hard right, and I watched him push the throttle forward. Both jets responded immediately, as if relieved to release the pent-up force that had held the craft on the ground. Within seconds we were airborne, blasting northeastward into the night sky, leaving the lights of Greenville, the Upstate, and all things familiar in our wake.

This was the sort of adventure the girls loved, especially when they were little. It should have ranked right up there with riding in the cockpit of the monorail at Disney World or having the first seat on the Mindbender at Six Flags. It should have illuminated their faces with excitement and exhilaration. But when I turned and glanced at Andrea and Karin, there was only apprehension reflected in their expressions.

And what must Lauren be thinking? She was not so heavily sedated that she couldn't comprehend the seriousness of the situation. Had she believed Karin and me when we had reassured her that she wasn't going to die? I wanted to reach across the aisle and touch her, but even the hand that wasn't broken was tucked tightly into the blankets to keep her as immobilized as possible.

The noise level was such that quiet conversation wasn't possible, and no one wanted to rouse Lauren from her intermittent dozing, so we sat in silence, staring out into the empty, dark sky. The cloud cover below us obscured any lights or landmarks that might have given us a clue as to our progress toward Baltimore. As far as I could tell, my family was adrift, lost somewhere in the universe.

I tried to follow our progress on a map in my mind's eye as we glided through the sky. Finally, a break in the clouds revealed the lights of a city below us. I reckoned it was Norfolk, just across the North Carolina-Virginia border. Then Jeff turned around from his seat in the cockpit to announce we were approaching Baltimore already.

"We're only a few minutes out," he shouted, so Karin and Andrea could hear him. "But we're going to have to circle for a while; BWI just closed. They're not telling me what's going on, so I can't give you an estimate of how long we're going to be up here. Just sit tight. I'll let you know as quickly as I find out."

Jim, the EMT, was leaning over Lauren, straining to hear something she was saying. I looked at Karin. At her widened eyes, I gave a shrug and held out my hands, palms up. Nothing to do but wait.

I twisted back around to see Jim preparing a hypodermic needle. Lauren had been without any medication for a while now. Knowing that she was in pain made the delay even more disturbing. Nothing I could do about that, either.

We lost altitude. Outside my window, the blanket of clouds lifted briefly, just long enough to reveal the Washington-Baltimore megalopolis glowing in its vastness, spectacular and intimidating.

Surely, somewhere out there, we'd find what we were looking for.

Jeff leaned back and called to us again. "Okay, folks. We've been circling about twenty minutes now. The tower just called. We're cleared to land. They never did tell me what the problem was, but that's a no-never-mind. Make sure you've got your seatbelts tight. We'll be on the ground shortly. Jim, get Lauren ready, okay?"

Jim tucked Lauren's blankets in even tighter to avoid any bounce that would cause her more discomfort. He needn't have worried. The landing was perfect, soft as a feather floating down into a puddle, without so much as a ripple.

Ours had been the only plane taking off or landing when we left Greenville, but at this huge airport, we were a mere speck taxiing amid behemoths. Starting and stopping as we cautiously proceeded toward the terminal, we waited to cross runways while giant airliners screamed by, blasting us with jet fumes. Before we even left the plane, I knew we were in a different world from the one we had left behind in South Carolina.

Eventually, our tiny craft was able to make its way through the cross traffic. We pulled up and parked at the private terminal among about two dozen other personal and corporate jets.

Jeff opened the door and motioned for Karin, Andrea, and me to follow him into the unseasonably warm, misty night. The jet directly in front of us, with an impressive family crest painted on its monolith of a tail, was the largest private plane I'd ever seen.

"Dodi Fayed," Jeff said in response to my amazed stare.

"Say what?" I looked at him as if he had suddenly spoken a foreign language.

"Dodi Fayed," he repeated. "You know, the guy Princess Dianna was engaged to, or was dating or something, over in England. That's his father's jet. He owns a department store over in London. I hear he flies his grandkids over here pretty regularly to shop at Toys R Us. Can you believe it? These people fly a jet across the Atlantic to take the kids to a toy store, like you and I would throw 'em in the backseat of the van and head for Walmart. It's a whole different world out here."

"You can say that again," I replied in a quiet voice.

He disappeared into the plane. A couple of minutes later Jeff, Jim, and Greg had Lauren safely on the ground beside us.

I bent down and whispered into Lauren's ear, "How was that plane ride, Chicken?"

"It was okay, I guess," she whispered back. "Can we hurry, Daddy? My leg really hurts."

"Yeah, we'll hurry. I see the ambulance coming around the corner. It won't be long now, I promise. We'll get you something to stop that hurting, okay?"

"Okay." She forced a smile that brought a lump to my throat.

The ambulance pulled up. We thanked the three jet jockeys while Lauren was carefully loaded into that vehicle. Karin and Andrea climbed in the back with Lauren and the ambulance attendant; I rode shotgun with the driver. There was only a small window between the driver's compartment and the patient area of the vehicle. I couldn't tell what was going on back there.

The driver was barely out of his teens, obviously of foreign origin, but he spoke perfect English. He even had the distinctive Maryland accent I had learned to recognize years earlier when I was a Clemson student. My freshman year roommate was a great guy from the DC area. There had been plenty of kids from up here who wanted to get far enough away from home to escape their parent's immediate grasp. Taken as a whole, they were a good group, Southern enough to know what grits were, Northern enough to think that we natives talked funny.

"I guess they explained to you that you're not going to Johns Hopkins, exactly." Our youthful driver glanced at me while we careened through heavy traffic on the dark, slick interstate.

"Yeah, Baltimore Hospital," I answered, never taking my eyes from the highway ahead. I shifted my body and pressed my right foot into the floor board, as if to brake, as we darted wildly across traffic lanes.

"The patient rep down in South Carolina who arranged all this for us explained that the doctor we came up here to see chose to put my daughter in that hospital rather than Johns Hopkins. I don't know why. It really doesn't matter to us. We wouldn't know one from another anyway. Are the two close? And about how long before we get there?" I unclenched the death grip I had on the right arm rest and flexed my fingers to restore the circulation.

"We're getting close, maybe ten, fifteen more minutes," the driver told us. "Baltimore's roughly across the street from the main campus of Johns Hopkins, the university, but it's a few minutes by car from Johns Hopkins, the hospital."

He swerved onto an off-ramp and onto city streets that were either cobblestone or asphalt, which had suffered badly from the temperature extremes experienced in this part of the country. We whizzed past block after block of old brick row houses, convenience stores with unfamiliar names, and snow evacuation route markers that looked remarkably like the hurricane evacuation route markers so prevalent between Aiken and the beach. I felt a pang of homesickness and wondered how Lauren was handling the jostling in the back of the ambulance.

Finally, we pulled up at the ambulance entrance of a modern, medium-sized hospital. I jumped out of the cab and walked to the back as Karin ducked out of the rear of the vehicle.

"How was the ride back there?" I asked Karin.

"Rough. Really rough. Lauren's hurting; all that bouncing didn't help. We need to get her something for pain right away."

Our escorts seemed to know exactly where they were headed as they pushed Lauren's gurney through immaculate corridors with gleaming floors, onto stainless-steel elevators, and up to the west wing of the ninth floor. It was just past nine o'clock. The hospital in Greenville would have still been teeming with visitors, but this place was quiet. Other than staff, no one was roaming the halls. *Good*, I thought. *They run a tight ship.*

The trip ended in a large room, maybe three times the size of the hospital room Lauren had occupied in Greenville. One entire wall was an expanse of glass, from about the waist up, with a view of the Baltimore skyline. Three chairs, which converted into beds, were lined up under the windows, each already made up with a blanket and pillow.

The EMTs moved Lauren onto the hospital bed. As they made their way out, a smiling nursing assistant came in.

"We heard there would be three family members coming in with the patient, so I pulled these chairs in and made them up for you. Is that going to be okay?" Her smiling face and eager-to-please attitude eased our apprehension.

"This is really nice," Karin answered. "Thank you so much for setting this up for us. I'm worried about my daughter, though. I know we just came through the door, but can you get her something for pain? She's had nothing for quite a while, and with all the jostling in the ambulance, she's really hurting."

"Oh, sure. I'll let the nurse know. I'm certain she'll be in soon. If you need anything for yourselves, just let me know." She glanced at Lauren, lying stiffly, with her eyes squeezed tightly closed. "I'll ask her to hurry," she whispered.

Then she backed through the door into the hallway, leaving the four of us alone…profoundly alone.

I stacked our three small suitcases in a corner. The room had obviously been originally designed as a semi-private, which accounted for its size. The only television was a tiny, seven-inch set bolted onto an adjustable bracket that swung over the bed, intended for patient viewing only. At the moment, television wasn't high on Lauren's list of priorities.

I sat at the foot of one of the cots and watched the other three members of my family. While Karin wiped Lauren's face with a cool washcloth, Andrea gently stroked her arm. Their gentle touch did nothing to relax Lauren's rigidity. A big clock on the wall opposite Lauren's bed clicked off the seconds.

Fifteen minutes passed; no nurse came.

"I'm going to find somebody," I said.

Karen nodded.

I strode through the door and made my way to the nurse's station. A young woman sat behind the desk, intently working at a computer.

"Good evening, ma'am," I said, summoning every ounce of Southern genteelness I could muster. "I'm Mike Tarrant. My daughter Lauren came in a while ago, sort of an emergency case from South Carolina. She's in room 942."

"Yes?" The nurse's gaze never left the computer screen.

"Well, first of all, I want to thank ya'll for the really nice room. That's a beautiful view. And the young lady who pulled in those three chairs and set them up as cots for us, that was very thoughtful. We sure do appreciate it."

Still no response from the nurse.

"But Lauren's gone for a long time now with no pain medication," I continued. "I don't know if you've had a chance to look at her information yet, but she's had four surgeries in the past week and a half, the last one just yesterday morning. Is there any way you can get her something right away?"

"She's not in the computer yet. I can't do anything until she's in the computer." She still hadn't looked at me. For all she knew, she could have been conversing with a leprechaun.

"Do you have any idea how long before she's in the computer?" I asked with great humility and respectfulness.

"They do that downstairs. I have no control over it," she replied, maintaining complete focus on the screen in front of her.

"Oh…okay. Well, please, as soon as possible. She's in a lot of pain."

"As soon as she's in the computer, Mr. Tarrant." She made no attempt to hide the exasperation in her voice.

I shuffled back to Lauren's room and whispered the situation to Karin and Andrea, still at Lauren's bedside. With clenched teeth and set jaw, tears trickled down the side of Lauren's face from her tightly shut eyes.

I sat back on the chair, chin in hand, elbow propped on my knee, and watched the clock click off another thirty minutes before I headed back to the nurse's station.

The same nurse was behind the desk—standing now.

"I'm sorry to keep bothering you," I said, "but it's been another half-hour and still no medicine for my daughter. She's in torture. Can you please check to see if she's in the computer system?"

This time the nurse looked at me before stepping over to the computer. "No, she's not in there yet."

"Who do I need to talk to downstairs? I don't want to make a bad impression from the get-go, but this is not going to continue. We didn't bring our child this far to have her suffering for hours."

At that, a petite lady with salt-and-pepper hair, cut into a neat wedge, appeared from an office behind the station. She looked at me and spoke in a calm voice. "Give me ten minutes. I'll have someone there."

"Thank you, ma'am." For some reason, I trusted her.

Eight minutes later, a third nurse was in Lauren's room, inserting an IV and administering precious relief. When Lauren fell asleep, the other three of us collapsed, exhausted, onto the cots.

Bright lights abruptly pulled us awake. I sat up and reached for my glasses on the window ledge behind me. The bright blur of the room focused. I glanced at the big clock: 5:45 AM.

"I'm sorry to wake you." It was the petite, gray-haired nurse from last night. "Dr. Baxter is making his rounds. I expect he'll be here in a few minutes. I thought it best to wake you all now." With that, she quietly disappeared, closing the door behind her.

Our wake-up call hadn't come a moment too soon.

Seconds later, with Karin, Andrea, and me still seated on our cots and blinking from the bright light, the door flew open with a bang. Like the commander of a conquering army, a tall, middle-aged, bespectacled man marched into the room. A regiment of residents, uniformed in white lab coats, scurried behind him, trying to keep up with his pace. He halted beside the startled Lauren, who, like us, had apparently been sound asleep seconds earlier.

"I'm Bobby Baxter," he boomed. "I've looked at your charts. You're not going to lose your leg."

"What?" Lauren began, groggy, yet frightened. "How do...?"

Then she screamed. An agonizing, ear-shattering scream of pain, unlike anything I'd ever heard from either of my children.

Karin and I jumped to our feet.

Andrea crossed the room at lightning speed. She inserted herself between her now-sobbing little sister and the residents, who had Lauren's injured leg lifted at almost a ninety-degree angle.

"Put her leg down! Now!" she commanded the startled group. "How dare you come in here, without even introducing yourselves, and manhandle a person like a piece of meat! This is my sister. There's a human being at the end of that leg. She's been through enough in the last two weeks. Back off!" Andrea held her defiant stance beside Lauren's bed, standing guard between the residents and her sister.

Carefully, the residents placed Lauren's leg back onto the pillows and stepped back.

Karin and I looked at each other, slack-jawed. Where on earth had that come from? This, from our quiet, reserved, lady-like older daughter?

Dr. Baxter jumped in to reassert his authority. "Okay, let's take a deep breath and start over, shall we?"

"Yes, let's *all* take a deep breath and start over." Andrea reaffirmed her control of the situation.

"Let me reintroduce myself," Dr. Baxter started again. "I'm Bobby Baxter. I'm the doctor you flew up here last night to see." Then, turning to Andrea, "And I gather you are the patient's sister?"

"Yes, I am." Andrea was still fully in control. "These are our parents, Karin and Michael Tarrant."

We stood on the opposite side of Lauren's bed. Arms folded, Dr. Baxter looked from us to Lauren. "I really don't have adequate time to discuss your case this morning. I'd like to come back this afternoon, say around four o'clock, and meet with you, your sister, and your parents and go over in detail what we're going to do to save your leg."

Lauren didn't answer, still too shocked and hurt to speak.

So I answered. "I don't expect we're going anywhere. We'll see you at four."

With that, the doctor started toward the door. The resident regiment parted to allow him to pass, then filed out the door behind their leader. No further attempt to touch Lauren's leg, or even look at it, was made.

"Oh, my gosh, Michael!" Karin turned to me, pale and still sleep disheveled. "What have we gotten into?"

There was no time to contemplate her query. The door swung open again almost immediately. This time, the disinterested nurse from the night before entered, carrying a tray with a can of Ensure, an empty glass, and a paper pill cup.

She ignored the three of us surrounding Lauren's bed, and with great authority spoke to the now shell-shocked Lauren. "Good Morning, Miss Tarrant. These are your morning meds." She popped the top of the can of Ensure and poured the thick, brown liquid into the glass. "You'll be taking all of your medication with Ensure from now on. You need the nutrients. Water won't be necessary."

I looked down at my shoeless feet, clad still in the navy blue socks I had put on the day before in South Carolina and had slept in all night. My mind conjured up visions of Lauren two weeks earlier, in the recovery room in Greenville, struggling to swallow the concoction that an orderly had directed her to drink, and unable to keep it down.

"I don't think I can swallow pills with that," Lauren croaked. It was the first time she'd tried to speak since her rude awakening and ensuing scream.

"I'm quite sure you'll manage." The nurse stood watching as Lauren swallowed each pill, one at a time.

As soon as she'd finished and the nurse left the room, Karin poured the chocolaty brown stuff down the drain and filled a glass with water. Lauren gratefully drank it and sank back onto the bed. We'd been awake for less than ten minutes, it was still dark outside, and already the day was exhausting.

Karin and I huddled away from Lauren, in the little hallway by the bathroom.

"Let me wash my face. Then I'll go downstairs and see if I can find us something to eat," I said. "After that, I'll scout around for a hotel nearby. We can't all stay in here like a bunch of vagrants. Maybe I should call Medway Air Ambulance and see what it would cost to fly us all back down to Greenville. What do you think?"

"It couldn't hurt." Karin turned her head to look at our daughters. Andrea stood over Lauren, wiping her sister's face with a wash cloth.

"But what about what Baxter said?" Karin turned back to me. "So far this place has been miserable. But he did say he could save Lauren's leg."

"Well, there's no way we could get out of here before four o'clock this afternoon," I replied. "I don't think Lauren's in any shape to travel today, anyway. But it can't hurt to contact Medway, just get some info."

Within a few minutes, having made myself somewhat presentable, I stood waiting for the elevator, my mind wrapped in doubt, second-guessing our decisions. A voice from behind me pulled me back to consciousness.

"You're doing the right thing."

I turned to see the source of the statement. It was the same nurse who had awakened us right before Dr. Baxter came in.

"Ma'am?" I replied.

"You're doing the right thing," she repeated as she walked up beside me. "You just looked so lost in thought. I imagine that if I were in your circumstances and had just met Dr. Baxter for the first time, I'd be wondering if I hadn't made a huge mistake."

"You're a pretty good mind reader." I managed a wry smile. "As a matter of fact, I'm on my way downstairs right now to call the air ambulance company about taking us back to South Carolina. You think I should wait?"

She returned my smile. "It's no secret that Dr. Baxter's bedside manner needs work. But I'll tell you this: if one of *my* children was ever seriously hurt like your daughter is, I wouldn't have anyone but Bobby Baxter taking care of her. He's one of the best in the country, if not *the* best. How did you find him?"

The elevator arrived, but we let it go while I explained the circumstances that had brought us to Baltimore. It was obvious that she was on her way home at the end of her shift at 7:00 AM, but this lady was so genuinely concerned, it didn't seem to matter that our conversation stretched close to a half hour.

"What an amazing story," she said when I finished. "What a brave and determined family you all are."

"Lauren's the brave one. The rest of us are just desperate," I replied. "By the way, I'm sorry; I haven't introduced myself. I'm Mike Tarrant. My wife is Karin, and our older daughter is Andrea."

"I'm Betty. Betty Freedman." We shook hands.

"I'm the resource nurse for Nine West," Betty said. "I don't do much direct patient care. I'm responsible for assigning nurses to patients, so I'd really be interested in your initial impressions...besides your first encounter with Dr. Baxter and company."

"I don't know, Betty. It's different up here. I guess there really is such a thing as Southern hospitality. The folks back in South Carolina, a lot of them anyway, seem to use a little more courtesy and diplomacy. I shouldn't be making that comparison. We just got here late last night. The nurse's assistant who set us up with those cots in Lauren's room couldn't have been nicer or more eager to please. But then there was that nurse who was on duty last night and early this morning."

Betty had a knowing look in her eyes as I continued. "If it hadn't been for you, I don't know when Lauren would have gotten that pain medication. I can only imagine how badly she was hurting. Lauren doesn't complain unless she's really in trouble. I understand procedures and protocols, but sometimes you have to step outside the box and make things happen. It's just human decency."

Betty shook her head. "She's a traveling nurse. You won't see her again."

"I appreciate that," I replied. "Thanks for being so interested and concerned. You came along just at the moment I needed a friend."

A warm smile lit her face.

"Maybe I won't call that air ambulance company just yet," I said.

Betty pushed the call button and stepped into the elevator. "You put that number away, Mike. Lauren's where she's supposed to be."

Something about Betty made me believe she was right.

As I retraced my steps back to Lauren's room, Becky's words from years ago abruptly popped into my mind: *The Lawd don't let nothin' happen that He cain't make good come of it.*

Then, hesitantly, for the first time in days, I said a silent prayer. *Lord, I'm trying to work through this on my own, without bothering you. I just don't want us to lose touch, okay?*

By four o'clock that afternoon, I had braved the showery but unseasonably warm weather, checked into an adequate hotel room across the street from Baltimore, and moved our luggage.

Lauren was fast asleep when Dr. Baxter entered, right on time, dressed in green scrubs. Roughly the same age as I, he looked like one of my best friends from high school who was also, coincidentally, named Bobby. Both had lean builds and the same sort of rectangular face. I hadn't seen my friend in years, but I could imagine him now with thinning hair, a graying mustache and glasses, like Baxter.

Karin knew my friend, Bobby, also. She had met Bobby before she met me, and even dated him. It had gotten pretty serious between the two of them, but it was through Bobby that Karin and I met. Now the resemblance that Baxter held to an old friend put me curiously at ease with him. I wondered if Karin noticed the resemblance too and felt more comfortable.

We followed Dr. Baxter to a small conference room down the hall, while Andrea assumed the role of her younger sister's guardian.

"We got off to a shaky start this morning," the doctor began as we sat down around a small, round table in a secluded waiting area. "But I don't think Lauren was hurt as much as she was startled." Though he started off defensively, the sharp edge that Dr. Baxter had displayed earlier had noticeably dulled.

"You don't know Lauren, yet," I said. "She doesn't scare easily. That was a howl of pain, not fear or surprise."

"Lauren and I will have ample opportunity to become better acquainted over the next several days. If she's anything like her older sister, then I believe you when you say she doesn't scare easily. I just want to clear the air right up front. Like I said, it's regrettable that we started off with an incident, but I don't want that to define our relationship.

"You all have come a long way and are doing everything you can to save Lauren's leg. That's what I'm about too, and that's what we need to focus on, agreed?"

"Agreed," Karin said for both of us.

With that out of the way, Dr. Baxter got down to business. Diagramming on a notepad, he reviewed Lauren's injuries and the consequences of the infection in painful, graphic detail. Finally. he began to describe his plan of action.

"I've been at this for a long time," he said, dropping his pen to the table and looking over the top of his glasses at Karin and me. "I've learned a few things over the course of years. I know one thing for sure about infections of this kind in a joint: infection loves motion. If we're going to kill it, we have to hold it still, so I've got to completely immobilize Lauren's leg. To do that, I'm going to put it in an external fixater. I'll need to insert a set of three or four screws through the skin, directly into the femur, and another set of screws through the skin, directly into the tibia."

He picked the pen up again and sketched a picture of a long device with a set of three screws at the top and three more at the bottom. Each set of screws held a bracket that in turn held a cross-bar, perpendicular to the screws. The cross bars were connected by two parallel steel bars that would stretch from near the top of Lauren's thigh almost to the ankle. Unlike anything I'd ever seen or imagined, the diabolical device was medieval, straight out of a chamber of horrors. I glanced at Karin. From the look on her face, she was equally appalled.

Dr. Baxter sketched and described the device with the verve and enthusiasm of a Chevrolet salesman illustrating the features of a brand-new Corvette.

"It's not as bad as it looks," he said in response to the shocked expressions he encountered when he looked up from his notepad. "I do these things every week. They work. Lauren will get used to it."

"It looks so…painful," Karin uttered between clenched teeth.

"I assure you, it's not painful. The only concern Lauren will have is keeping the screw insertion points clean. That means using peroxide and a Q-tip twice a day to clean them. No big deal."

"How long will she have to have this thing?" I asked.

"Three months," he answered. "And she'll probably have a port for antibiotics, too."

I closed my eyes and shook my head. I felt Karin grab my forearm and squeeze it.

Dr. Baxter paused, rolled his eyes toward the ceiling in thought, and leaned back in the chair. "I tell you what. I have a patient, a young woman a little older than Lauren. She fell off a jet ski in the middle of Chesapeake Bay. Lay there in the water with an open fracture for several hours while her friends went for help. The Coast Guard finally picked her up with a helicopter. She developed an infection that went to the bone—very nasty. She wasn't my patient initially. She came to me as a last resort, like Lauren.

"She's in a halo right now. It's not quite like the fixater Lauren's getting, but it might be a good thing if she could talk to Lauren before the operation. She's one of the most upbeat, determined individuals I've met. The odds were against her keeping her leg, but she wasn't about to give up. I'll call her and see if she's able to come by tomorrow. I'd like the whole family to meet her."

Dr. Baxter stood up. "But right now, let's go explain the plan to Lauren."

The conference ended on far better terms than when we had begun. But as we approached the door to Lauren's room, I worried about Lauren's reaction to Dr. Baxter, and especially to his plan of attack.

We found Lauren awake when we walked in, with Andrea seated on the bed beside her. At Dr. Baxter's approach, Andrea relinquished her position, but she kept a wary eye on him as he explained his strategy. With a confidence now tempered with compassion, Dr. Baxter's approach and explanation contrasted dramatically with that of the early-morning encounter. As he laid out the plan, Andrea turned to Karin and me, eyes wide, silently sharing our initial shocked reaction to the scope of the treatment.

Feverish, Lauren remained mute, looking through sunken eyes at the doctor. She nodded affirmatively when Dr. Baxter asked if she understood, displaying neither surprise nor dismay. It was as if she had resigned herself now to whatever fate blew her way.

Dr. Baxter left with a warning that, since her surgery was on an emergency basis, Lauren would have to be worked into his operating schedule, and so nothing would occur before late the following day. That meant the next morning would begin an entire grim vigil without food or anything to drink for my sick, broken child. When she asked for a chocolate milkshake after Baxter had departed, I was only too happy to find one.

I stepped out of the hospital into the waning sunshine of the late-autumn afternoon. Brilliant red leaves still clung to the branches of the trees that dotted the sidewalks in front of the tightly packed townhouses and businesses. Walking in the fresh air, I contemplated again the wisdom of our decision to bring Lauren to Baltimore.

I had underestimated the physical and emotional toll the trip was costing Lauren. It was hard to tell if her withdrawal was a physical response to conserve strength, an emotional retreat brought on by the realization of the seriousness of her own condition, a surrender to the foreign surroundings and people, or a combination of all of it. No matter, it was clear that she had hit a new low. She could not gather the strength to speak even to Robbie during his frequent phone calls.

Any lingering thoughts I might have entertained about returning to South Carolina were out of the question. Lauren's condition simply would not allow it. Still, I selfishly longed for the familiar graciousness of "our people," and the subtle confidence of being on home turf. A fortnight had passed since Karin and I had stepped out of the house for supper, yet there was still no apparent end to this journey that had been thrust upon us all.

I turned a corner, following a hospital security guard's directions to the only burger joint within walking distance. The sidewalks became busier with people leaving work. From all appearances, everyone around me knew exactly where they were going and how to get there. I envied them their bearings.

Awash now with homesickness, I quickened my pace and searched the street ahead for any sign of the place where I'd find Lauren's milkshake.

Where the heck is this place? I thought. *I can't be lost. Figure it out. I'm supposedly intelligent, got a college degree. Can't I use the brains God gave me to follow simple directions? Do I need help with everything? What am I supposed to do, pray for help finding a milkshake? I need divine help driving. I need divine help falling asleep. I need divine help finding a hamburger joint that's just down the street. Am I a little old lady who thinks she's talking to Jesus every afternoon, or a grown man with a family depending on him?*

I turned another corner and saw the neon sign, "Tampers, Burgers and Shakes," flickering above the sidewalks. Donning a stony expression, I went in, picked up four chocolate shakes and carried them purposefully back to my family.

Though we had a perfectly adequate hotel room close by, Karin, Andrea, and I chose to spend the night on the three cots in Lauren's hospital room, ostensibly because each of us felt that Lauren might need us during the night. Truth be told, it was each of us who needed to be in Lauren's presence.

Mercifully, the medical staff had orders to keep Lauren heavily sedated that Wednesday. It fell to us three to wait all day for Lauren to be taken to surgery. We paced the floor and watched the clock slowly tick off the minutes.

The appearance of a young woman at the door roused us from our soporific watch. "Hi, I'm Kim. Dr. Baxter asked me to stop by."

Karin was first to get to the door. "Please come in. Excuse my whispering. We're letting our daughter sleep until they're ready for her in the OR."

Kim smiled and stepped in confidently, seemingly ignoring the hobbling device that surrounded her right leg. Thirtyish and of a hardy build, she wore a shirt and shorts specially made with a zipper along the outside of the right pant leg.

Lauren slept on while we whispered introductions.

"Dr. Baxter told us what happened to you," Karin said softly. "I'm sorry for everything you've been through. How are you doing now?"

"Well, as you can see, I can walk." Kim smiled proudly. "I'm out of a wheelchair, I don't have to use crutches. And I have my own leg. But I can tell you this: I wouldn't be standing here if it weren't for Dr. Baxter."

"How'd you find him?" Andrea asked.

"My first orthopedic surgeon recommended him," she replied. "I went through about eleven operations, but when the infection went into the bone, he sent me here to Dr. Baxter. I'm from the Eastern Shore, so I'm close by. Anyway, this is the third halo device I've had, and it's going to be the last. Since the accident, I've had twenty-one operations. I've got one more to go, to get this thing off."

I found myself looking Kim straight in the eyes, to keep from staring at her leg and the apparatus that surrounded it.

Perhaps recognizing my uneasiness, she leaned over and pointed to one of the screw insertion points. "See? There are two screws on either side up here"—she pointed just below her knee—"and a couple of others down here." She pointed just above her ankle. "I know it looks painful, but it really isn't. It just stings a little when you clean around the screws, but you get used to it. Keeping those screws clean is not easy, though. I've had a few pretty good infections from not being diligent enough. Probably cost me a couple of extra surgeries along the way that I might have avoided if I'd been a little more careful."

Karin looked at me. I knew that information had registered big time with her.

"People stare a lot, but you can't blame them," Kim went on. "That's a lot of metal and wire, not a pair of bell bottoms. They give you a wide berth, though, when you're walking down the street. People don't want to bump into me, and I'm glad for that."

I glanced over at Lauren, hoping she had not been roused. She lay facing away from us, her brown curls flowing across the pillow. Dr. Baxter was right about Kim. Her extraordinary attitude and determination were inspiring and encouraging. But at the moment, I knew Lauren would focus more on the physical than the mental. I was relieved to see that she remained fast asleep.

"I wanted to keep my leg," Kim continued, "because there's so much I want to be able to do. I climb scaffolds and work with piping for a living. I love the outdoors. I have a couple of dogs that love the outdoors as much as I do. I knew from the start that the freedom of having my own leg, my own independence, was worth fighting for. And I'm just about to win the fight. I don't care how my leg looks. I just want a leg that works."

The evidence of Kim's fight for life and limb was forever etched in the scars borne by her beleaguered leg. With no apparent self-consciousness, she showed us how a portion of the calf muscle had been rotated to the front of her shin in a complex procedure to aid the cure of the infection and restore mobility. Kim bore her scars with the courage of a conquering gladiator.

But twenty-one surgeries and two previous external fixaters had left grisly evidence of her many battles.

We chatted for at least an hour. Kim sat down, propping her steel-clad leg on a short stool placed in the middle of our conversation circle, unintentionally making it the focal point. She told details of her accident, the agonizing, lonely wait in the waters of the bay and her amazing rescue. She spoke in glowing terms of Dr. Baxter and his stubborn resolve to save her leg, and ultimately, her way of life. She left us impressed and encouraged by her attitude and courage. At the same time, though, her visit introduced in each of us a new, heretofore unrecognized, dread.

After Kim left, Andrea was the first to verbalize it. "Kim's awesome. I wish I had half her guts and determination."

She stood at the foot of Lauren's bed and turned to make sure her sister was asleep. Then she lowered her voice and continued. "But, oh, my gosh! I can't believe what she's had to go through. Twenty-one surgeries and she's not even done yet. Sure, it's been over the course of a couple of years, but it works out to almost one surgery every month! What kind of quality of life can that be?

"And...all that...metal stuff! I've never seen anything like it. I don't care what anybody says, it has to hurt." Andrea paused, looked at her sister, and whispered, "I'm ashamed to say this, but ya'll saw Kim's leg. The extent of disfigurement is, well, more than I expected. I know vanity should be the least of our concerns right now, but, well, she's my little sister and she's always been so beautiful, and so perfect."

A tear trickled down her cheek, but Andrea wiped it off with the back of her hand and continued. "Lauren doesn't just walk. She *dances* everywhere she goes. When we cheered together in high school, I used to look down at the other end of the squad, and there was my sister, the one with the highest kicks and the tallest jumps. At home, she still skips around the house. Her beautiful legs are a part of who she is. When you alter something that is so much a part of a person, when you take away something of beauty that's always been a part of her, that changes her whole being, doesn't it? And you know Lauren's going to worry about how Robbie will handle this. We have to care about how Lauren's going to take all this emotionally. We have to help her handle it. I'm her big sister. I have to help her. But how can I help her handle it, when I can't even handle it myself?"

At that, the tears could be held back no longer.

No sweet, Southern ladies came to take Lauren to the OR that evening. Instead, a solemn orderly showed up around six o'clock. In a now peculiarly familiar ritual, we followed our groggy daughter's gurney down the elevators and corridors leading to the surgery suites. We kissed her one last time when we could follow no further then returned to the empty hospital room to wait in nervous, dyspeptic silence.

Almost five hours later, Dr. Baxter, though looking exhausted, bounded into the room. He spun a chair around backwards, straddled it, and began the briefing. He reported that everything went pretty much as expected: a lot of infection in the quadriceps had to be removed. He reiterated the massive bone loss then warned us of additional transfusions and a continued waiting game. We smiled when he said that there would be no antibiotic port necessary. Everything would be oral upon Lauren's discharge.

"Your surgeon in South Carolina...Dr. Moore? He's a sculptor!" Baxter said. "The antibiotic spacer he put in place of the missing bone was carved to resemble the missing bone so closely, only a sculptor could have done it! I'd like to meet the man someday."

We smiled again.

"You're going to have to help Lauren get used to that fixater," he warned. "We'll give her a day to rest. Then physical therapy will come in on Friday and start showing her how to move with it. It's big, it's awkward, and it's going to be scary at first. But it's the best way to save Lauren's leg. The best way to help Lauren not be afraid of it is for *you* all not to be afraid of it."

Despite the lateness of the hour and the grueling day the man must have endured, he talked with us for another hour while we waited for Lauren to arrive from recovery. We talked about the Clemson versus Maryland game coming up on Saturday. He talked about his family; we talked about ours. He talked about what he liked to do when he wasn't working, and we talked about what we like to do back home. He finished by telling us that if all went well, we'd be home in a week.

If all went well.

Sometime after midnight, Lauren was returned to us. Each successive surgery extracted an ever-higher toll on our beleaguered child, and each time it was a toll she was less able to pay. Standing over her, I desperately wanted to take her place—to let her stand and walk and let me handle the suffering.

Lauren was in torment. Her only relief from the intense pain was to self-administer the morphine as often as the machine would allow, which was every seven minutes. She'd doze for a few minutes after each hit, then the pain would wake her again.

When we could no longer bear to see her in agony, we gently pried the device from her fingers, set up rotating two-hour shifts, and—against every hospital regulation—the three of us took turns pushing the button for her.

The Lawd don't let nothin' happen that He cain't make good come of it, I thought as I sat beside Lauren's bed, holding the morphine pump in my fist. With one eye, I watched the clock tick off seven minutes then pushed the red button that released the medicine. In the darkness and quiet, the seconds ticked off like slow water torture. With my other eye, I watched the door, ready to drop the morphine pump on the bed should a nurse enter.

To heck with there being a reason for everything, I thought. *And to heck with hospital rules. There is no reason for this kind of agony. My child is innocent. Why must she endure this misery? Why must Karin and Andrea endure this? And why must I? What ultimate good can ever come of this? I'm guilty only of loving my children. Can hell offer any more hideous punishment than a father having to endure the suffering of his child?*

Finally, the morning light filtered into the room, making the steel framework that surrounded Lauren's leg apparent under the covers. At eight o'clock, I called the contractor working on the remodeling at home. I asked him to build a wheelchair ramp and have it ready by the following week, though I would not allow myself to believe we'd be home by then to use it.

True to his word, Dr. Baxter gave Lauren the day to recover. "Recovery" meant another transfusion, massive doses of intravenous antibiotics, and bouts of nausea and intense itching. The tremendous pain that immediately followed surgery abated. That evening, Betty Freedman, who at this point had practically adopted us, brought doughnuts and pastries for Karin, Andrea and me, while Lauren slept.

"I think Lauren's had a good first day," Betty said quietly. "Has she seen the fixater yet?"

"No," Karin replied. "She's been so out of it today. Actually, none of us have seen it." Karin looked at the long rectangle that was Lauren's leg under the white sheets and blankets.

"Be prepared to help Lauren through this," Betty warned, "because she'll have to face it tomorrow." Then she smiled and backed out the door. "Good night, my favorite South Carolina family."

As Dr. Baxter had promised, Friday morning a vivacious, young physical therapist pushed a wheelchair into the room and began the arduous process of helping Lauren become mobile. Karin, Andrea, and I gathered around the bed, knowing step one would be to introduce Lauren— and us—to the steel device that was now integrant with Lauren's leg.

"So, Lauren, are you ready to see it?" the PT asked.

"No," Lauren answered truthfully, tears welling. "I don't want to look at it."

Our younger daughter had started the day a little less sick, as far as the effects of the infection, but a lot more injured from the effects of the surgery. She existed as a veritable human pin cushion. Each day there were either transfusions going in or blood samples going out, and always nightly shots in the stomach. Restarting IVs were agonizing. Her petite veins would collapse, nurses would get frustrated, and Lauren would end up getting stuck over and over again. She accepted it all without a whimper, but this was too much. Wasn't being impaled enough? Must she be forced to scrutinize her wounds, as well?

"I wish you didn't have to see it, Lauren, but you do." The therapist was kind but adamant. "You can't go home until you've looked at it and touched it, because you have to pick it up to move your leg. I'm going to pull back the covers and show your mom and dad and sister, and then you can look at it when you're ready, okay?" She looked from us to Lauren and back again. "Here goes."

She gently pulled back the sheets to reveal Lauren's leg, swaddled in bandages, as it had been for almost three weeks. But now that fragile, delicate limb supported a bulky metal frame that impaled her leg at three places on her thigh and three places on her lower shin. Though similar in concept, the device was nothing like the halo we had seen on Kim's leg earlier in the week. This was much bigger, made of heavy steel. Six thick, gauze-wrapped screws pierced the skin and provided a sturdy support for the fixater, which held her leg in a hyperextension.

With my non-medical background, it was unlike anything I had ever seen or could have imagined.

Within seconds, with both faces drained of color, Karin and Andrea looked up. Our eyes met. Lauren lay semi-propped on her pillows, eyes shut.

"Maybe we should give her a little longer," I pleaded with the physical therapist. "Maybe this afternoon, or even tomorrow."

"No!" Lauren commanded. She twisted so that her left arm provided support and struggled to sit up. "No, I'll look at it now."

The therapist raced to brace Lauren's back and pushed her into a sitting position. While she held her there, Lauren studied the fixater from one end to the other. Beads of sweat gathered on her forehead, and the therapist suggested she lie back down.

"I'm all right," Lauren protested. "Just show me what I have to do. Please."

While Karin moved to support Lauren's sitting position, the therapist placed one hand on the crossbar that connected the two steel rods that ran along either side of Lauren's leg. "I'm going to lift your leg the way you'll do it when you want to move. I'll be very gentle; I'm not going to hurt you."

With that, she raised Lauren's leg from its position on the bed, as if she were lifting a suitcase by its handle. Reflexively, I sucked in air, drawing looks of strong disapproval from the others in the room.

Despite the fact that it looked excruciating, as if the screws would pull right out of Lauren's leg, there was no change in Lauren's expression, no sign that the movement had caused additional pain. From that point on, Lauren seemed to tap into a reservoir of strength from a source unknown.

The next several days were consumed with physical therapy sessions. Lauren was now so frail and exhausted that a few steps with a walker were all that could be hoped for. Negotiating stairs, a big concern because of what she would face when she returned home, required an extra person to hoist her hyper-extended leg.

Dr. Baxter held daily examinations for any signs of a return of the infection. Karin, Andrea, and I nonchalantly busied ourselves elsewhere while he peered at Lauren's leg. Then with each "all clear" announcement, we breathed a collective sigh of relief. Despite her progress, Lauren remained stoic, almost emotionless, not daring, it seemed, to hope that she'd be released, lest she be crushed by disappointment again.

Evenings provided short but welcome relief when Robbie called or when Betty spoiled us with nightly snacks. We remained camped out in the hospital room each night, using the hotel room across the street only to shower and change into "fresh" garments that had been worn maybe only once before. We'd crawl into our cots, Andrea and Karin still shod, and in the darkness talk back and forth across the room like the Waltons.

"What's the first thing you want when we get back home?" Karin inquired in the dimness one evening after everyone was tucked in.

"Sweet tea," came the first response, from me.

"To wash my hair with shampoo, instead of the dry stuff they use here," was Lauren's wish.

"I want to pick up Boo and let her lick me all over my face," Andrea said.

"You know what I want to do?" Karin asked.

A voice in the dark answered, "What, Mama?"

"I want to sleep without my shoes on!"

We laughed until we cried.

On Monday morning, Dr. Baxter switched Lauren from morphine to little capsules of a drug none of us had heard of: OxyContin.

"This is powerful stuff," he explained to Lauren. "You will become addicted; I just want you to know that up front. You will not be able to take yourself off this drug. You shouldn't even consider doing so for many weeks. When it is finally time to discontinue it, you'll need to do so under the direction of your doctor back home. Never, *ever*, under any circumstances, should you break a capsule in half to reduce the dose. These capsules must not, I repeat *must not*, be broken. To do so is extremely dangerous, and can, in certain circumstances be fatal. Am I clear on that with all of you?"

We nodded, and the doctor continued, "I'll provide a full report for you to take down South with you when you leave... tomorrow." He flashed a smile, searching our faces for a reaction, then continued. "I figured since Maryland kicked Clemson's rear in Saturday's football game, you guys would want to get out of town gracefully, and as soon as possible."

"Hey, one win, once in a blue moon, and these guys figure they can gloat," I quipped back, unable to contain my grin.

"Who's your doctor down there?" The doctor quickly resumed his professional demeanor. "Are you going back to Dr. Moore in Greenville?"

"I'd like to go back to Dr. Moore," Lauren responded. "But I'm not going back to Clemson, obviously, and it's a long drive from Aiken to Greenville."

"My sister works for one of the area hospitals," Karin added. "I've asked her to help us locate a practice that can take Lauren's case."

"Okay," Baxter answered. "I won't address the letter to anyone specifically, but as soon as you know, give my office a call and let me have the name of the physician down there. You'll need to act quickly, though. Lauren's going to need to establish home health care right away, within a couple of days at the most, for maintenance of the fixater."

The doctor left with a few more words of medical advice, spiced inappropriately, in my opinion, with cracks about turtles being able to outpace tigers.

That evening I made plane reservations—fully refundable—for the four of us for the following day. Like Lauren, I was not to be caught off-guard again.

The next morning, Tuesday, exactly three weeks since the accident, Dr. Baxter officially released Lauren from the hospital. But he had some sobering final words.

"I would be remiss if I let you go with any misconceptions about your condition, Lauren. While I see no sign of infection now, there's no guarantee that it won't reoccur without warning at any time. I know of one case where a nine-year-old girl contracted an infection in an open fracture. The infection was apparently treated, but in fact lay dormant for over sixty years. At the age of sixty-nine, the infection reappeared and the woman subsequently lost her limb. I'm not saying that will happen to you, but I want you to be aware of potential outcomes."

Lauren sat stone-faced, the smile that she had worn for a brief moment replaced with an intent gaze.

"As for where we go from here," he continued, "you are leaving with a serious injury that will have to be addressed as soon as your condition allows. You will have to make some difficult choices. None of the alternatives are especially attractive, but at least we have, I believe, been able to provide you with alternatives. You still have your leg.

"There are many who would say that in a case such as yours, the optimum outcome would be amputation. I would argue that maintaining your natural leg, even if it's immobile, is a better outcome than an above-the-knee amputation. I'd rather be able to get up in the middle of the night and get myself to the bathroom without putting on a prosthesis first. I think most people would agree with me on that. But it is still an option."

The doctor went on. "There has been mention of an al-lograft, using bone from a cadaver to rebuild some of the bone that you've lost. That's an extremely difficult procedure in your case, but I believe it may be possible. I'm not sure where you would have it done, but I would probably be willing to attempt it should you decide to return to Baltimore. However, I also believe that the best you can hope to achieve in mobility is less than a thirty-degree bend of your knee. If you were to achieve that, it would be more painful than you could bear. I think you'd be back here, begging me to fuse your leg.

"Which leads me to what I think is the best alternative for you, under the circumstances."

He paused. At this point, whatever joy I had allowed myself to feel at the prospect of returning home had been wrenched away. Despite all my resolve to the contrary, I had allowed myself to be sucker punched once again. My wife's beautiful green eyes shone with tears. Andrea, arms crossed in front of her, had turned to face the Baltimore skyline, shining through the window.

Lauren, though, remained as she had been, her eyes fixed directly on Dr. Baxter, taking in his every word with no visible sign of emotion, as if he were speaking only of a fictional textbook example.

The doctor began again. "In my opinion, knee fusion will provide the best long-term outcome. That means, of course, that your leg will not bend. It would be fused at a slight angle that would allow you to walk. Your right leg would be somewhat shorter than your left, but I think it's your best chance for a pain free life."

"I realize these are not the best life options for a beautiful twenty-one-year-old girl, but this is your future, as I see it."

Focused intently on Dr. Baxter, Lauren lifted her head. Her voice resonated with a strength and confidence that belied her broken body. "Then you don't know my God."

And, neither, I feared, did I.

Chapter Seven

Pray and ask God for everything you need, Always give thanks.
—Philippians 4:6

WITH THE WIND blustering around him under a gray, chilly November sky, the cab driver leaned against the silver Lincoln limousine. He stood with both feet on the threshold of the open driver's door, flicking a lighter as his cupped hands shielded the cigarette in his mouth. When at last it lit, he glanced at his watch and impatiently looked over the roof of the limo and surveyed the cars, horns blaring, shifting in and out of the drop-off zone at the Baltimore-Washington International Airport.

Karin stood guard over our luggage on the adjacent sidewalk. Held in place by Andrea, a weak, frightened, and helpless Lauren, with her outstretched right leg, sat sideways across three quarters of the backseat.

My frantic, twenty-minute search for a wheelchair that could accommodate Lauren's special needs had proven fruitless. In desperation, I rushed a worn and dirty, flat luggage cart up to the car. I wiped the sweat from my eyes despite the chilly breeze.

"Michael," Karin shouted from the sidewalk. "What is that for?"

"It's for Lauren," I shouted back to be heard above the wind and the drivers, who honked and gestured at us constantly. "I can't find a wheelchair that will work. I figured she could sit flat on this and I'd roll her into the airport."

"Oh, my gosh!" Karin shouted back. "She can't be pushed on that thing. You've got to find a wheelchair."

A skycap approached, probably intending to find out why the cab hadn't moved on. But when he understood the situation, he left then returned within minutes with a wheelchair that would accommodate Lauren's leg. Together, the skycap, cab driver, and myself negotiated Lauren into the wheelchair and out of the foul weather and foul language that surrounded us.

I fumbled with luggage as we picked our way through the crowded terminal. Andrea pushed Lauren in the wheelchair. Karin carried the walker while clearing a path in front and to both sides so the crowd wouldn't bump into Lauren's fragile leg, which extended precariously in front of her. The only garment big enough to cover the metal fixater was the largest pair of green scrubs that Betty could find at the hospital before we left. The pants engulfed the rest of Lauren's tiny frame, accentuating her appallingly frail appearance.

With the luggage checked, we approached the security gate with dread.

"My daughter was just released from the hospital," Karin said. She rolled the wheelchair to the metal detector. "She has a metal device attached to her leg that cannot be removed. What do you want me to do?"

"I gotta see it, ma'am. Follow me." The guard motioned them to follow her behind a screen. Several minutes passed before they emerged.

"That wasn't pleasant." Karin directed her comment my way as we hurried to the gate.

I had booked first-class seats for Karin and Lauren, and coach for Andrea and me. We began to board as soon as they called for passengers needing special assistance. I rolled Lauren down the jet way and as far into the 757 as possible. The aisles were too narrow to allow the walker to pass, and Lauren was too weak to use it, anyway. I wrapped my arms around Lauren's waist, picked her up as high as I could, and carried her to her seat in the front of the plane. I had asked for a seat on the aisle on the left side of the plane. When I tried to set Lauren in her assigned place, she didn't fit. The right armrest on the seat prevented her from placing her rigid leg into the aisle. I stood with both arms clamped around my daughter's waist while the flight attendant rushed to figure something out.

"Daddy," Lauren whispered as we stood there, "I think I'm going to pass out."

"Oh, my gosh, Chicken Little." I looked around. Karin was directly behind me. "All right, we're going down right here in the aisle, okay?"

Karin backed up, the other passengers now boarding backed up, and I began to ease Lauren down.

"Wait," the flight attendant called. "Put her right here." She motioned to the first seat behind the bulkhead. The bulkhead wall didn't extend quite as far to the right as a seat would have, allowing barely enough room for the fixated leg to fit. We set Lauren in the wide leather chair and reclined it as far back as it would go. I lifted her foot so her hip could settle in the seat while two flight attendants scrambled to build a makeshift ottoman out of pillows and blankets, then fetch a Coke and a wet paper towel.

With Lauren settled in the only seat in the 757 that could accommodate her, the fainting spell was averted. First class wasn't full; the flight attendants invited Andrea and me to move up to the seats directly across the aisle from Karin and Lauren before the plane took off.

We'd made a complete spectacle of ourselves, but I couldn't have cared less. We were on our way home!

Across the aisle, I saw that Lauren had fallen asleep almost before we were off the ground. Seated in the window seat beside our sleeping daughter, Karin kept an eye on the wobbly tower of pillows and blankets that held the injured leg.

Though it was still early, I already felt worn out. Andrea must have felt the same; we pushed our big leather seats back, savoring the peaceful interlude before we landed in Atlanta. Somewhere over Virginia, I allowed myself to slip into that semi-conscious state that precedes sleep.

Andrea nudged me awake. "Daddy? What are we going to do when we get to Atlanta? They're supposed to meet us at the jet way with a wheelchair, right? They know to get one that will support Lauren's leg, don't they? What about when we get home? Have you talked to the medical supply place? We've got to have a wheelchair waiting on us when we drive up. Without it, the only way we'll get Lauren into the house is to carry her, and then she won't be able to move around. By the time we land in Atlanta, pick up the rental car, and drive to Aiken, it'll be close to five o'clock. I don't want that place to close up before they deliver all the stuff Lauren's going to need tonight."

My older daughter's eyes, so like her mother's, searched my face for reassurance. Andrea had selflessly put her own life on hold for almost a month, even postponing the scheduled starting date of the job she had landed in Augusta before Lauren's accident. The extent to which Lauren relied on the physical and emotional support of her big sister was obvious. I realized how much Karin and I counted on her quiet strength too.

"This whole thing stinks, doesn't it?" Andrea continued before I could respond to her concerns. "Until now, I'd never given much thought to what handicapped people have to go through every day. I've taken so much for granted. I mean, look at the struggle Lauren went through just to get in and out of a car. And getting on the plane? Practically impossible. Yet millions of people go through that and more every day, and for the most part, they make their way though life without complaining."

She paused for a long time, looking beyond me at the broken girl across the aisle.

"Do you think it's better to have been born handicapped, Daddy, and never know what life without a disability could be like?"

I could only shake my head.

We waited for everyone else to exit the plane when we landed in Atlanta. I carried Lauren to a wheelchair waiting, as promised, in the jet way, then dashed off to pick up a rental car while the girls headed for the baggage claim and the restroom. Using the bathroom on the plane would have been impossible for Lauren, and she had fretted that she'd not be able to hold out for the almost two-hour flight. She'd made it, but now it was a matter of urgency.

I picked up a Cadillac, the only car the agency had with a back seat big enough for Lauren's leg, and circled around the airport to the passenger pickup. Seeing no handicapped parking, I stopped at a point where the sidewalk crossing was level with the walk surrounding the building so the wheelchair could be rolled close. Hopping out of the car, I searched the throng for signs of my family. Within a couple of minutes, an Atlanta airport policewoman sauntered in my direction.

"You'll have to move the car, sir," she ordered.

"My daughter was just released from a hospital up north," I replied as she approached. "She's hurt and in a wheelchair. I don't see anywhere else that I can roll her wheelchair close enough to the car to get her in."

Without a word, the policewoman pulled out a pad and a pen and started writing. Then stuffed the paper behind the windshield wiper.

"What is this?" I asked, pulling the paper from behind the wiper and unfolding it. "It's a ticket. You wrote me a ticket! I told you my circumstances, and instead of offering advice or assistance, you wrote me a ticket. It's not even a warning. It's a *ticket!*"

I stood looking at the woman, incredulous.

"If you don't move your vehicle right now, I'll write you another one," she replied over her shoulder as she strolled away.

Blood boiling, I slid behind the wheel, put the car in gear, and pulled back into traffic. Each circle around the passenger pick-up took several minutes. I strained on each pass to see the girls. Finally, on the fourth pass, I spotted them. I had no choice but to pull back to the same place where I had received the ticket.

I put the car in park, jumped out, and ran around to get Lauren in as fast as possible. But moving her leg without hurting her was a task that required all three of us. The same police-woman approached as Karin and Andrea were lifting Lauren out of the wheelchair. I hung halfway in the car, stretched across the backseat to lift and guide Lauren's leg.

"If you don't move that vehicle immediately, I will ticket you again!" Sprawled as I was across the backseat, she shouted her threat at Karin, Andrea, and Lauren.

"What?" Andrea shouted into the backseat over the traffic. "What's she talking about?"

"I can't tell you now," I shouted toward the girls. I scrambled backwards off the seat and straightened by the driver's door. "Slam the trunk and move Lauren back to the sidewalk. I'll circle, and we'll just have to somehow get Lauren in down there." I motioned to a point behind us as I put a foot into the car.

"Oh, no, you don't, Daddy!" Andrea commanded in a roar. A crowd began to form on the sidewalk beside us. "You are not moving this car."

Flames seemed to shoot from Andrea's eyes as she approached the cop.

"Can't you see my sister is handicapped? She's been hit by a car and spent most of the last month in hospitals. She is badly hurt. You show me anyplace else where we can get her into a car. What's the matter with you?"

The crowd drew closer. An elderly man joined in.

"Yeah, what kind of a human being are you?" he jeered at the cop. "Can't you see how bad that girl's hurt? There's nowhere else they can go to get her in the car." He stopped, looked around, and realized he had the gathering crowd's backing. With added confidence, he took another swing. "You're a disgrace to the City of Atlanta!"

Ignoring the show of support, Andrea continued to address the now-stunned member of Atlanta's finest. "I'm putting my sister in this car," she said, eye-to-eye with the woman. "My father's driving us away from here, and you're not writing any ticket."

Certain now that we were all going to jail, I darted into the backseat and grabbed Lauren's leg while Karin and Andrea lifted her in. That done, I threw the bags in the trunk, the girls jumped in, and I floored it out into the traffic. A glance in the rearview mirror revealed the crowd still glaring at the policewoman as she shuffled back from whence she came, framing a picture of Southern hospitality at its best...and worst.

In the backseat, leaning against the tigress that was formerly her sister, rested a smiling Lauren.

For the next couple of hours, we sailed east in our rented luxury, through the Georgia hills veiled in the evergreen of pines. Spanish moss draped the hardwoods lining the wide Savannah River and waved a welcome as we crossed the bridge into South

Carolina late that overcast November afternoon. Twenty minutes later, we pulled into our driveway. Home, exactly three weeks late from our dinner out!

Moments earlier, a cell phone call from the medical supply company informed us that they were only minutes away, so we waited in the car and let Lauren sleep. When the van pulled up, we took our time to gently move her into the wheelchair. We were home, where there were no bustling doctors or nurses, no blaring horns, no rude cops, no cold, impersonal institutions. There was just a comfortable, ordinary house where children had grown up, and people loved each other and could help each other heal.

We opened the gate and stepped into the backyard, where, true to the contractor's promise, a ramp running almost the length of the house waited to raise the injured family member into sanctuary.

We flung wide the double doors on the deck at the top of the ramp and rolled Lauren's chair through the opening. Clearing a path so the wheelchair could travel through the remaining clutter, we marveled at the metamorphosis. The rooms that had been stripped bare had been rebuilt and reequipped. The scars and marks and bumps and dings of the past had been erased. Everything old was new again.

There was a tangible energy about the place, an exhilaration that brought renewed vitality to our injured child. Lauren's smile, the one that had been ever-present until three weeks earlier, returned to its rightful place. It was more than just good to be home; it was euphoric. We were back where we belonged, back where good things happened. Where, if we needed one, maybe even a miracle could happen.

By the end of that joyous evening, I had quaffed several glasses of sweet tea, Lauren's curls had been washed with real shampoo and water, Andrea had been thoroughly licked by Boo, and Karin was tucked into our own bed, wearing no shoes!

And for the first time in a while, I remembered to say my prayers.

A Pennsylvania transplant once told me that November was South Carolina's gift to its residents for sweltering through the heat and humidity of the long summer. Accordingly, by mid-morning of our first day home, glorious Carolina sunshine poured into the house, further brightening our spirits, still elated from the previous night's homecoming.

Two nurses from the hospital's home health care service came by to clean the pins on Lauren's fixater, in the process teaching Karin to do the twice-daily task. Not even that painful procedure seemed to dampen Lauren's happy mood. Friends and family stopped by with food and good cheer. Time passed quickly between helping Lauren move around, straightening and reorganizing the post-construction mess, welcoming visitors, and answering the many phone calls. It was bedtime before I had time to tell Karin about a telephone call I had taken while she and the girls had been entertaining company.

"Remember that orthopedist Lauren has an appointment with tomorrow? The one your sister found for us...Dr. Hines? Well, a lady from his office called late this afternoon while Bobby and Patsy were here."

"Really," Karin answered. "What did she want?"

"She said that when Heidi contacted them about taking Lauren's case, they hadn't realized how unusual her injury was. The doctor learned the whole story when he reviewed Lauren's records from Baltimore today. Now they're concerned about taking Lauren on as a patient, unless we can assure them that Dr. Hines will be the one to perform Lauren's future surgeries."

"What?" Karin turned from pulling the covers back on the bed. "How could we do that? We don't even know what surgeries she'll need, or when. I've never heard of such a thing! What did you tell her?"

I yanked the comforter back on my side. "I told her we couldn't do that, for the same reasons you just said. I said that Dr. Hines had come highly recommended; we'd heard he was the best-qualified doctor in this area to handle a case like Lauren's, so I couldn't say that he wouldn't be the one to do any future operations. I couldn't guarantee that he *would*, either. The only thing I could guarantee was that when the time came, we'd do whatever's best for Lauren."

"So what'd she say?" Karin asked, climbing into bed.

"She said in that case, they'd not be able to accept Lauren as a patient."

Karin's eyes widened. "What about Lauren's appointment tomorrow? Dr. Baxter warned us to get her to a specialist down here immediately. The infection could come back! She's got to be monitored!"

"I know," I replied. "I told her if they backed out on us now, they'd be putting us in a real bind, potentially jeopardizing Lauren's recovery. I think I got through to her, because she said she'd speak with Dr. Hines, and they'd call us back in the morning to either confirm Lauren's appointment or tell us to find someone else."

"Good grief!" Karin muttered, sitting in bed with her knees pulled up. "Now we've got that to worry about."

I put my arm around my wife and pulled her close. "Let's just wait and see what happens in the morning."

For the second night in a row, I remembered to say my prayers.

We weren't left hanging for long. Dr. Hines' office called early the following morning to confirm Lauren's appointment for three o'clock.

Chapter Seven

In the hospital, minutes had often seemed like hours. But at home, there was much more to be done than time to do it. The house constantly buzzed with activity and people. Though most of the remodeling was complete, there were still painters touching up here and there, men finishing up carpet and tile, others making final adjustments to kitchen and bathroom plumbing and appliances. At any given moment, there might be four or five different people working.

We'd negotiate Lauren in her wheelchair around their work. Sometimes I'd catch them warily watching us help Lauren maneuver the stairs, a cumbersome process. It involved her sitting on a step, then pushing herself up one step at a time, while someone held her fixated leg level, carefully avoiding putting pressure on the screws that went completely through the bone.

Medicine schedules had to be followed carefully, and proved time-consuming as well: no dairy products for an hour on either side of the Cipro, OxyContin every six hours, anti-acids at bedtime, anti-nausea as needed, and on and on. It added up to an extensive and complicated regimen. With the kitchen cabinets not completely in order and the large volume of prescriptions, Karin had organized a little drug store on two Lazy Susans on a kitchen counter.

Dr. Hines' office was about an hour away, so as the clock approached two that afternoon, I grabbed a plastic bag and scooped up all the prescriptions to take with us. While Lauren waited in her wheelchair downstairs, I met Karin in our bedroom.

"Here's the medicine," I said, dumping the bag on the bed. "Make sure we're not missing anything."

Karin examined each prescription and placed it back in the bag. When there were no more bottles on the bed, she looked at me.

"Where's the OxyContin?" she asked.

"Didn't you just count it?" I replied.

Karin frowned. "I didn't see it."

She looked up when she'd inventoried the bag for a second time. "It's not here, Michael. Did you check in the bathroom?"

I dashed to both bathrooms upstairs, then checked Lauren's bedside tables and dressers. I ran downstairs and checked the kitchen cabinets, the refrigerator, even beside the couch in the den.

"Nothing," I announced as I returned upstairs. "I checked the whole house. It's not here. How long since Lauren's had a dose?"

"Not very long," Karin answered. "I'll check the note pad. I don't think she's due for several hours, anyway. Who's still here? Besides us, I mean."

"Nobody," I replied. "The last one I saw leave was that nice kid who was working on the carpet at the threshold from the dining room to the kitchen...right by the counter with the Lazy Susans. That's the kid you gave the extra carpet to, right? And the one who was so concerned about Lauren and asked you all those questions, too. You don't suppose he could have stolen the OxyContin, do you?"

Karin bit her lower lip in thought. "I don't know. But you know what else is missing? My piggy bank. It was hidden in the back of my closet. I noticed it was gone when I went in for my jacket. I must have had at least a couple of hundred dollars worth of change in it. The only workers who would have gone in there would have been the guys who were putting down the new carpet."

She paused again. "You paid for that prescription when we left Baltimore, didn't you?" "How much was it?"

I looked down, concentrating. "Over three hundred dollars, just for the OxyContin alone. But what good would it do anybody? I never heard of the stuff until all this. All I know is that Baxter said it's highly additive, and the stuff works. So if

Lauren doesn't take it when she's supposed to, she's not only going to be in tremendous pain, but she's also going to start having withdrawal symptoms."

"If he did take it, then how cruel! He saw how badly hurt Lauren is and knew what she'd been through. No wonder he was so interested in how she was doing," Karin mused out loud, disgusted. "He had to know she'd be in torture without that medicine. Now, if he or someone is selling it on the street, they know Lauren has to have that medicine. What's to stop them from coming back here looking for more, maybe when we're asleep, or no one is home?"

Karin ceased her rumination. "Lauren's waiting. We've got to go or we'll be late. It's a good thing we're on our way to the doctor. All we can do is explain what's happened and get a refill. We can call the police from the car. Just make sure you lock the house, Michael, and set the alarm!"

"Just great," I fumed as we walked downstairs. "The doctor doesn't know us from Adam's housecat. He's already hesitant to take Lauren's case. Now, we meet him for the first time and give him this story about somebody stealing hundreds of dollars worth of painkillers from right under our nose, and immediately ask him for more."

This was Lauren's first excursion out of the house since we'd come home. Even though it was only a doctor's visit, we had planned to keep it light and have some fun on the way, maybe stop for an ice cream cone or milkshake. But discovery of the theft had put us behind schedule, and the phone call to file a police report on the missing drugs lasted almost all the way to the doctor's office, precluding any conversation in the car along the way.

The waiting room was full when we arrived, packed with people of all ages, some with casts on their arms, some on crutches or with canes. I parked our daughter in her wheelchair at the end of a row of chairs. Karin and I took seats beside her. Lauren, wearing oversized, tear-away warm-up pants to cover the fixater, flipped through *People*. I noticed some in the waiting room discreetly peering over their magazines at the pretty but frail girl who had just come in and at the bulky device on her hyper-extended leg. Others stared openly. Burying her nose deeper in the magazine, Lauren crouched low in the wheelchair.

After a few minutes, an elderly lady leaned forward and touched Lauren's good knee.

"What happened to you, honey?" she asked.

"I was hit by a car while riding a moped at Clemson," Lauren replied politely.

"Well, bless your heart, dahlin'. I sure hope you're better real soon."

"Yes, ma'am. Me, too. Thank you." I noticed the end of Lauren's nose turn red as she spoke. She quickly returned to her magazine.

I hoped Dr. Hines would know something about the importance of emotional healing, as well as healing bones.

He did. Gentle, self-assured, kind, and jolly, Dr. Hines won our hearts and our confidence; he and Lauren hit it off immediately. There was no mention of his earlier reluctance to accept Lauren as a patient. He happily wrote a prescription to replace the stolen OxyContin, and he promised to remove the cast from Lauren's hand when she returned the following week.

The return trip home was quiet. We had much to think about.

That evening, a police investigator stopped by to take a report on the burglary, but offered no hope that the perpetrator would ever be apprehended. With a copy of the police report in hand, I drove to Kroger to pick up the new prescription. A song came on the radio that I recognized as one of Lauren's favorites from Young Life:

"Light the fire in my soul, Fan the flame, make me whole,

Lord, You know just where I've been, so light the fire in my heart again."

Alone in the car, it was safe for me to sing out loud. Abruptly, like a rogue wave in a calm sea, emotion washed over me and I choked on the words. I clicked off the radio and shook my head to regain control.

Where did that come from? I asked myself. *A lot's gone down in the last forty-eight hours, but I'm handling it.* I ran through the list in my mind. *A discouraging prognosis from Dr. Baxter, and a glimpse of the obstacles—including curious strangers—my daughter faces for the rest of her life as a handicapped person. Then, an inexplicable hassle from a local doctor, so that I had to practically beg him to take Lauren as a patient, followed by theft and betrayal from a person we had befriended. I guess that's a fairly substantial list. But I'm handling it. I don't need to go whining to God for help. He gave me strength and intelligence and expects me to handle the bad with the good. And that's what I'm doing. I'm okay.*

I pulled into a parking place and noticed a postal service drop-off box right in front of the car.

That reminds me. I better make sure Bobby took care of mailing those bills like I asked a couple of weeks ago. I shut off the car, leaned across the front seat, and ran my hand through the pocket of the passenger door. Then I checked the pocket of the driver's door as I got out. *Good, both empty. I've got enough going on without having the phone or the power shut off for non-payment.*

Early Friday afternoon found Lauren settled in an over-sized chair and ottoman in the living room. Fresh air and autumn sunlight poured in, illuminating that famous Lauren smile.

"Robbie just called, Daddy," she said as I plopped onto the couch. "He's on Whiskey Road. He'll be here in five minutes."

"Who's Robbie?" I teased. "Oh, ain't he that guy you complained was always hanging around you at Clemson? That boy who's such a pest?"

"Oh, yeah. That's him," Lauren teased back in her classic style. "Why don't you go out in the yard and stop him before he comes in? Send him back where he came from so he won't be botherin' me no more! I don't need him hangin' around down here too!"

The exchange was short and silly and so characteristic. We broke into raucous laughter, both tickled more by the glimpse of a carefree, hope-filled Lauren than the humor of the conversation.

Later, Karin and I sat on the front porch steps and watched Robbie push Lauren down the street, out for a spin in the wheelchair.

"There go the same two kids we watched run up a mountain a month ago," Karin sighed wistfully. "Boy, life can turn everything upside down in a second, can't it? You think you know how everything's going to turn out, but you don't."

I could only nod. They turned the corner, and we watched until Robbie's Tiger Paw baseball cap disappeared through the trees.

"Lauren's lucky to have him," I said.

"He's lucky to have *her*," Karin replied.

We decided that Saturday night would mark the beginning of a week-long celebration that would begin with the

Clemson-South Carolina football game and continue through Karin's birthday, which would fall on Thanksgiving Day. Robbie had gone back to Clemson for this, the 100th meeting of the two arch rivals. Other friends had gathered to keep Lauren company, among them Mary DuPree, a Kappa sorority sister, a Young Life leader, and family favorite.

Always the biggest game of the season, this year the Clemson-Carolina game promised to be huge. South Carolina was coming in on a four-game losing streak. After starting the season like gangbusters and looking like a lock for a third straight bowl game, Coach Lou Holtz now needed this win to salvage his season and become bowl eligible. Plus, Carolina won a year ago, twenty to fifteen. If they could clinch this game, it would be the first back-to-back win in over thirty years and a disaster for Clemson's Tommy Bowden.

Clemson had five losses under its belt as well, but three of those losses had come against teams ranked in the top twelve in the nation. After last year's miserable loss to the Gamecocks, Bowden would be looking to make sure the cocky chickens from the Columbia coop would have nothing to crow about.

ESPN was carrying the game live. By kick-off time, everyone had gathered around the television. Things didn't look good for Clemson by the end of the third quarter as South Carolina struck for two, third-quarter touchdowns to go ahead twenty to thirteen. A dozing Lauren woke up in the fourth quarter—about the same time as the Tigers—to watch Clemson's new quarterback, Charlie Whitehurst, get Clemson back on track. Whitehurst completed five passes on two drives as Clemson rallied to win twenty-seven to twenty. In the process, they secured bragging rights as the state champion and a likely trip to the Tangerine Bowl. The Clemson fans swarmed the field at Death Valley, taking out the goal post in front of Howard's Rock.

There's nothing like being in Death Valley for a big win. You're more than a mere spectator; you're an integral member of the team. On a key third-down play, when the players on the field look up in the stands and signal the fans to stand up and make noise, it's up to you to make the first and ten by screaming your head off. Winning against South Carolina is always vindicatory, no matter how many times we've beaten them in the past.

That night it felt good, personally good, gut-level good, to be on the winning side, even though we were miles away from the game. Though our celebration was a small one in front of the TV set, for those of us gathered there, the taste of victory—*any* victory—was especially sweet.

Over the weeks leading up to Christmas, there were other small victories to savor. As he had promised, Dr. Hines removed the cast on Lauren's hand before Thanksgiving. Though her wheelchair would remain Lauren's primary mode of transportation, removal of the cast allowed her to progress to crutches for short trips around the house, ditching the tedious, plodding walker.

That same week, Andrea started her new job in Augusta, in an office this time, instead of an airplane. She seemed happy to end the work day at the same place where she started. I went back to work after a month's absence. I found my appointment calendar still opened to October 29, and I perused all the "essential" meetings and deadlines that had been missed. The generosity and selflessness of dozens of coworkers had not only made my extended absence possible, but had also rescued me from a suffocating backlog that would have kept me in the office and away from home.

Karin and Lauren established a routine of sorts. The sky-high doses of antibiotics, coupled with a boilermaker of other drugs, caused Lauren to start each morning extremely sick to her stomach. Mother and daughter worked as a team to quell nausea, take care of personal hygiene, dressing, negotiating stairs, cleaning fixater pins, and dispensing medicine. Then, while Lauren napped, Karin worked to clean and reorganize the left-over remodeling mess, fix meals, keep up with chores, and decorate for the holidays. On sunny afternoons, she made time to take Lauren out for a wheelchair spin. If the weather wasn't nice, they'd watch a movie or television show together, play cards or a game, or just read.

Dinners were a nightly reunion for the whole family. We hadn't been together on a routine basis since our younger child left for Clemson and our older child left to test her wings at United. Keenly aware of how close we'd come to losing one of our own forever, we rejoiced in the present, choosing not to dwell on when, or if, or how our wounded one would ever walk again.

But in the deep darkness of midnight, vestiges of the trauma Lauren had endured dared to return. Almost nightly, she woke in fright from bad dreams of nurses standing over her with needles, or being strapped to an operating table, unable to move, with masked doctors looking down at her. Never prone to nightmares as a child, these were numerous, vivid, persistent, and horrifying. So for a while, Lauren and I traded places at bedtime. Now, when the nightmares came, she could reach out and touch her mother—aka healer, best friend, and dragon slayer!

Thanksgiving Day arrived on Karin's birthday. With the extended family gathered at our house to celebrate and feast on turkey, birthday cake, and ice cream, we had much for which to be thankful, as well as ample cause for celebration.

The birthday girl took a seat at the head of the table. Lauren sat at the end. I sat on the corner to Lauren's right, with her fixated leg resting in my lap. Also seated around the table were Mark (Karin's nephew), Andrea, Granddad (Karin's father), and Senior Heidi, Mature Heidi, and Young Heidi. Boo waited with great expectation under the table.

Karin's mother, Prussian by birth, English by marriage, is Heidi. Karin's sister, daughter of Heidi, is Heidi. And Karin's niece, daughter of Heidi, granddaughter of Heidi, is Heidi.

Ambiguous reference is a way of life in the family; we've dealt with it for years.

The festive table sparkled with Karin's finest china. Crystal and silver sat on a pristine white table cloth, enhanced in the center by a pine-cone turkey perched on a nest of glossy green holly scattered with red Nandina berries. Shimmering candles bordered the conifer turkey north and south, while a banner over the door proclaimed, "Happy Birthday."

Everyone was all smiles, especially Lauren. The most social member of the family, she always delighted in the noisy hubbub of holiday merriment. Plenty of that was going on as the meal began with noisy chatter, passing platters, and carpet-marring splatters.

At some point well into the meal, the commotion lessened as we set our minds to the task of cleaning our plates and obtaining seconds.

It was during this interlude that Young Heidi spoke up. "I'm dropping out of college," she announced. "I've decided to become a beautician."

Eating ceased, forks poised in mid-air. You could hear a pin drop. Everyone looked around for a moment. Then all heads turned toward Mature Heidi, mother of Young Heidi, anticipating her reaction.

But it was Granddad, never at a loss for words, who responded first. He enunciated each syllable of every word perfectly, as he always did, in his proper, British accent. "What sort of technician, Heidi? There are many different varieties of technicians, you know."

I leaned forward, peering around Mature Heidi, who was seated on my right, and into Granddad's ear. I looked for signs of his hearing aid. Noting nothing there, I leaned back, confident that the entertainment was about to begin.

"No, Syd," Senior Heidi corrected. "She didn't say 'technician.' She said 'mortician.'" Then turning to Young Heidi, she continued. "Heidi, whatever in the world would possess you to want to leave college and become a mortician? Mind you, I'm certain you can do well financially, but it seems to me it's a business that's passed on from generation to generation within a family. Certainly no one in this family has ever been in that business, not in England, and without a doubt, not in Germany. But, Michael"—she turned to me with suspicion—"perhaps someone in your family here in South Carolina?"

"Oh, no, not me," I answered innocently. "You all know I'm a descendent of Francis Marion, the Swamp Fox. We're war mongers. No one's ever been in the funeral-home business."

Lauren's eyes met mine, her mouth agape and curved into a roguish smile.

"Michael!" Karin glared at me from the other end of the table. Then she turned toward her parents. "Mum, you and Dad both—"

Mark, the brother of Young Heidi, interrupted. "Sounds to me like a good profession for you, Heidi. I always knew you'd drive me into an early grave. I'll probably be your first customer."

Karin tried again. She waved her arms in front of her above the table. "No, wait, everyone. That's not—"

She was cut short again, this time by Young Heidi. Karin leaned back in surrender, folding her arms in front of her.

"Mom," a wide-eyed and incredulous Young Heidi interrupted. "How can you let this go on? You know I told you this is what I wanted to do. Why can't you support me in front of all these people?"

"Well, of course I support you," answered Mature Heidi. "But why bring it up now? There's a time and place for everything."

"I thought you'd stand by me, that's all." Young Heidi pushed back her chair, tossed her napkin on her plate and left the table.

"I'll go check on her," Mark said, also leaving the table.

"Oh, good grief! Excuse me, I'll be right back," exclaimed Mature Heidi. She left the room too.

"Well," said Granddad, looking straight ahead at the empty chair formerly occupied by Young Heidi. "I'm still waiting to learn what sort of technician Heidi has decided to become."

"Oh, Sydney!" said Senior Heidi. She dropped her fork onto her plate in exasperation.

A shared glance twinkled between Lauren and Andrea. The two sisters, reduced to tears of laughter, could contain themselves no longer.

I shot Karin a sheepish grin, and along with our children, we dissolved into much needed, long overdue, hilarity.

The weeks leading up to Christmas sped by as fast as they do every holiday season. In addition to the usual trickle of Christmas cards, the mail was packed with get-well wishes from Lauren's Kappa sisters, Young Life leaders and kids, and old friends from high school—even some that neither she nor we were aware that we knew. Karin posted each one on a "Wall of Healing," providing transfusions of encouragement to all who stopped there.

Though Lauren remained consistently cheerful, Karin and I found it necessary to visit the Wall of Healing frequently. Any stray rash or bump, no matter how small, appearing anywhere on our wounded daughter, sent us into a tailspin of worry that the infection had returned. Careful to share our concerns only with each other, we intently studied the messages from Hallmark, searching in vain for enduring reassurance.

By early December, the six weeks since the accident had brought about drastic changes in the comfortable, secure world my wife and I had come to enjoy. Over the past decade, we had scarcely noticed the transition in our responsibilities from nurturing small children to befriending nearly grown daughters. We had grown accustomed to allowing each to make her own decisions, trusting that, should a wrong choice be made, no permanent damage would result. We could relax our grip. We no longer needed to tuck them under our shielding blanket of parental protection. Even though they were often out of sight, we believed that they, like us, lived in a kind, forgiving world, where no lasting, irreversible harm ever befell one of our own.

The weeks since the accident revealed our betrayal by our own naivety, mine more so than Karin's. After all, I had allowed, even encouraged, the acquisition of the moped. The benevolent world that I imagined was ours never existed. Now, nearing Christmas, Karin and I struggled to fathom our roles as parents in this new reality.

With a mother's wisdom, Karin realized the importance of keeping Lauren involved in the activities she enjoyed before the accident. Together, she and Lauren set a goal of Lauren attending the Kappa Kappa Gamma Christmas formal in Clemson as a "coming out" party of sorts. It would be Lauren's first trip to school since her accident; a milestone in her physical recovery. Just as important, it was a test of emotional strength, though to this point her resolve, determination, and faith remained unshakable.

For Karin and me, a social occasion that should have been of no concern to the parents of a twenty-one-year-old college senior was, in this new reality, a matter requiring our direct involvement. Besides the fact that her room in the house she shared off campus was up a steep, narrow set of stairs, Lauren still required nightly assistance. Karin was best able to provide this, so we booked a room at the Hampton Inn.

We arrived in Clemson about noon on the day of the dance. Karin and I dropped Lauren off in the care of her delighted roommates. Then we made our way to the Clemson Police Department to thank the men who had helped Lauren after the accident.

"Come on back." The officer swung open the door to the back of the department when we explained who we were and why we were there. "Sergeant Phillips worked your daughter's accident. He's on his way to the station right now. I'm sure he'd want to meet ya'll. Just have a seat."

Minutes later, the door swung open and the officer on duty greeted a tall, thirtyish man with a crew cut.

"Bill Phillips, these are the Tarrants. Their daughter is Lauren, the girl you helped back in October. She was in that moped wreck in front of Bowman Field."

"Oh, yeah! How are you, Mr. and Mrs. Tarrant?" He shook hands with both of us. "I'm glad to finally meet you. We spoke several times on the phone." The man's face lit up as he spoke, obviously pleased to see us in person. "How is Lauren doing?"

"She's doing okay," I answered.

"She's here in Clemson right now," Karin added.

"She's back at school?" A look of disbelief crossed the officer's face. "That's incredible!"

"Oh, no…no. I didn't mean she's back in school," Karin corrected. "We brought Lauren up here so she could see her friends and roommates before Christmas break. Michael and I wanted to meet you and let you know how grateful we are to you for helping Lauren that night."

"I was just doing my job," he replied modestly. "I'll tell you, I've been doing this kind of work for seventeen years, and I've seen a lot of accidents. But I've never seen anything like what happened to your daughter. When I saw how she was laying there on the street and her leg and all…" he paused and drew a deep breath. "Well, I actually stopped in my tracks for a second. Then when I got to Lauren, she was so calm. She wasn't crying; she wasn't afraid. What an amazing, brave girl."

"Would you like to meet her?" I asked. "Her house is just down the street, across from Fike Field House. I know she'd like to meet you."

"Yes, I would. I'd very much like to see her again. I'll be off in about forty-five minutes. Would it be all right if I met ya'll there?"

"Sure," I answered. "We'll see you there shortly, then." We shook hands again, and Karin and I turned toward the door.

"Hold up a second," the sergeant called. "I hesitate to mention this, but there are pictures, you know, of...of the accident. I can show you, if you want to see them."

I turned to Karin. Her expression was solemn. My mind flashed back to that first night in Lauren's room in the Greenville hospital, when I lay on the cot and begged God to stop my imagination from torturing me with images of what my child must have suffered. At the time, I thought He had immediately answered my prayer. Now I wondered if I had just had the mental fortitude to redirect my thoughts. Whatever the reason, the images had ceased and had not returned since. Yet, I knew at some point I'd need to understand more of what actually happened, for insurance purposes if nothing else. But looking at actual pictures....

Sergeant Phillips must have noticed our distress. "You might take a look at the damage to the other car." He paused. "We have pictures of the moped too, but it was so disintegrated there's almost nothing to see. The whole accident scene is available. It's up to you. I just thought I'd let you know."

"Why don't we take a look at the car?" I responded.

Sergeant Phillips led us to a room of white filing cabinets, where he located a large manila envelope of 8 x 10 color photos. He pulled the pictures from the envelope and stood facing us, flipping through the photographs so we could see only the backing. Finally, he handed Karin two pictures. She passed one to me and studied the other.

The photograph revealed a well-used, run-of-the-mill, white minivan. The passenger door had been severely folded in; the rear door jam was exposed like a massive knife blade that ran the height of the automobile. A wide, red streak began there, parallel to the ground, flowing the length of the van and finally angling up toward the roof.

Doubtless, the automobile had, by now, spent a day or two in a body shop and emerged no worse for the ordeal.

Karin put the picture down without a word. She looked at me, then closed her eyes in an unsuccessful effort to stifle a shudder.

I felt my cheeks redden as I turned to Officer Phillips. "Do you know if the driver, the grad student from China…" I paused and sank my teeth into my tongue before continuing. "Do you know if he was ever charged or fined?"

"Yes sir," the policeman answered, diverting his eyes from mine. "He was charged with failure to yield and paid a twenty-five dollar fine."

Karin grabbed my forearm, digging in her nails.

"I see," I said. I felt the pit of my stomach catch fire.

Less than twenty-four hours later, I stood by the huge, white columns on the portico of Sykes Hall on the Clemson campus. Before walking into the Registrar's office to withdraw Lauren from the school she loved so much, I looked out at Bowman Field. Its green expanse contrasted with the barren, leafless hardwoods, locked in December's bitter grip. They were scattered like giant, monolithic tombstones on the hillside beyond, sloping up to the alumni center. Somewhere amidst that scene, my child had lost a vital component of the physical framework of her life. Worse, a well-planned and prepared-for future had been forever altered in a split second, leaving a void filled with sickness, pain, and uncertainty.

Last night, looking frail but so pretty in her most elegant, over-sized, tear-away jogging pants, Lauren had been whisked to the ball in the backseat of our big Buick, with a proud Robbie as coachman and chauffeur. The couple returned around midnight, with Lauren happier and more vibrant than she had been since the accident. She shared the events of the evening with Karin and me, like a middle-school kid after her first school dance. It was nearly 2 AM before anyone went to bed.

This morning, however, I knew Karin was back at the Hampton Inn with Lauren, helping as best she could while her child vomited, the price for revisiting life as it used to be, even if peripherally, and for only a moment.

I turned and stepped into Sykes Hall.

The Lawd don't let nothin' happen that He cain't make good come of it.

Yeah. Right, I thought.

Chapter Eight

*"For I know the plans I have for you," declares the Lord, "plans
to prosper you and not to harm you, plans to give you hope and
a future."*

—Jeremiah 29:11

THE VERDANT FRONDS of the palms lining King Street
rustled in the December sea breeze as Mary DuPree stepped to
the middle of the pedestrian crosswalk and raised two crutches
crisscrossed over her head. The Christmas traffic on Charleston's
narrow, three-hundred-year-old main street obligingly ground
to a halt. Wheeling Lauren before him, Robbie hurried across
the intersection. Mary DuPree lowered the crutches and then
bounded across the south-bound lane to join her friends. Having
patiently waited, the traffic then politely resumed in this, the
most well-mannered city in America.

This annual shopping trip to Charleston was as much
a Christmas tradition as pizza on Christmas Eve or playing
charades with Grandma and Granddad on Christmas night. This
year we were determined that no tradition would be unobserved.

Every holiday ritual brought with it a comforting normalcy, an illusion that nothing had changed since last year.

As the season progressed, Lauren spent more and more time in her chair by the fire in the living room—our resident Tiny Tim. Robbie spent much of his Christmas holiday at our house, squeezed into the oversized chair with his girlfriend, watching hushed football games as Lauren became increasingly sensitive to sound. On those evenings when Robbie was back in Tega Cay, Andrea would come home after work and cuddle into the chair with her little sister, holding her while she dozed.

New Year's Eve found Lauren and Robbie quietly playing cards at home with Karin and me, avoiding the noise associated with our Southern custom of welcoming the New Year with firecrackers and Roman candles. But by mid-morning on New Year's Day, the house was jumping with plenty of company.

I stood at the kitchen counter, carving a big ham Karin had just taken out of the oven when Lauren hobbled in from the living room, clearly aggravated.

"Daddy! Oh, my gosh! Are you ever going to put that electric knife down? It sounds like you're running a chain saw in here. If I ever get a house of my own, no way will there be an electric knife in it. That thing has run continuously since Thanksgiving."

Before I could respond, the wall phone rang behind Lauren.

"Good night! A person needs hearing protection to live in this house!" She grumbled and crutched away down the hall, seeking a more peaceful setting.

"Happy New Year!" I greeted whoever was on the other end of the phone line.

Andrea's voice answered, "Hi, Daddy. Happy New Year!"

"Hey, Chicken! How was the party last night with the Augusta crowd?" Without pausing for an answer, I continued. "Did you get the message we left? We need you to pick up some sour cream on your way home. Hurry up! We'll be eating in an hour or so."

"Daddy, I didn't go to Augusta. I'm in Charlotte." Andrea's voice was controlled, as if counting down to a rocket launching.

To my aggravation, I noticed that the kitchen was suddenly filled with people. All the Heidi's and Karin, even Granddad, milled about like a group of impatient spectators awaiting the first burst of New Year's fireworks. They'd not have to wait long.

"Charlotte?" I repeated. "Charlotte, North Carolina? What in the world are you doing up there?"

"Daddy, I'm engaged!" Andrea blurted.

The first sky rocket went up; it was awesome.

"Engaged?" I shouted. "Engaged to be *married*? To whom?"

Everyone in the room stopped and turned in my direction. Karin's face glowed crimson then rapidly faded to ashen, like an expiring burst of fireworks.

"I'm at Bo and Jackie's, Daddy," Andrea replied. The tension in her voice ratcheted up a notch. "Marc flew here from Colorado. He gave me a diamond last night. He asked me to marry him, and I said yes."

Marc and Andrea had been in a series of serious on-again, off-again relationships for years, since Andrea was a freshman in college. The last break-up had come about the same time Andrea had decided that flying wasn't for her and had returned home.

Good looking and athletic, Marc rode a baseball scholarship from his home in Boulder, Colorado, to the University of South Carolina at Aiken, two institutions separated by sixteen hundred miles in distance and light years in philosophies. His meeting our cheerleader daughter was inevitable.

He wasn't a bad kid, but the culture clash between the two of them sporadically overrode their mutual attraction. Brought up in the Front Range of the Rocky Mountains, in the very neighborhood of the University of Colorado, Marc appeared baffled by our Southern conservatism and the closeness of our family.

Like flying, there must have been an element of excitement and mystery about this boy from a place and society so different from our own that attracted our older daughter like a moth to a flame. Over the past several years, each break-up and subsequent reconciliation had drawn Andrea closer and closer to that flame. The resulting burns became more and more devastating emotionally and even financially. Karin and I had always stepped in and swept up the ashes, doing what we could to restore our daughter.

Now, I could scarcely believe my ears. Andrea was informing me that she had set a flight path for a final conflagration. I already had one daughter physically injured so badly that no one knew how to fix her; I was not of a mind to sit back and watch the emotional devastation of the other one.

"Hold on while I switch to the portable phone," I said, struggling to keep my voice under control. My live audience in the kitchen watched in silence as I grabbed a cordless phone and stormed out to the driveway. Karin followed me.

"Have you lost your cotton-pickin' mind?" I yelled as soon as I reached the cooler air and relative privacy of the outdoors. "What are you, some kind of glutton for punishment?"

Even as the words were forming in my head, I knew I should have paused, used some psychology, played it cool. But only a few short weeks had passed since the last time I had been caught off guard by the slings and arrows of outrageous fortune. Though I had sworn not to let it happen again, I felt myself being sucked into another cruel vortex.

Karin stood beside me, shivering in the brisk air, with no jacket and just a thin blouse, while I begged, pleaded, reasoned, and threatened at ever increasing decibel levels.

Andrea was not to be dissuaded.

"I'm coming up there," I finally announced. "I'm leaving right now. You're going to explain to me face-to-face why on earth you're making a decision of this importance in haste."

"No, Daddy," Andrea responded. "Don't do that. It won't change my mind, and it will serve no purpose whatsoever."

"Michael, calm down," Karin demanded as I felt my face turn red with desperation. Though she hadn't been on the phone, the content of the conversation was crystal clear.

"You're going to give yourself a heart attack. Just let it go. There's nothing you can do about it. Tell her good-bye for now. We need to go back in." Then she repeated, "There's nothing you can do about it."

Andrea overheard our exchange

"Mama's right, Daddy," she said. "I'm sorry to break the news to ya'll like this, but I didn't want to lie to you. I know this is not good timing. And I don't want to hurt you or Mama. Tomorrow I'm coming back to Aiken. Marc is coming with me, and we can talk more then. I'll give work two weeks notice, then I'll find a job and a place to live here in Charlotte until we're married. We haven't set a date, but we've agreed that Lauren's recovery comes first. I don't want to do anything that might get in the way of her getting well as fast as possible."

I hung up and followed Karin back into the garage, where we sat on the stairs to regain our composure before facing the concerned gathering that awaited us in the house.

"Well, Happy Stinkin' New Year," I said between clenched teeth as we sat side by side in the chilly garage.

"Pretty lousy timing, huh?" Karin answered.

A couple of minutes passed in silence, then Karin spoke again.

"You know, there are a couple of ways we can handle this. We can choose to be upset and angry...and we have every right to be. Their relationship has not been pretty. And it's been you and I who have paid the price, literally, more than once."

"Or?" I prompted, anxious to hear any alternative.

"I know you want to go up there and yank her back, because it's the only way we can be sure she won't get hurt. I want to do that too, just like I want to go back two months and stop Lauren from going to that meeting at the Hendrix Center on October 29."

Karin turned away and gazed across the cars parked below us on the garage floor and out to the bare-limbed dogwoods lining the driveway. Then she went on. "But, we can't stop Andrea from making this mistake—if it *is* a mistake—any more than we can go back in time and protect Lauren. Even God lets His children make choices, Michael."

She sighed. "So now we have a choice. We can choose to let this destroy our relationship with our daughter, or we can choose to accept the situation with grace and give it to God. I'm thinking we've got enough on our plate right now. I choose to give this one to God."

With that, Karin had reached into the tornado swirling about me, grabbed me by the collar, and pulled me to safety. I was not sure this situation was of sufficient importance to merit God's personal attention, but Karin's tender logic was beyond argument.

"One thing's for sure," I said, gently turning my wife's pretty face around so we were nose-to-nose, "I made the right choice when I chose you. We'll make it a happy new year, despite it all, together."

She gave me a quick kiss.

"Come on," she said. "Let's go break the news to everybody, then sit back and watch the fireworks!"

When his daughters are small, riding his shoulders or cuddled in his lap while he reads a bedtime story, no daddy can bear the thought of someday giving his precious little girls to some certain-to-be-undeserving boy, at a wedding that costs about the same as the Porsche daddy will never be able to afford. Alas, the day that undeserving boy asks for his daughter's hand is dreaded indeed.

That's why God invented the teenage years. After a decade of drama, the prospect of children leaving the nest and starting families of their own becomes considerably less traumatic. So the meeting with Andrea and Marc, though no episode out of a fairy tale, was at least cordial.

Andrea showed off her diamond before she and Marc left. Then, as I watched the two of them drive away, the challenges and turmoil of the teen and college years faded away. All I saw was my Annie, the little girl who rode my shoulders and watched TV in my lap, riding away with her choice that would shape the rest of her life.

I longed for a simpler time.

For the next few days, while Andrea prepared to move to Charlotte, Lauren became uncharacteristically surly, to a worrisome degree. When Dr. Hines suggested a bold move at her appointment, the first week in January, she eagerly agreed. Karin and I, though, were hesitant.

"I want to remove the fixater," Dr. Hines announced after the x-rays were taken. "I want to do it soon, within the next two weeks if we can schedule it that quickly."

He looked at Lauren as he talked. "I'm convinced that if we don't allow some movement, the chances of you ever moving your leg are very low. I want to take the external hardware off and remove the internal spacers so that, with physical therapy, we can bend your leg and break up the scar tissue."

Lauren agreed, but Karin and I exchanged glances. I knew Dr. Baxter's recommendations were echoing in her head as loudly as mine.

"When we left Baltimore, Dr. Baxter told us the fixater should remain until at least the middle of February," I began with some hesitation, keenly aware of Dr. Hines' ownership issues regarding Lauren's case. "He told us that motion was an infection's best friend. Are you sure it's not too soon to begin allowing movement?"

"How old is Dr. Baxter?" Dr. Hines bristled, confirming my fear that he would take my question as a personal affront.

"He's about my age, I guess." I responded. "Maybe a little older."

"I only ask because older doctors are often more conservative in their approach to orthopedics than those of us who have completed our studies more recently. I'm convinced the infection is history. But just to be sure, I'm going to keep Lauren on Cipro for three more months. And I'm going to schedule the procedure at our outpatient surgery center. I don't want her exposed to the potential of picking something up in the hospital."

All three of us must have looked surprised, because Dr. Hines quickly went on.

"This is a simple procedure. Nothing like what you've been through with any of your past surgeries, Lauren. You'll come in early, we'll take the fixater off, make a small incision to remove the spacers, and you'll be ready to go home after lunch. Then we'll get you into our physical therapy center a week after that and see how much mobility we can get."

The tension of moments earlier faded as this offering of hope sank in.

"I'm ready right now," Lauren said, smiling brightly at Dr. Hines. She felt more comfortable with him than with most of the doctors and nurses she'd met over the past couple of months. Her mood brightened.

"But I also want to get off the OxyContin," she continued. "It's making me feel weird, like I'm being dragged down to a place I don't like. I wake up in the morning, and the only thing that motivates me to get out of bed is knowing there's a pill waiting. I hate that feeling. So, how do I go about getting off this stuff?"

"Cut your dosage," came Dr. Hines' quick reply. "Just break the pill in half."

Karin and I looked at each other again. Baxter had warned us of grave consequences if an OxyContin tablet were broken.

This time Karin spoke up. "I hate to keep invoking the name of Dr. Baxter, but before leaving Maryland, he cautioned us against breaking an OxyContin."

To our relief, Dr. Hines seemed to take no offense. "Then extend the interval between each dose. It shouldn't be a problem. And you won't need anything that strong following this next procedure."

For the third time, Karin and I exchanged glances.

"Look," the doctor said, rolling back in his chair for a moment's deliberation, "I'll give Dr. Baxter a call, tell him what we're planning, and see what he thinks. If he has any problems with it, we'll play it his way. But I'm positive he'll agree this is the best way to proceed."

He hugged Lauren and shook hands with Karin and me. The girls headed for the restroom while I checked out at the front desk.

"Michael! It's Lauren! Come quick!" Karin's voice rang out from the opposite end of a long hallway, a good one hundred feet away. I dropped the pen I was using in mid-stroke and sprinted down the hall, bursting into the ladies' room. Lauren lay unconscious in the middle of the floor. Nurses rushed in behind me.

Karin cradled Lauren's head while I brought wet paper towels. One nurse took Lauren's vital signs; another held smelling salts under her nose.

Lauren recovered quickly.

"Just a little weak," the nurses said. "Nothing to be concerned about."

As we drove home, it was obvious that her earlier, more optimistic frame of mind had been replaced by the familiar and disturbing melancholy. The fainting spell served to underscore how frail Lauren was physically, but this deepening sadness was more disturbing. Whether it was Robbie heading back to Clemson, Andrea moving to Charlotte, the post-holiday lull, two and a half months on morphine and OxyContin, the uncertainty of ever being able to walk again, the realization of a life-time of disability, or a combination of everything, Lauren was being reinjured right before our eyes.

Neither Karin nor I knew how to stop it.

"I'm taking Lauren out for breakfast in the morning," Karin whispered to me when we went to bed late that same evening. "The house is too quiet with Robbie gone and you at work. The Christmas decorations are down; things are January bleak. Maybe we'll go to IHOP and then look around in Barnes & Noble. I don't know, just anyplace that's not a doctor's office and doesn't remind her that more surgeries are coming up. I just want her to have a playful day."

By 9:30 the following morning, Karin bustled up and down the steep stairs that led from the house to the garage. After packing Lauren's wheelchair in the trunk of the Buick, she left the door at the top of the stairs ajar while she ran back

inside and up to the bedroom, getting ready to help Lauren out of the house.

Waiting in the living room, Lauren pulled herself up from the couch with her crutches, hobbled through the kitchen, then paused at the open garage door.

As if responding to a command from a voice that only she could hear, Lauren suddenly shifted her weight to the left crutch. Her left hand grabbed the right crutch, jerked it from under her arm and sent it flying to the garage floor below.

Tears born of months of frustration, anger, and drug-induced emotion streaked down her freckled cheeks.

"I'm...so...sick...of this!" she shouted between great, gulping sobs. The words echoed into the emptiness below her.

The tears subsided, she straightened as best she could, then using her right hand, she gripped the left crutch and ripped it from its place.

With her support gone, Lauren swayed over the empty space of the staircase.

The weight of the fixater on her right leg rocked her forward into the void. Her body tilted toward the open chasm.

At that instant, from behind, an arm clad in a pink cotton sweater shot between Lauren and the nothingness before her, seized her around the waist, and pulled her in and down to the floor.

There they stayed for the rest of that morning, mother and daughter, awash in tears, but safe for the moment in each other's arms.

Twenty-four hours later, Lauren, Karin, and I waited in the office of a psychologist specializing in Post Traumatic Stress Disorder.

"Really, ya'll," Lauren said, her face displaying none of the torment of the previous morning. "I'm okay. I'm feeling much happier today. I don't need to be here. This is a big waste of time. I'm sorry I freaked out yesterday, but like I've said a dozen times, I just went too long without an OxyContin. I know if I back off that stuff more gradually, nothing like that will ever happen again."

Lauren was right. Her spirits since the incident at the garage door had markedly improved, like sunshine's return after a spring thunderstorm has cleansed the air of pollen.

Before we could respond to her last-minute pleadings, the door opened. A trim, nicely dressed, middle-aged lady with shoulder-length brown hair entered.

"Hello, I'm Dr. Smith," she said, shaking hands with each of us. She had a kind face but a distant, professional demeanor. She seemed nice enough, but I knew Lauren's type—sweet, motherly—and I feared Dr. Smith wasn't it.

Once she made sure that Lauren wanted Karin and me to sit in on the session, the doctor jotted notes while she asked a series of questions focused primarily on the circumstances of the accident and the aftermath. Each question seemed to draw Lauren deeper and deeper back into the melancholy morass from which she had just emerged.

Finally, the questions ended. Pulling off her glasses, Dr. Smith leaned forward in her chair. "Lauren, based on your answers and my observations, there's no question that you are suffering from Post Traumatic Stress Disorder. That's no reflection on you, or your character, or your personality. Given what you've been through and are still going through, PTSD is to be expected."

Lauren sat emotionless, returning the doctor's direct gaze.

"I can help you deal with it. I can help you put this behind you. I'd like to set up a series of sessions. It may take a few weeks, it may take a few months, but I want to help you get through this."

Lauren shifted in her wheelchair, squaring her back and shoulders. With an uncharacteristic lack of deference, she responded, "I don't need psychological counseling. My parents have helped me get this far, and they can help me through this too."

Karin and I exchanged glances. Her eyes shimmered with tears, and I felt a lump rise into my throat.

No, Chicken Little, I thought. *Mama and I can't help you with this. We're not qualified. We don't know anything about depression or counseling. This is too serious.*

I wanted to speak, but I was mute with emotion.

The voice in my head continued to plead silently.

Please let this lady help you. Let someone who knows what they're doing help you. We love you too much. I can't stand to see you suffer anymore than you already have.

But Lauren left no doubt as to her intentions. "I don't want to come here again," she concluded.

Unlike me, the counselor appeared to be taking Lauren's dismissal in stride.

"Lauren, you've been through so much, and you're suppressing this experience. That's okay for now. But sooner or later, these specters you're burying are going to come back to life and demand that you face them. Whether you deal with it now, or ten years from now, at some point you *will* have to deal with it. I think it would be healthier if you dealt with it now, while help is at hand."

In tears now, Lauren would hear none of it. "My faith in Jesus has brought me this far. He will help me, along with Mama and Daddy. I don't need counseling. I just need Him. I don't want to come back."

We filed out of the doctor's office and rolled our wheelchair-bound daughter to the car and, as usual, positioned her in the back seat. The three of us sat in silence as I negotiated through the parking lot maze and out onto the busy street.

"I was doing better before I went in there and that lady made me relive the whole thing." Lauren's poignant cry broke the silence. "I'm not crazy, and I don't want to be treated like I am. I'm just sick of having these nails going through my leg, and I'm sick of feeling crummy all the time. I'm sick of not being able to walk. I'm sick of having to depend on someone else to even move! I'm sick of being placed into the car like a baby, or an invalid, or an old lady."

Now the recollection of the nightmare, dredged up during the session with the psychologist, completely overwhelmed her. "I just want to be who I was before. I just want to be *me* again!"

Flooded with emotion, I could no longer drive. I pulled into a shopping center parking lot. Karin moved into the back seat of the car and held Lauren while she cried.

They sat huddled together, two of the three people I love most in the world, absolutely wretched.

My feeling of powerlessness was immeasurable. *How many times and how many ways*, I thought, *can a father's heart break?*

We were a pathetic trio, parked in front of Pier One, trapped in a nightmare, while normal people carried on the business of normal lives right outside our car windows. There was no indication that anyone noticed the meltdown occurring in their midst, but at length I decided we should move away from this spot.

The lights in the parking lot flickered on, warding off the darkness falling around us. But as we turned in the direction of home and moved away from the meager light of the parking lot into the depth of the oncoming night, Lauren seemingly moved beyond depression to capitulation. As her sobs subsided, so, it seemed, did her desire to fight anymore.

With that realization, I found myself more scared than I had been since Lauren's accident. There had been a tangible enemy, infection, to fight when Dr. Moore had predicted amputation. We could see the infection, target it, declare war on it, and ultimately see physical evidence of victory.

But this enemy was insidious. It couldn't be seen, or smelled, or touched, or heard. Existing only in the mind, it was potentially more devastating than anything Lauren or we had ever faced.

We cannot go home like this, I thought. With Karin still holding Lauren in the backseat, I felt as if we were the only three souls in the universe, desperately needing help with no where to turn. *There's got to be a pill or something. There's got to be something that'll help us through the night.*

I dialed our family doctor on my cell phone. The answering service picked up and suggested that emergencies at this hour were best handled at the hospital.

I hung up. *That's not gonna work.*

In the rearview mirror, Lauren lay like a lifeless rag doll against Karin.

"What about the Aurora Pavilion?" I whispered as we approached Aiken. "It's a mental health clinic, isn't it? Do you think they could do anything? Should we at least ask?"

"We've got nothing to lose," Karin whispered back.

Minutes later I pulled up under the portico of the clinic. I left Karin still clinging to Lauren in the back seat and walked into the clean, brightly lit building.

"Hello," the nurse called as I approached the reception desk. "Can I help you?"

What on earth am I doing here? I wondered before I answered. *There is no way these people can do anything tonight. I'm as naïve as I am desperate.*

The nurse was waiting for a response. She looked puzzled but still smiled at me.

"I...uh...I have a family member, who was in a bad accident several weeks ago. She...uh...just came from a really stressful doctor's appointment, where she got some...uh...some bad news," I fumbled. "She's sad and depressed. My wife and I don't know how to help her. We were...uh...passing by here and thought...well...maybe you all could help. But I guess...without seeing her...well, there's probably nothing you can do."

My stammered explanation surely convinced the nurse that I needed help more than the mysterious "family member" of whom I spoke.

"We'd certainly like to help you, sir," she replied. "But you would have to bring your family member in."

"Yes, I know. I'm sorry. That's not possible. I'm sorry I wasted your time. We'll be okay tonight." I felt my face flush bright red as I backed toward the door. "If we need you tomorrow, we'll call you. Thanks again. Sorry to have bothered you."

The three of us made our way home in shared misery. Mercifully, Lauren fell asleep in her big chair by the fireplace. While Karin made dinner, I went out to retrieve the mail and pick up the garbage cans I had placed by the curb that morning. As I trudged down the driveway, it occurred to me that, as far as I could recall, I had never been in a more horrid mood in my life.

I pulled the usual junk out of the mailbox, along with a couple of delinquently delivered Christmas cards, which did nothing to cheer me. Standing under the street light above our mailbox, I ripped open an official-looking letter from our insurance company.

Dear Mr. Tarrant,

This is to inform you that you are two months in arrears in your homeowner's and automobile insurance payments. Payment within 48 hours is required. Otherwise, we will terminate all policies on your account, notify the South Carolina Department of Transportation, and your mortgage holder...

What? Impossible, I thought.

Karin had written the check to the insurance company, along with all the other bills, the day Lauren had been hurt. She had placed them in the front pocket of the car door, intending to mail them that night. Granted, we had forgotten about them amidst the turmoil of Lauren's accident, but my brother had retrieved the mail from our car and posted it for us, albeit ten days later. I knew that for a fact, because I had looked in the car door pocket only a few days earlier to make sure nothing had been left. And I had written checks for the current bills just a couple of weeks ago, when we got home from Baltimore.

An outlet opened for my pent-up fury. Tomorrow, I'd call that insurance company and read them the riot act!

Standing alone in the dark in front of our house, the letter from the insurance company in my hand waving in the cold wind, I looked up into the starless, overcast sky and shouted a curse for anyone listening to hear. Before turning and storming back inside, I sent the garbage can clattering across the street with one swift kick.

The following morning dawned as gray and dismal as my mood. A cold drizzle sprinkled the windshield as I drove through the bleak January landscape to work. At 9:00 AM, as soon as our insurance agent's office opened, I called to launch my attack.

The office receptionist picked up after several rings. Mustering what meager self-control I still possessed, I explained the situation.

"I'm sorry, Mr. Tarrant," she explained in a sugary southern accent, "but if the Atlanta office doesn't receive a payment for the past month, even if they do receive a payment for the current month, they won't credit your account for either payment. Since you've already written the checks, but the first one is apparently lost in the mail, I'm afraid you'll have to stop payment on both checks, then bring in another check for both months to make sure your coverage doesn't lapse."

My black mood having sapped my last ounce of stamina, the tongue lashing I had relished the night before went undelivered. I pulled on my jacket and braced against the wind and drizzle as I began a ten-minute trudge to the credit union to do as I had been instructed.

Walking through the gloomy, blowing mist, every bone in my body ached as if from a bad case of flu. This, I thought, must be how Lauren feels all the time. The physical aching was surpassed only by the emotional agony.

As I walked, my thoughts turned blacker. Every fear I had been suppressing, every doubt that I had buried in my subconscious, now came tumbling to the forefront of consciousness.

What have we accomplished in the last two months? I thought. *Sure, Lauren still has her leg, but will she ever be able to bend it? Dr. Baxter said it would take a miracle for her to be able to bend her knee to thirty degrees. Even if she could, it would be so painful that she would beg to have it fused. So, what has this all been for? How can she ever have anything close to a normal life with a leg that's stuck straight out? She'll hardly be able to attend any sporting events and sit in an arena seat; she'll have a heck of a time getting into any theatre, or on an airplane or bus or public transportation. Riding a bike, one of her greatest passions, is forever out of the question. She won't even be able to sit normally in a car.*

And what about playing with future children? She won't be able to kneel beside the bathtub and bathe her baby. She won't be able to sit in a school cafeteria and watch a play. For that matter, she won't even be able to sit in a chair without something to prop her leg on, or without raising her hip and twisting into a contorted position.

The flood of dark thoughts continued pouring in, unrelenting.

So here's what I've managed to do for my child, the voice in my head hissed.

My efforts have put my child in the position of facing a life of constant aggravation, inconvenience, and pain. Maybe she'll decide that she'd rather have her leg amputated, after all. Maybe she'll decide that life with a prosthesis would be better than having a shapeless limb that won't bend. If I had left things alone, she would have at least been spared the agony of making a horrendous decision like deliberately choosing to amputate her leg. It would have just been done. There would have been no choice.

By now, she could have been well on her way to facing a new reality, healing, and learning how to move about on an artificial limb. Instead, she's endured six surgeries already, with a certainty of more to come, with little hope that she'll be any better off than she is right now. She'll be faced with making a choice that no one should ever have to make. And, whichever way she chooses, both paths end in a disabled, disfigured, frustrating, painful life. I could have at least spared her the misery of having to choose which path she must follow.

I walked on in the foul weather. Water clung to the needles on the pine trees that lined the sidewalks like an icy shroud. If there were other people about, I didn't notice. Once again, I was utterly, completely alone.

Finally, I reached the credit union. As I pushed open the double doors, the events of the past weeks merged in my mind, forming a suffocating whirlpool of surgeries, unknown doctors and strange procedures, distant hospitals, unfamiliar people, amputations, infections, thieves in our home, police, morphine, ambulances, flashing emergency lights, wheelchairs, walkers, dashed plans, wrenching doubts, searing pain and paralyzing fear. They swirled into a giant vortex, sucking in everything and everyone in its path.

At its very core, spinning and dropping lower and lower, was our precious child. I stood helplessly by, watching the horror play out, now utterly without hope, and powerless to do anything to rescue her.

The doors slammed shut behind me. The noise jolted me back to the business at hand. I stepped inside and glanced at the tidy row of Plexiglas cubicles. All but one was occupied by a familiar member-services representative, each with a customer. The one available customer service rep was a young woman whom I had never seen before. I walked in, not caring whether or not I was helped by someone I knew. I was beyond help anyway. I sat down in front of her without a greeting.

"May I help you?" She spoke more to the computer terminal than to me.

Great, I thought. *This lady's going to be really interested in cutting me some slack.* "Yeah. I need to stop payment on a couple of checks."

"Okay," she said. "Are they sequential?"

"No. They were written several weeks apart." I pulled the checkbook out of my back pocket.

"That's too bad," she said. "If they were sequential, we'd only have to charge you twenty dollars, but since they're not, we'll have to charge you for two separate stop payments, so it'll be forty dollars."

"Forty dollars!" I shouted. "No way am I going to pay forty dollars because my insurance agent, who has had my business for twenty-five years, has some stupid rule about not depositing checks received out of sync or some such nonsense. Let me borrow your phone."

She handed me the phone across the desk, and we looked at each other for the first time. Younger than I, her short, dark hair framed a kind face that held no hint of a smile. Apparently, my abruptness and sorry mood were evident.

I punched in my insurance agent's number. To my surprise, he answered on the first ring.

"Hey, Joe. Is that you? This is Mike Tarrant. Since when do you answer the phone down there? In the twenty-five years I've been with your agency, you've never answered the phone yourself."

"Oh, I do occasionally, Mike," he responded. "You just haven't had the good fortune that you're encountering today."

Yeah, right, I thought. Before I could get to the point of my phone call, Joe continued.

"Mike, how's Lauren? I heard she was in a really bad wreck. We've been praying for all of ya'll. Can you tell me what happened?"

I tried to cut my answer short, but Joe responded to each statement with genuine concern that led to additional questions and explanations. I found myself pouring out the whole story of everything that had transpired over the course of the last two months, including Dr. Baxter's dismal prognosis. I shared my fear that Lauren now faced tougher times than what she'd already been through.

After several minutes, I glanced up at the young customer service rep and mouthed an apology for tying up her phone for so long. She responded with a "don't worry about it" shake of her head and wave of her hands. She made no pretense of diverting her attention elsewhere; it was obvious she was listening to this story as intently as Joe was on the other end of the phone.

Thirty minutes later, I completed the chronology of the sorry events of the recent past.

"Well, bless Lauren's little heart, Mike," Joe said. "You know we'll be thinking about her. And if there's anything I can do, you just let me know. Listen, forget about that stop payment on the check you mailed to Atlanta. I'll take care of those folks up there. But you better stop payment on that lost check from last month while you're in the credit union.

"Mike, one last thing before you go. Write this name down: Rob Boyd, B-O-Y-D. I don't have his number, but he's in the phone book. He's a lawyer and a friend of mine. With all that's happened, you need to talk to him, just to make sure all the bases are covered for Lauren's sake."

I scribbled the name on a scrap of paper and stuffed it in my pocket, then thanked Joe and hung up. With a throbbing headache now amplifying my misery, I apologized to the credit union rep for tying up her phone and taking a half hour out of her workday.

"I'm so sorry about your daughter, Mr. Tarrant, and all she's going through." Her attitude one of concern. "I was in a pretty bad wreck too, when I was in college."

In my current state, I could not have cared less about hearing this stranger's story, but she had afforded me the courtesy of using her business phone for an inordinate length of time. I had little choice but to feign interest.

"Really. What happened?"

"I was a freshman at Lander, in Greenwood," she began. "It was Christmas break, and I had just finished my last exam. I was so anxious to get home and start the holidays that I packed up my car and started driving in the middle of the night. It was after midnight when I left, I'm sure. I was coming south on US 25. Are you familiar with that road at all?"

I nodded, and she continued.

"Then you'll probably know exactly where I was when the accident happened. Do you know those big brick entrance gates that are on both sides of the road about halfway between Greenwood and Edgefield? They look like the gates to an old plantation. There are four of them, two facing northbound traffic and then a couple of miles later there are two more, facing southbound traffic. They sit out there in the middle of nowhere."

"Yeah," I said, ignoring my pounding head as I became more interested in her story. "I've seen those gates all my life and wondered why they were there. As far as I can tell, they don't serve any purpose.

"There's an old cemetery half-way between the two gates," she explained. "I guess the family had them built years and years ago as a tribute, or else to let people know when they were nearing the cemetery. I'm not sure. Anyway, like I said, it was late; I had been cramming for exams for days, and my car was packed with stuff from my dorm that I was taking home for Christmas. There was no room for anyone else to ride with me. Even the front seat was packed out. I was exhausted. I must have been doing about sixty miles an hour when I fell asleep at the wheel."

She had my full attention now.

"Oh, no!" I shuddered.

"I woke up just before I hit the brick gate that sits on the left side of the road and faces northbound traffic. The police estimated I was still going about sixty, but to me, when it was happening, well, it was like everything was in slow motion.

"The gate was built with concrete blocks and steel rebar under the bricks. When I hit it, the gate exploded and my car was totaled. The concrete-and-brick wall brought it to a stop instantly.

"Fortunately, I had my seat belt on, which kept me from going through the windshield. But I was hurt badly. I couldn't move. It was the middle of the night, and you know how deserted that road is at that hour."

I nodded.

"There's only one house on that stretch of highway," she said. "It's just down the road from the gate I hit. It was a miracle. The lady who lived in that house was a nurse at the hospital in Greenwood, just coming home from work in the car right behind me. She saw the whole thing happen and was there almost immediately. I don't know what she did for me right then, but after she made sure I was alive, she raced to her house and told her husband to call an ambulance. Then she raced back to me.

"They had me back at the hospital in Greenwood in less than an hour and rushed me straight into surgery. I had broken both my legs and the elbow in my right arm. My legs were in pretty bad shape, but the orthopedic surgeon said my elbow was the worst break he had ever seen.

"But all that's just background. Here comes the part I want to tell you. The surgeon told me and my parents that I'd never be able to bend my arm again. He said it would probably have to be fused, because I wouldn't be able to stand the pain if I tried to bend it. He said the best case would be that my arm would hang pretty much useless by my side, just able to swing from side to side and forwards and back. Almost what they've been telling you about your daughter's leg. But watch this."

She stood up behind her desk, lifted her right arm out to her side and then bent her elbow and touched her shoulder.

"See, Mr. Tarrant. They told me the same thing! But it wasn't true. When the doctor told me I'd never use my arm again, I knew he was wrong. I absolutely knew I'd use my arm again. I went to physical therapy knowing that I would bend my elbow, even though the physical therapist didn't agree. I worked hard for months. I never doubted that I'd use this arm.

"I still have trouble with my legs from time to time. Some day I'll probably have to have knee replacement. I'll face that when the time comes. But I'm all right, and I've known since the moment I hit that brick wall that I'd be all right."

She paused and looked me in the eye with unshakeable conviction. "Your daughter is going to be all right too. She's not going to lose her leg or have it fused. Everything's she's been through will not be for nothing. I guarantee it."

I sat in astonishment. How could this young woman, whom I had known for less than an hour, relate a story so similar to

Lauren's as to be almost unbelievable? How could she deliver this astounding prognosis with such unwavering assuredness?

She wasn't finished.

"I'm going to tell you how I knew from the minute I hit that brick wall that I would be okay. In fact, I wasn't even scared. What I'm about to tell you is something I've told only a handful of people besides my parents, because most people would think I'm crazy if I told them.

"I don't know you at all, yet I feel compelled to share this with you, and I know you won't think I'm crazy."

I was now riveted to her every word.

"I told you I was alone in the car," she said. "But when I woke up just seconds before I crashed into that wall, I looked at the passenger seat and saw a man riding with me."

She paused for a moment as if searching my face for a reaction, then went on.

"He looked at me and didn't say a word. I looked at him, and he told me without speaking that I would be all right. He told me I would be hurt, but that I would not die, and I would ultimately be all right. And I was no longer afraid. I calmly turned my head and watched as my car ran into that wall."

"Who was it?" I responded, incredulous. "Who was that man? Did you recognize him?"

"It wasn't anyone I had ever seen before, and it certainly it wasn't anyone I've seen since. I'm convinced it was an angel."

She smiled. "Now you see why I don't tell many people. No one would believe me, and just about everyone would think I'm crazy. But I know you believe it, and I know I was meant to tell you my story today."

Stunned, I looked at her for a few seconds. "What's your name?"

"Jennifer," she answered.

"Jennifer, I wish I could tell you how I felt when I walked into your office a little while ago. I was at the lowest point in my life, completely without hope. I carried the weight of all the horrific things that have happened over the last couple of months. I was convinced that everything we had been doing to help Lauren was ultimately, in some cruel twist, going to do no more than make her life one of even more torment.

"But you did something in the last few minutes that all the doctors and psychologists haven't been able to do. You gave us hope! I know now that God didn't bring us this far just to abandon us. There's a reason that all this is happening; God has something in store for Lauren. And you were God's messenger. In the span of a few moments, I have moved out of a pit of despair to the absolute assurance that Lauren will be all right."

She smiled, and I smiled back. I wanted to come around her desk and hug her, but I just thanked her and walked out into cold. The mist and drizzle had stopped, but I scarcely noticed the weather.

I took the same path back to my office, but without the aching, dark thoughts and overwhelming feelings of despair. In their place was not merely hope, but an assurance—an absolute certainty—that we were part of a plan that God had for our family.

Even more astounding was the realization that God had been aware of my thoughts, my most private and unspoken feelings and fears. I was so overwhelmed that—had it not been for the people around me on the sidewalks—I would have dropped to my knees in worship and awe.

Instead, for the first time in weeks, maybe for the first time in my life, I truly talked to God.

"Lord," I prayed as I walked, "You know everything. You know every thought, every fear, and every joy. How incredible is Your power. How merciful, how compassionate You are. At my lowest point, you stepped in. I will tell others. I will tell my family. I will trust You in everything for the rest of my life. I don't know what I've done to deserve this intervention, but I will not squander this gift."

I blew past my office and hopped in the Bronco, taking an early lunch and heading for home. I couldn't wait to share my experience, to share hope with everyone, especially with Lauren.

Robbie had driven down that morning, and I found Lauren huddled with him in her big chair by the fireplace. She had been asleep when I left for work. I now found her in no better spirits than when I had kissed her goodnight the night before.

No matter. I couldn't wait to share my story. I gathered Karin with Lauren and Robbie in the living room. They listened while I told them every detail.

When I finished, Lauren managed a smile. "I hope you're right, Daddy. I'm glad you feel better. But right now, I still feel pretty miserable."

"That's okay for now, Chicken," I said. "But remember this, for whatever reason, I have been 'called to the Principal's office.' I know without a doubt that you will be all right. I will no longer harbor worry and doubt. It is now my job, my duty and privilege, to be the one who knows this story has a happy ending, and to make sure you all don't forget it."

Back at work that afternoon, I considered the "coincidences" that had brought about my encounter with Jennifer. First, Karin paid the bills on the very day of Lauren's accident. They were left in the car-door pocket for an extended time period, then my brother mailed every bill except the insurance payment. The late notice from the insurance company arrived on the very day Lauren's depression reached crisis stage. Our insurance agent knew of Lauren's accident before my phone call to him that morning. Had he not answered the phone personally when I called from the credit union, I would not have recounted Lauren's story to anyone else at the agency. How else would Lauren's story be told in front of a complete stranger, who just happened to have suffered an amazingly similar accident, with an equally dismal prognosis, and ultimately obtained a remarkable, miraculous recovery? Had God choreographed every detail?

At home that night, Lauren smiled more than we'd seen in the last several days. She even asked for a chocolate milkshake, a sure sign that she was feeling a little better. Out of ice cream, I jumped in the Buick and drove up to Kroger. As I got out of the car at the grocery store, I dropped my cell phone in the car door pocket so it wouldn't be in plain sight. Then I got the ice cream and drove home.

I pulled back into the garage, reached into the car door pocket, and felt the cell phone...and something else.

It was a long, stamped envelope, addressed to State Farm Insurance. Tucked inside was a check Karin had written to State Farm, dated October 29.

How many times had I searched that car door pocket? How many times had I found nothing there?

The next morning at work, I left my office as soon as the credit union opened and retraced my steps of the day before. The wretched weather from the day before was now only a memory. The bright morning sun promised another Deep South mild winter's day.

I could hardly wait to thank Jennifer again, and to tell her about my discovery of the missing State Farm check. I wanted to tell her how much her story had meant, not only to me but also to Lauren and the rest of the family. I wanted to establish a link with this young lady; I wanted to find a way to keep her involved in Lauren's recovery.

Finding her office empty and dark, I went to the customer service rep in the office next door.

"Hi," I said. "I was in here yesterday, and a young lady, Jennifer, was working right next door to you. You know who I'm talking about?"

"Oh, sure," the rep answered.

"Is she here? I need to talk to her."

"No, sir. She's not here today."

Disappointed, I asked, "Will she be back on Monday? It's pretty important."

"No, she won't be back on Monday," the rep said. "In fact, she won't be back at all. She's what we call a floater. She comes to the branches when we're short handed or have something special going on. She's never been here before yesterday, and I doubt she'll ever be at this branch again."

I walked back out into the sunshine and looked up into the bright-blue, cloudless sky.

The Lawd don't let nothin' happen that He cain't make good come of it.

Becky, you were right all along, I thought.

Awestruck, I shouted for anyone listening to hear. "Becky was right! Becky was right! Oh, Praise God, Becky was right!"

Chapter Nine

And we know that all things work together for good to them that love God, to them that are called according to His purpose.
—Romans 8:28

THE FINAL NOTES of "Amazing Grace" rang in the high arches of the First Baptist Church as the crimson-robed choir took their lofty seats at the front of the cavernous sanctuary. It was packed to capacity on this, the first day of revival. As a six year old boy, I squirmed past my father's trousered legs and my mother's skirt and stood on tiptoes at the end of the pew, straining for a better view.

With my white shirt buttoned tightly at the neck, the red-and-blue striped clip-on bow tie bit into my throat. Mid-day approached outside; the July heat radiated into the unair-conditioned church through the open windows. Mama picked up one of the pew fans, with a picture of Jesus in the Garden of Gethsemane on one side and *Compliments of George Funeral Home* printed on the other, and mercifully stirred the stifling air around me.

As a rule, the eleven o'clock hour on Sunday morning found me stretched out on the pew, with my mother's lap for a pillow and Daddy's for an ottoman. The heat in combination with the soporific monotone of our pastor usually provided an excellent environment for a late-morning nap, not only for little boys but for a fair number of grown men, too. But on this day, the anticipation of change and renewal charged the congregation like the electrification of the atmosphere just before lightning strikes.

All eyes followed the visiting reverend as he approached the pulpit. Tall, slender, and youthful, with a full head of hair, his appearance set him apart from our own rotund, bespectacled deacons and pastors, comb-overs striping their shiny bald heads.

The preacher pulled a red bandana from his inside coat pocket and mopped his already perspiring brow. Then he let the rag hang from the edge of the pulpit. Holding tightly with both hands on either side of the podium, he began in earnest his efforts to save souls.

"Brothers and sisters," he boomed, "we are all on a journey. Some of us are on the straight and narrow pathway that leads home. But there are many of us, many of you right here in this church, who are on another road, a road that leads not to the home of our heavenly Father, but a road that leads straight to the eternal, scorching fires of hell! It is to those I have come to speak."

At that, he grabbed the red bandana and waved it over his head.

"I'm standing by that road right now," he shouted, waving his bandana as a warning. "I'm pleading with you to turn back, warning that you're on the wrong path. Brothers and sisters, there is but one way to avoid damnation, and that way is Jesus Christ!"

Even at the tender age of six, I had heard all I needed to hear. It was hot enough being stuffed into a starched shirt and leather shoes and socks on a South Carolina summer. No way did I plan to spend eternity in that kind of misery, or worse. I determined right then that if Jesus was the only way out, then Jesus it would be.

Nevertheless, it was only at my mother's insistence that I grudgingly gave up two weeks of precious, barefoot freedom each summer to attend Vacation Bible School. The cookies and Kool-Aid were insufficient compensation for the mandatory verse memorization and Bible drills, where the first kid to find a called Bible verse claimed a special prize each day: bola paddles, yo-yo's, and the like.

We sang "Jesus Loves Me," and I'd try to believe it. But I could never get the picture of that revival preacher out of my mind, waving that sweat soaked bandana in warning as I marched down the road to perdition. If Jesus truly loved me, why did I live in fear that someday there was at least a possibility He might allow me to burn in eternal fire?

For four decades, until God's choreographed plans to gain my attention culminated with my meeting Jennifer in the credit union, the foundation of my religion had been based primarily on fear. But on that day, in the midst of turmoil and despair, God reached down and touched me so powerfully that I finally realized...I am *His* child. He loves me like...a son.

At that moment I abandoned my religion...in exchange for a relationship.

Like the morning sun restores the blush of daylight to the somber tones of night, the spark and fire of Lauren's indomitable spirit gradually returned later in January. Slowly, the numbing veil of the OxyContin lifted as she tapered off the drug. As her next surgery approached, Lauren had managed to free herself entirely from the medicine's potent grip.

Early one Saturday morning, Karin and I were reaching for coffee mugs in the kitchen cabinet, when we heard the familiar thump of Lauren's crutches coming down the hall. Not a morning person, Lauren smiled brightly as she entered and greeted us both with a hug, then maneuvered into her place at the kitchen table.

"How ya' doin' this morning, Chicken Little?" I asked with a morning croak in my voice.

"I'm doin' great! This is going to be a great day!" Her smile broadened.

"Who are you?" Karin teased as she joined us at the table. "And what have you done with our Lauren?"

"It's me, drug free," Lauren replied.. "For the first time in I don't know *how* long, I woke up without thinking about taking a pill as soon as I got out of bed."

"That's great, Larnie Jane!" Karin said.

"Yeah, but I've got even better news," Lauren continued. "Are ya'll ready for this?"

We nodded.

"The infection is gone!" she exclaimed. "The seratia marsupial, or whatever it's called, is no longer in my leg. It's gone. The infection has left the building!"

With a smile, then a puzzled look, Karin and I glanced at each other. Then we looked back at Lauren.

"Last night," Lauren explained, "I went to bed with a clear head. For the first time in months, I could really think. It was like cobwebs had formed in my head while I was on OxyContin. Then suddenly, somehow, they had been completely swept away.

"Before I said my prayers, I started going over in my mind everything that has happened, not just to me but to all of us, since the accident. A lot of it is painful and a lot is bad—especially the nightmares, for me. They're almost worse than the real thing."

She paused and turned away from us to the bright sunshine flooding through the bay window, but she couldn't conceal the glistening the recollections brought to her eyes. In a moment, though, the smile returned and she went on.

"Anyway, with my newly recovered faculties, I started thinking about my favorite verses from the Bible. I went through them in my mind, and one verse kept coming back to me over and over again. 'You have not, because you ask not.'"

She paused. "So I asked.

"I couldn't ask that the accident never happened, because what's done is done. But I could ask Him to take the infection away. I told God how badly I wanted to walk again and to use that to better serve Him. I prayed that if there were a way His will could be done and the infection removed from my leg, then please let it be so."

Now Karin's eyes shimmered with moisture as she, like Lauren moments earlier, turned to face the sunshine and draw composure from its brilliant, morning warmth. She quickly turned back. Her hesitant but hopeful smile urged Lauren to continue.

"I finished my prayer and almost immediately felt a tingling in my leg. It was like nothing I had ever felt before. My whole leg just came alive, not with any kind of pain, but with this... sensation. I knew it was the infection leaving me. God answered my prayer right then and there. And He wanted me to know it. He wanted me to know that He had heard my prayer! I don't know why. I don't know exactly what plan He has, but I know without question the infection that threatened my leg, even my life, is gone...forever!"

Lauren beamed with confidence and joy. Karin and I sat with mouths agape. Several moments passed in amazed silence.

I was the first to recover from what we'd just heard.

"You know what, Chicken Little? A few weeks ago, if you'd told us what you just told us, I'd have believed it. But I'd have believed it mainly because I desperately wanted to believe it. More than anything in the world, I want you to be well and healed."

My voice croaked, but not from the early morning hour this time. I looked to the sunshine to regain control, found myself and continued.

"But with everything that's been happening to this family lately, especially with all the evidence that God is at work here, I not only *want* to believe it, I *do* believe it. I believe God answered your prayer, and what you felt was God at work."

Karin looked at Lauren. "I believe it too. It's a miracle, Larnie Jane."

We celebrated with French toast, bacon, and orange juice. Then Karin and I abandoned chores and spent the day rejoicing in the healing of our child.

But despite the evidence of God's mercy and grace that had been showered on us in recent days, I couldn't shake the lingering, nagging voice in my head that whispered, *It's not true. None of it's true. You only believe it because you want to believe it.*

"I don't care if I'm heading into another operation," Lauren declared a few days later. Karin and I were driving her to the outpatient surgery center in the chilly, pre-dawn hours. Andrea had come down from Charlotte and rode with her sister in the backseat.

"I can't wait to get rid of this ex-fix and to get to work at physical therapy. For the first time since the accident, I can start doing something to get myself well, to help with my own recovery. You know what I mean? So far, I've been like a spectator, watching everyone else work for my recovery. After this, I can begin to make things happen myself. I can begin to take charge of my own healing."

Lauren's restored confidence bolstered our spirits, but the three of us still sat in nervous silence in the cramped waiting area while our daughter underwent another operation.

As always, Karin, after some time had passed, gave voice to exactly what I had been thinking.

"What if Lauren's wrong? What if the tingling she felt in her leg was the infection beginning to rage again? What if they find the infection has returned?" she fretted. "Dr. Hines said this was a relatively simple procedure, but it's taking so long. Everyone else who was here this morning has left. What if something's gone wrong? This is an outpatient surgery center; they're not equipped for emergencies."

"Worry about nothing, pray about everything." I tried to answer with confidence and took my wife's hand. But the clamminess of my own hand betrayed my anxiety.

Didn't God just grab you by the shoulders a few days ago and show you He's in control—that He knows what Lauren and your family are going through? I thought. *Didn't He reassure you that as long as He's in control, everything will be all right? So why are you so worried?*

Because I'm still new at this! I argued with myself. *I'm like a child who needs constant reassurance.*

Another hour passed. Finally, a man in green scrubs and shoe covers approached, carrying a large plastic bag filled with screws and rods of various lengths and designs.

He smiled. "Lauren's doing fine. It's taking a little longer than expected because there was so much hardware to remove. I have it here in this bag."

Andrea stepped back as I cautiously peered into the sack.

"Dr. Hines asked me to bring it out to you all," he continued. "He thought maybe Lauren would like to have it as a souvenir."

"Uh...no. Thanks, anyway," Karin answered. "I'm quite sure Lauren will be happy to never see any of this again. But what about the infection?"

"I'll let Dr. Hines answer those questions," he replied.

Then lowering his voice, he added, "Oh, heck! It'd be cruel to keep this from you any longer. I know how worried ya'll are. Dr. Hines won't mind if I tell you this much. There is absolutely no, none, zip, zero, *nada*...no sign of any infection!"

At that, tension that had been building on Karin's face all day melted into a smile. Andrea relaxed into a chair.

I felt warmth returning to my fingers and a blush of shame redden my face. *What will it take to finally break me?* I thought. *Why am I so afraid to believe?*

Several hours later, with her leg now supported from hip to ankle by a removable, black metal and Velcro brace, we wheeled Lauren into our home instead of a hospital room. She was no longer a human pin cushion. All the prescriptions were oral, including an additional antibiotic, cephalexin, as well as the reintroduction of Lauren's old friend, OxyContin.

Another surgery completed, one massive infection defeated, yet still no plan for how Lauren could ever walk again.

But somehow, at that moment, none of us doubted that she would.

Since Lauren's accident, well-meaning folks had offered a wide range of advice to Karin and me—some solicited, some not, some valuable, some not. One valuable piece of advice, to contact a lawyer, had been offered by Joe Ferguson, our insurance agent, on that fateful morning when I met Jennifer at the credit union.

Some time later, I met the man Joe had recommended, Rob Boyd, and introduced him to the family. Though all of us, especially Lauren, were initially cautious and skeptical about involving an attorney, Rob quickly earned our trust through his genuine concern and mutually shared values and common sense.

"You're going to have to meet the man who caused the accident, Mike," Rob warned. "Because he's from a foreign, Communist country, the usual legal recourses for a serious accident such as this are going to be hampered. Nonetheless, I need to set up a deposition. How do you feel about meeting this man face-to-face?"

We were meeting in Rob's office downtown. I sat in a comfortable, high-backed chair across from the attorney's desk, which was piled high with books and documents. Rob waited patiently while I attempted to develop an acceptable answer to his question.

"How am I supposed to feel about meeting a guy who crippled my child?" I finally asked.

We left it at that.

The deposition was held at an office in Greenville, only days after Lauren's surgery to remove the fixater. Rob and I arrived early and took seats at the empty conference room table.

What do I do when this guy shows up? I thought. *Am I supposed to stand up and shake hands, like I'm pleased to meet him? Why not just stand up and slap him on the back? Tell him how glad I am he decided to study in the USA, and how especially happy I am that he picked Clemson.*

I brought my thoughts under control. *The Lawd don't let nothin' happen that He cain't make good come of it.* I focused on Becky's wisdom. We waited. I believed that now with all my heart. Still, though, God's ways remained a mystery.

Xiang Liu, along with the attorney his insurance company was required to provide, finally entered. I stood and shook hands first with his attorney, then with Xiang Liu. His hand was small, in proportion with his frame. It was the hand of a scholar—smooth and cold. He wore thick glasses and only a hint of a smile.

A secretary entered and turned on a tape recorder. In rapid succession, Rob fired questions to the obviously uncomfortable, intimidated man. The line of inquiry was, by and large, financial in nature. Xiang Liu frequently asked Rob to repeat the question before answering in barely audible, and even less understandable, English.

The drilling lasted no more than twenty minutes, after which the secretary gathered her equipment and left the room. Both attorneys then excused themselves to confer in the hallway.

I was left alone with Xiang Liu, whose actions had forever altered the lives of the people I loved most and had inflicted suffering upon my innocent child.

I looked at him. He returned my gaze then quickly diverted his eyes to the table between us. Silence hung heavy in the air.

"Why did you come to the United States?" I asked abruptly. The fragile silence between us shattered like a smashed mirror.

He looked up, and to my surprise, smiled brightly. His face held an unmistakable look of relief and genuine appreciation that I would choose to speak to him.

"Because you have best technology in world," he replied, his eyes shining. "Nowhere else can I learn what I can learn here."

Though taken aback by his response to my scant display of kindness, I resolved to continue my line of questioning. "Why did you choose Clemson? Weren't there other schools in the United States you could have gone to?"

"Clemson offered me and my wife most money," he replied haltingly. "We both offered graduate assist...assistantships. No other schools would."

What are we doing? What is this country doing? I wondered. I forced my mind back under control to prevent my thoughts from whirling off in a direction I didn't want to go. "Will you stay in the United States after you and your wife receive your doctorates?"

"Oh, no," he answered. "We go back to Shanghai. Our families there. China is our home. We must go back to our own country."

He smiled again—an innocent, genuine smile.

The lawyers reentered, said a few insignificant words, and the meeting was adjourned.

I left with a profound feeling of something being amiss, but it wasn't with Xiang Liu any longer. But for the grace of God, any one of us could have been Xiang Liu, an innocent player in a world that humans only pretend to understand.

Anger and resentment hurt no one but me and my family. Recognizing at last that we are blessed beyond measure to live in a country where we can know the true and living God, I determined never to lead my family down a path of bitterness again.

Lauren began physical therapy on January 31, a cold, cloudy Friday morning. The one-hour drive from our house to therapy was spent in silence, contemplating the approaching challenge. As I pulled under the portico of the steel-and-glass building to let Lauren and Karin exit into its meager shelter from the chill breeze, the exterior temperature display in the car warned it was only thirty-nine degrees at mid-morning.

Where is spring? I thought, trudging into the building to catch up with my wife and daughter. Just behind me, an elderly lady, stooped and struggling with a walker, labored to reach the door. The icy wind parted her thin, white wisps of hair. While I held the door for her, a middle-aged man pushing a young woman in a large wheel chair, her head cradled in padded headrests, rushed toward the sanctuary of the building. As they passed through the open door, the man, looking bone-tired, uttered a barely audible thank you, but the young woman only stared blankly ahead.

*There, but for the grace of God...*I thought.

Another day, another waiting room. Lauren sat across from Karin and me, dressed in a Clemson sweatshirt and black tear-away pants, nervously twirling that brown curl between her thumb and forefinger.

Too anxious to focus on anything in particular, Karin waited quietly, hands folded in her lap. I flipped through the same *Field and Stream* I had picked up a dozen times in various waiting rooms over the course of the last several weeks, reading the same sentence in the same article until with a sigh, I tossed the magazine back onto the stack.

Finally, Lauren broke the silence. "I don't know what's wrong with me. I've been waiting for this day for weeks, but now, I'm asking myself, 'What am I doing here?' My leg is missing so much bone that it's like an insect's leg with this brace for an exoskeleton. Most of my quadriceps is gone, lost to infection. Dr. Hines says it's still too early to be looking for a doctor who can rebuild what I've lost, if one even exists."

She sighed. "It makes it kind of hard to imagine any goal I'm supposed to be working toward."

Lauren stopped for a moment and twirled her lock of hair with increasing fervor.

I clenched my teeth and racked my brain for an adequate response, but it wouldn't come.

A solitary tear rolled down Lauren's cheek. "Plus, for some reason I just don't want to be put back into a lot of pain."

Obviously afraid the tear might be discovered by someone other than her parents, Lauren quickly wiped it away with the back of her hand.

"But what's worse is, I'm afraid everything Dr. Baxter predicted is about to come true. The therapist is going to release the lock on this brace and try to bend my knee. What if Baxter's right? What if I can't budge it? After all, it's been locked straight out for three months. Even if I hadn't lost bone and muscle, it would be inflexible. I can't *really* expect it to move, can I?"

Karin didn't hesitate with a reply. "Do you remember what you said when Dr. Baxter told you that fusion of your leg was the only remedy?"

Lauren shifted in her chair and stopped twirling the curl. "I said, 'You don't know my God.' I was about as doped up as a person can get, and I don't remember much of anything about Baltimore. But I do remember that."

"And haven't you spent the last few years working with Young Life, convincing kids that with God, *all* things are possible?" Karin continued.

Lauren nodded.

"Well, today, *you* begin to achieve all that is possible."

Lauren's lips curved into that familiar, confident smile. A watery sparkle returned to her pretty green eyes.

I looked at the woman I married, who never ceased to amaze me with her courage, faith, and common sense, and I felt the tension in my jaw relax.

Called back moments later, Lauren crutched down the hall, with Karin and me following. The receptionist led us into the lair of the physical therapist. The large room contained some special equipment, but mostly just familiar, everyday objects like steps and ramps and narrow doorways with high thresholds. They were innocent things that the able hardly notice, but stumbling blocks that vex the disabled on a daily basis. A glass wall of windows running the length of the room bathed the area in brilliant morning sunshine, while a stereo system blasted The Beach Boys singing "California Girls," infusing the room with energy.

A diminutive young woman in a white shirt and khakis approached Lauren.

"Hi, Lauren. I'm Anna. Welcome to physical therapy. Boy, have we heard a lot about you! It's great to finally meet you." A liveliness and warmth radiated from her.

Just the type person Lauren will take to, I thought.

Yet, despite the cheerful room and Anna's upbeat personality, Lauren, as if subdued by finding herself amidst the incongruous juxtaposition of objects for the able and the disabled, momentarily seemed to lose her confidence.

"Hi, I'm Lauren," she said, eyes downcast. She leaned on her crutches so her right hand could reach up and twirl a lock of hair. "These are my parents."

We shook hands, and Anna introduced the other staff members in the room.

Then she turned to the business at hand. "Dr. Hines has taken a special interest in your case, Lauren. We've met with him extensively to map out your physical therapy course. To say that you've impressed him with your attitude and determination would be an understatement.

"I have to admit," Anna continued, "I've not seen an injury quite like yours, but few physical therapists have. I'm sure it comes as no surprise to you that most people who have been similarly injured have lost their leg.

"We're going to start out on the course we've developed and see how far we can get. If we hit a roadblock, we'll regroup and try again another way. I hear you're a fighter."

Anna paused. She had to be thinking that Lauren, propped on crutches, still twirling that curl, and looking closer to fourteen than twenty-one, looked like anything *but* a fighter.

"I want you to understand that we're in this with you for the long haul. Come what may, we're not going to give up—as long as you don't, either."

Lauren looked up. Straightening on her crutches, she let the curl rest.

"I won't quit." Lauren returned Anna's eye contact, her response now that of an iron-willed young woman. "I will walk again."

And so, recovery began.

Lauren sat on a therapy bench, leg stretched out before her, as Anna carefully removed the brace. With her tiny but strong fingers, she dug into Lauren's upper leg, kneading, stretching and breaking up scar tissue. She kept up a constant stream of conversation, asking questions about life at Clemson, family, boyfriends, favorite movie stars, future career plans—anything that focused attention away from the painful process.

Lauren returned the chatter, sometimes stifling a grimace, sometimes wiping away tears with the back of her hand, but never complaining.

The brace was replaced, and two hours of non-weight bearing exercises followed. As each one finished, Anna lavished encouragement. The two of them quickly melded into an energetic team, working their way through as many of the devices as Lauren's injury would allow.

Karin and I watched with a mixture of excitement and trepidation.

Finally, the pair ended up back at the therapy bench where they had begun. Anna unlocked the knee joint on the brace. As if the click of the brace unlocking were their cue, the other physical therapists quickly gathered around, watching with interest.

"Okay, Lauren," Anna said. "Here's what you came for. Swing to your left and let your left leg hang off the side of the table."

Lauren's quick compliance left her performing a virtual split on the tabletop.

"Now," Anna continued in a calm, quiet voice, "while I support the back of your right leg, you move it over, off the side of the table. Don't worry. I'm not going to let go."

Slowly, painfully, Lauren twisted her body to the left, until she was seated with both legs in front of her. Anna still held the out-stretched, injured limb.

"I'm going to hold your leg under your thigh, like this," Anna said, holding the back of Lauren's right thigh, "and I'm going to catch under your calf with my other hand, like this."

Karin and I exchanged glances.

Lauren looked up at us, then around at the small group peering down at her. Tears once again glistened in her eyes.

Okay, I thought, preparing myself for the worst. *Here goes. If it doesn't bend, I've gotta stay upbeat. I can't let Lauren or Karin see the disappointment on my face. Oh, Lord, please. Please let Lauren's leg bend at least a degree or two. Please don't let Dr. Baxter's prediction be true.*

I held my breath and reached for Karin's hand.

Gently, almost imperceptibly, Anna began to lower the right leg. A second passed. Lauren grimaced with pain as the weight of her lower leg pulled at tissue that hadn't moved in months. Another second passed, and still another.

And then, like the minute hand on a clock, all of us realized the brace was no longer at a 180 degree angle. Maybe only a degree or two less, but it was no longer straight!

No one spoke.

Anna dropped the calf a little more, and the leg followed. More, and the leg followed. Still more, and the leg followed.

"Oh, my gosh!" Lauren cried, pushing with all her might, her face red. "Oh, my gosh! It's bending! It's bending!"

Quickly, still supporting Lauren's calf, Anna moved her hand from under Lauren's thigh and grabbed an instrument to measure the angle. She compared those results to the read-out on the brace itself.

"Thirty-eight degrees, Lauren!" she shouted. "Glory hallelujah! Thirty-eight degrees! Your first day in physical therapy and you got thirty-eight degrees, eight degrees more than they predicted you'd *ever* get."

The group surrounding Anna and Lauren broke into applause. I looked around and saw that even the other patients were applauding.

"It doesn't hurt," Lauren replied, ecstatic. "It's tight; it feels a little weird. But it doesn't hurt."

"That's awesome! Dr. Hines won't believe this! I can't wait to tell him. There's no stopping you now, girl!" Anna hugged Lauren. Both girls wiped away tears.

I hugged Karin, and everybody hugged everybody. We rejoiced all the way home.

Back at physical therapy the following Monday, Lauren hit forty-five degrees, then on Wednesday she hit forty-nine. On Friday, she hit fifty-six degrees, right before her regular weekly appointment with Dr. Hines.

Like us, Dr. Hines was elated at Lauren's progress. Unlike us, he was not ready to discuss a path forward.

"So what do you think, Dr. Hines?" Lauren asked. "Anna is great, and I'm working as hard as I can. When will we be ready to talk about how we can go about getting me walking?"

"Let's not get ahead of ourselves and lose sight of what we're accomplishing right now," Dr. Hines cautioned. "There's plenty of time. We'll get to the next step soon, but what that step is depends a lot on how well you continue to progress."

Later that same afternoon, we found ourselves heading up US 25, past the huge brick gates on either side of the road where Jennifer, from the credit union, had her accident years ago. We wound silently through the hills and pines of the Sumter

National Forest en route to Clemson to drop Lauren off with her roommates and a weekend return to the life of a college coed.

It should have been a joyous trip, one of rowdy celebration. After all, the curse had been broken. In spite of massive injuries, Lauren's will had prevailed; she'd once again beaten the odds and confounded the experts. But as we followed the sliver of highway past Greenwood into the still, bare hardwoods of the upstate, what little conversation there was dwindled with the daylight. The three of us slipped into our own thoughts.

"Something's not right." Lauren spoke as the highway curved through the little town of Hodges, cutting right through the middle of a cemetery, whose population of deceased townspeople appeared greater than that of the current, living residents.

"What do you mean?" Karin asked.

"Today, I hit a milestone. I'm on my way to spend the weekend with my best friends, and Robbie is going to be so proud of me. I'm getting stronger every day. I'm moving my leg, on my own, more than Dr. Baxter ever guessed I'd be able to. And I've only been in physical therapy a week. Just one week!"

Lauren paused in thought as just beyond the car windows twilight blanketed the fields, freshly plowed in anticipation of the seeding that would soon follow. I waited for my daughter to finish her thought, wondering if she and Karin had been silently contemplating the same concern as I. Finally, she continued.

"Yet, Dr. Hines still doesn't want to talk about any options for rebuilding my leg."

"That's exactly what's been bothering me too." Karin twisted against the shoulder harness to look at our daughter in the backseat.

"That's funny, because I've been chewing on that as well," I said. "Don't get me wrong. I really like the man, but he's sure slow to discuss the long-term path. To tell the truth, I can't forget that conversation I had with his office manager, back before the very first appointment, when she asked for a guarantee that Dr.

Hines would be the one to perform whatever procedures would be done, if any could be done, to enable Lauren to walk."

"He keeps saying I'm not ready," Lauren added. "That's probably true. But I'm ready to know what we're going to do and have some idea of how we're going to do it."

Never one to waste time, Karin seized the moment. "What law says we have to wait on Dr. Hines? Let's figure something out ourselves. We've got another hour or so with nothing else to do. Let's come up with a plan."

An hour later, we pulled up next to Robbie's shiny, black Ford Ranger in the Cracker Barrel parking lot on I-85 in Anderson, with a fresh plan of action.

Leaving the restaurant after dinner, Lauren headed for the parking lot ahead of everyone. Since she had been unable to bend her leg enough to fit into the passenger seat of the Ranger, we usually traded vehicles with Robbie on weekends when Lauren visited Clemson.

"Toss me your keys," she called back to Robbie. "Let's ride in a truck."

Propping herself on her crutches to free her right hand, she skillfully caught the keys as they sailed from Robbie's hand to hers. Then she headed for the passenger door of the Ranger.

"Now, watch this!" she called.

Lauren opened the truck's door. Then putting her left hand behind her and holding both crutches with the right, she hopped up on the seat and swung her left leg in. She grabbed her right shin with both hands and pulled her leg into a bend sufficient enough to sit in the little pickup.

"Watch out, I'm back!" she called as she slammed the door closed. Smiling and laughing, Robbie jumped into the driver's seat, and the happy pair headed up the road to Clemson.

The following Monday morning found Karin working her cell phone from the car, while Lauren worked at physical therapy. Karin's first call was to Maryland and Dr. Baxter.

"I can't believe it!" Dr. Baxter exclaimed when he returned Karin's call later that day. "Considering that Lauren has practically no supporting bone structure and has sustained massive muscle loss, achieving an almost sixty-degree range of motion after only a week of physical therapy, with little or no pain, is truly miraculous. I could not be happier for her."

He went on. "With that level of progress, I'd say she's an excellent candidate for an allograft. But frankly, I wouldn't want to attempt it myself, not since that joint has obtained such a degree of mobility. She needs somebody with very specific experience, and there aren't that many of them in the country. I do know a couple of colleagues you should contact. One is here at Johns Hopkins, the other is closer to you, down in Charlotte. If you get in to see one or both, you'll need the medical records and x-rays I gave you when you left Baltimore. You'll also need the latest x-rays taken since the fixater was removed."

Before the phone call ended, Karin had names and contact information for both doctors, which she shared with Lauren and me that evening.

It had been another dreary winter's day, with a chilly, intermittent rain. I found myself longing for spring and warm May evenings spent outdoors, breathing the fragrance of Confederate Jasmine. But for the moment, I was content with the family gathered in front of the fireplace, mugs of hot chocolate with marshmallows in hand, listening as Karin gave details of what she had learned earlier in the day.

"I haven't called either of the doctors Baxter recommended," she said after relating the details of their conversation. "But I did talk to Donna Hudson at Best Doctors. By day after tomorrow, she said we'd have a list of specialists to contact."

She paused. "But there is a bit of a problem."

Karin tightened her lips and looked from me to Lauren and back again. I sensed another brainstorming session about to begin.

"How are we going to get the latest set of x-rays?" she asked. "I don't think we're off base in thinking that Dr. Hines hasn't done anything much, so far, toward determining what needs to come after physical therapy. I don't get the impression that he would encourage us to go out on our own like this either."

"But I do feel that Dr. Hines wants what's best for Lauren. I'm just afraid he may be convinced that *he's* what's best for Lauren and there's no use looking any further."

Karin stopped for a sip of hot chocolate.

Man! I thought, gazing down at my empty mug. *She can make stuff look so good and last so long.*

"I'm not sure it would be wise for us to tell Dr. Hines what we're up to," she continued. "I'm not saying we should lie to him. What I am saying is, let's handle this quietly ourselves. Maybe I'm wrong, and Dr. Hines is actively looking at all the options. Maybe we'll all come to the same conclusions eventually. That would be great, and I hope it happens."

"I don't want to do anything to upset Anna, either," Lauren added. "She's become more than just my physical therapist. She's my friend. I wouldn't want to do anything that might hurt her feelings, or worse yet, get her in trouble with Dr. Hines. After all, he is her boss."

"So we're all in agreement. We'll keep this search to ourselves," I said. "That brings us back to where we started. The x-rays we need are in Dr. Hines files. How do we get them without upsetting anybody and without jeopardizing Lauren's relationship with Anna?"

No one spoke for a minute or two. Then Karin took a final, delicate sip of hot chocolate and set the mug in a coaster on the side table.

"We have a relative in the business, don't we?" she asked. "Michael, your cousin Jason is a well-known radiologist in the same town as Dr. Hines. He has been interested in how Lauren's getting along. What better way to explain Lauren's recovery to a radiologist than to show him the actual x-rays. At the same time, we'll have another expert's opinion that might give us more options in how to proceed and who to contact."

I carried the suggestion to its logical next step. "After Jason's looked them over, he may have some recommendations of his own. At that time, we're free to do with the x-rays as we choose."

"Isn't this sort of deceitful?" A worried look crossed Lauren's face. Could the two people who were the foundation of the family's integrity be hatching a plot rife with deception?

Karin pounced on the question. "We're not being deceitful at all. The fact is, those x-rays were bought and paid for by this family, and they belong to you, Lauren. We don't owe anyone an explanation as to why we want copies, or what we intend to do with them. But given Dr. Hines' sensitivity about your case, I think it's appropriate to be judicious in what information we share. The intent is not to deceive; it is to independently ensure that whatever course of treatment is decided upon, it's based on the best medical advice we can find and not on anyone's ego."

Twenty-four hours later, Jason had reviewed the x-rays and had made duplicates of the duplicates so multiple doctors could be contacted simultaneously.

"I wish I could do more, Michael," Jason said when he completed his review. "I wish I could tell you who Lauren should see, but her injury is so unusual. I think your best bet is to follow the leads Dr. Baxter provided."

Once again, Karin contacted Donna Hudson at Best Doctors. In short order, we had a list of orthopedic surgeons with specialization in trauma to lower extremities and bone grafting, and ranked by their peers as the best in the country.

So the search began. Though we admitted to feeling a little intimidated initially, after the first few phone calls, we felt comfortable talking to doctor's offices in distance places. The staff at each practice was concerned, professional, and genuinely interested in helping…with one exception.

As one might expect, the one exception was a hospital in a far-away place, upon whose streets few genuine Southern boys had trod: New York City. By the luck of the draw, it fell to me, not my more sophisticated and cosmopolitan wife, to contact a famous hospital located in the midst of that metropolis of mythical proportions.

Also as one might expect at such a large institution located in such an important city, I encountered difficulty in reaching an informed party. But I persevered, and when at last I reached my contact, I began to pour out our story as quickly as my South Carolina-bred tongue could accommodate. About half way through, the New York lady on the other end of the line interrupted.

"We're a private hospital in Manhattan."

Her terse announcement and her Bronx accent gave me pause.

This ain't gonna go good, I thought. "Yes, ma'am. I know that."

"Then you should also know that this is an expensive hospital, and New York is an expensive place," she said. "If your daughter became a patient here, you and your family would need a place to stay, probably for several weeks. And it's very expensive here."

"I don't care how much it costs," I answered, peeved but trying to remain respectful.

"In addition," she continued, "we do not accept insurance. We are strictly private pay. We do not file insurance claims, and we may require a deposit equal to the cost of the procedure before admittance."

"You don't accept Blue Cross/Blue Shield?" I asked.

"We don't accept insurance of *any* kind," she said in a tone of disgust. "We're strictly private pay. And any orthopedic procedure will be very, *very* expensive."

"Well, ma'am, as *I* said, I don't care how expensive you are. If you're the only place in the world that can fix my daughter, then we'll do whatever we must to get her fixed. I tell you what, I'll check with everyplace else first, and we'll call you back as a last resort."

Satisfied that she had successfully repelled a Rebel invasion, she said goodbye and we hung up.

Speaking to the cradled receiver, I added, "We're jus po' ole sharecroppers down in these here swamps, but I shore do 'preciate the information. Maybe if I sell enough gator hides this spring, I can afford to get my little girl fixed up."

Someday, I'd like to walk into that swanky building up there and see where all the rich folks go to get well.

Even with New York off the list, we still had plenty of leads. Within a week and a half, Karin had mailed packages to Cleveland, Boston, Baltimore, Gainesville, and Jacksonville, and to Rochester, Chicago, Charlotte, Atlanta, and Philadelphia.

Each package was affixed with postage and high hopes, then sealed with a prayer.

But one by one, each package found its way back to us, along with various words that carried the same message: "Sorry, we can't help you. Not within our area of expertise."

All except one.

On March 5, Dr. Jeffrey Kneece of a well-known medical center in Charlotte talked to us after he completed his examination of Lauren's leg. "I know you have an appointment with Dr. Bowles later this morning," he said. "He and I work together, and I usually see the patient first."

Replacing the brace, he pulled the last Velcro band tight then turned to face our three hopeful faces. "I'm not going to send you on to Dr. Bowles, Lauren. I'm afraid your injury is not one that fits into our area of expertise."

I glanced at Karin and Lauren. Their faces showed interest but not disappointment.

"The patients we see are frequently children who have lost bone to cancer," Dr. Kneece continued. "For them, an allograft provides a relatively quick return to mobility. Their injury is surgical, as opposed to yours, which is due to trauma. And sadly, because of the cancer, most of these kids have a limited life expectancy, so we can use bone from a cadaver, which doesn't hold up like 'live' tissue.

"The good news in your case is that you don't have cancer. The bad news is, your injury is complex because of the trauma and the infection. That doesn't mean that an allograft won't work for you. You would do better with live tissue from a donor. That gives your own bone a chance to heal into the donated bone, in effect, making it your own. You're not looking for a fast, temporary fix; you're looking for a fix that's going to last as long as possible.

"You need an expert in orthopedic trauma and reconstruction, in addition to bone transplants. There are very few who take on cases like yours. I know of only two in the country. One's in Seattle, the other in Denver. Both are associated with bone and tissue banks."

"Dr. Conner is in Seattle. His name's Ernest, but he goes by Billy. He's probably the most experienced man on the planet for this type of surgery. Dr. Reese, in Denver, is equally qualified, though he may not be quite as experienced as Dr. Conner.

"I'll get a referral letter off to both doctors this afternoon, with copies of your x-rays and case history. Today is the fifth. Give them until the fifteenth. If they haven't gotten in touch with you by then, call them.

"I'm sorry to send you away, Lauren. I wish we could help you here. But your injury is one in 100,000. I'm confident, though, that one of these guys will be able to help you."

Far from being disappointed, the three of us left in high spirits. For weeks, we'd been shooting in the dark. Now we had a specific target.

Good cheer prevailed as we met Andrea later in the day for a tour of her new office and new apartment. She'd landed a job with an insurance agency within a couple of days of moving to Charlotte. Marc had helped her find a nice one-bedroom flat in a safe area of town, close to her work.

Later, we grabbed hamburgers at Wendy's and started home. Andrea listened as we filled her in on Lauren's appointment with Dr. Kneece.

"It sounds promising," Andrea said as she dug her dainty fingers into the box of French fries, "but we still have no idea of what will be done and when."

"We'll just have to wait and see," Karin said.

"Oh," Andrea responded and fell silent.

"Is something on your mind?" Karin asked.

"Well, yeah…sort of. I want to go ahead and set a wedding date. But Marc and I have talked and we don't want to do anything that might get in the way of Lauren's getting well. That's got to be first priority. So we don't know what to do."

"It takes some time to put on a wedding," Karin said. "The sooner you get a date set, the better. I can't pull one off overnight."

Andrea dropped her half-eaten French fry on her napkin.

"You mean, you'd give us a wedding? Because…well…Marc and I haven't exactly handled our engagement and my moving to Charlotte…well, heck! Our whole relationship hasn't been what you and Daddy had…uh…hoped for."

I fought the urge to utter, *you can say that again*, and behaved myself while I listened to Karin's reply.

"Daddy and I have discussed it. We knew you'd be wanting to set a wedding date before long. Even though you and Marc have had your ups and downs and on and offs, you've been dating now for what...almost six years? Surely within that time you both must know what you want out of life and what you're looking for in a spouse. And your wedding day should be the most special day of your life. After all, it only happens once."

Karin let her last phrase soak in while she gave Andrea a stern but loving look across the table.

"Since it only happens once, Daddy and I want to give you and Marc a wedding that you can look back on. That is, if you want us to."

With tears streaming down her cheeks, Andrea could only nod. Finally, she recovered enough to respond. "It would mean more to me than anything in the world. Not just because I want a beautiful wedding, but because I'd know I have your blessing."

"What date are you thinking about?" Lauren asked, wide-eyed.

"We were looking at September 13. What do ya'll think?" Andrea answered.

Karin rolled her eyes up and thought for a moment.

"Hmm, September. An end-of-the-summer wedding. That gives us six months." She thought some more. "It'll be tight, but it's doable!"

"So," Lauren chimed in, "who's your maid of honor?"

"You are, of course!" Andrea exclaimed.

"As well I should be," Lauren answered. "Who knows? Maybe I'll walk down that aisle all by myself—without crutches."

Tears welled up again in Andrea's blue eyes as she shot out of her chair and ran to Lauren with a hug.

"That'd be the best wedding present anyone could ever get."

The two gaunt, haggard, shirtless men perched precariously on an eight-inch square platform ten feet above transparent, aquamarine water. Atop a pole anchored in the ocean floor, they fired pebbles from a slingshot at a ceramic bull's eye mounted fifteen yards away on a postcard perfect beach. Shot after shot missed the mark. Finally, a pebble launched by the older, scruffier of the two struck the bull's eye dead center. The target rocked backward, striking a lever that pulled a rope, which pulled a pin and allowed a primitive-looking flag to unfurl in the tropical breeze.

A crowd of equally grubby folks celebrated as if they'd just won the lottery. The only individual among the gathering who looked like he'd had a shower in a month presented them with an unbaited hook tied to a spool of flimsy fishing line.

Just then, the ringing of the telephone interrupted our Thursday night ritual, where Karin, Lauren and I gathered in front of the television to escape reality for an hour by watching unreal, reality television.

"Who dares to call while *Survivor* is on?" I hollered. I hurried to the kitchen and barked a slightly aggravated "Hello," into the phone.

"Mr. Tarrant?" the male voice asked.

"Uh, yes. This is Mike Tarrant," I answered, seeking to mitigate my initial brusqueness.

"This is Billy Conner at the Pacific-Northwest Medical Center. How are things down there in Georgia? Or is it South Carolina?"

"It's the Georgia/South Carolina border, actually," I replied. "We're okay. How are you, Dr. Conner?"

"I'm just wonderful, thank you. I'm calling to let you know that I received your daughter's referral from Dr. Kneece. I think we can help Lauren."

"That's fantastic, sir!" I was amazed that a doctor would take the time to personally call. "We've waited a long time and done a lot of searching to hear those words."

"Yes, I can imagine." Dr. Conner quickly got to the point. "I think Lauren is a good candidate for a fresh osteochondral allograft. By 'fresh' I mean one that has been recently procured. It provides a much higher rate of success because of the greater cartilage viability or 'aliveness.'

"Now keep in mind that Lauren does have a significant risk of infection because of her previous wound infections. Nevertheless, if you all are in agreement, I will put Lauren on a list at the Northwest Tissue Center for procurement. I cannot, however, secure a graft for her until I have the actual size of her femur. I need an accurate size of her good knee joint so I can measure the width of her normal knee. That film needs to be a plain x-ray with a marker for magnification correction. That's an extremely important factor in selecting a graft that will fit well in reconstructing Lauren's femoral defect."

"Dr. Conner," I interrupted, "can you hold for a moment while I write this down?"

"Don't worry about writing this down now. I'll put all this in a letter, because I also need any previous CT or MRI scans of her knee. I need a good bit of information, but I'll list it all for you."

"As soon as we receive your letter, we'll gather everything you need," I assured the doctor. I glanced at the calendar Karin kept on the kitchen counter and noted it had been eight days since we met Dr. Kneece.

"When would you anticipate the surgery taking place?" I asked.

"That's dependent on when a donor can be located," Dr. Conner replied. "It could take several months, possibly a year or even longer. It's impossible to predict."

"I'm sorry." I said. "Obviously, I'm not familiar with how a transplant like this comes about. I understood you procure the bone from the tissue bank."

"That's right," the doctor patiently replied. "But the 'fresh' tissue must closely match the dimensions and configuration of Lauren's good leg. Judging by the x-rays Dr. Kneece forwarded to me, it appears that Lauren has a slight frame, with relatively long bones. So an appropriate donor would most likely be female, preferably young, of similar size and stature to Lauren. There's no way to know when a donor that fits those requirements will become available."

At those words, a sudden flash of understanding left me dumbstruck.

"Mr. Tarrant, are you still there?"

Dr. Conner's voice brought me back. "Yes, sir. I'm sorry. Thank you so much for everything. You've given us real reason to be hopeful, and I can promise you that Lauren and my wife—the whole family—will be thrilled. We'll await your letter and respond just as quickly as possible. Thank you again, and you have a good evening."

Dr. Conner returned the goodbye. I hung up and walked back upstairs to the den.

"We're going to have to record the rest of *Survivor*," I announced in response to the girls' curious expressions. "I've got news."

Good news, as well as bad news, travels fast.

The following morning, the phone began ringing with family and friends. It happened to be my day off, and the early spring weather was too beautiful to spend indoors on the phone, so while Karin took Lauren to physical therapy, I decided to tackle some chores in the yard.

The landscape was alive with the fresh, fragile sprouts of spring. *First green is gold*, I remembered the poet saying. I walked under the delicate, new gold-and-green canopy of the deciduous trees growing on the hill in the backyard.

I stopped at a small water oak that looked just as it had late last summer. Normally evergreen, it had uncharacteristically lost its leaves in the August heat. Now its branches remained barren and lifeless against the pale blue sky, without so much as a bud. I ran my hand down the rippled, gray bark that covered the rock-solid wood beneath, until my palm caught on something sharp.

I pulled a thin, steel splinter from my flesh and watched as tiny, red droplets of blood formed in its place. Bending down for a better look, I found a long-forgotten steel cord imbedded in the tree. I had fastened it there probably fifteen years earlier, the upper end of a zip line I had strung through the woods for Andrea and Lauren. For years, the little tree had continued to grow, until the noose I had neglected to remove slowly strangled it. There was nothing to do now but cut it down.

I got my chain saw and felled the tree, trimmed off the branches, and cut the trunk into logs.

Good wood, I thought, as I hauled the logs to the curb to await pick up by the city's trash truck. *I have no use for it, but what a shame it will go to waste.*

The job finished, I stood on Lauren's wheelchair ramp, downing a bottle of water while I surveyed the gap the removal of the tree left in the backyard. I hadn't imagined the yard would look so bare, so incomplete.

Then I looked down at the structure I stood on. The long ramp stretched almost from one end of the house to the other. Though functional, it was not pretty.

How this yard has changed in just a few months, I thought. *Who would've thought the loss of one scrawny tree would be so conspicuous? Shoot. Who'd have thought we'd ever need a wheelchair ramp in the backyard? For one of our children, no less?*

Who'd have thought Andrea would up and get engaged without so much as a word, then move off to Charlotte, all in the matter of a few weeks? And Lauren, who should be at Clemson getting ready to graduate in six or seven weeks, instead may be waiting months or longer, just to have a chance to walk again?

I took a final swig of the water then hurled the empty plastic bottle across the backyard as far as I could, knowing I'd just have to pick it up later.

And who'd have thought that if my daughter is ever to have a chance to walk again, another father's daughter will have to die?

Oh, God! How can I pray for my own child to be healed if it means someone else will lose their own precious child? Of all that we've gone through in the past few months, Lord, this one I really don't think I can handle!

Water, or something wet, splashed my cheek. I wiped it off with the back of my hand as I grabbed a rake to clean up the last of the debris from the dead tree.

Midnight found me writhing in bed, my mind whirling just as it had been all day.

"Will you please settle down and go to sleep?" Karin couldn't hide the sleep-deprived aggravation in her voice. "You've been flipping and flopping like a fish out of water for over an hour. You're keeping me awake. What's the matter with you? You've been acting funny all day."

"Sorry," I said, rolling over to face my wife in the darkness. "I'd get up and go to the den, but I can't because Robbie's spending the weekend on the couch in there. And I'm too tired to get up and read. I'll try to settle down."

"You didn't answer me. What's been up with you today?" Karin insisted.

"I can't get this transplant business out of my head." I said, rolling onto my back. I reached behind my head and flipped my pillow to the cool side. "And I'm worried about another surgery bringing the infection back. I know...worry about nothing, pray about everything. I try, but sometimes—"

"You know what Lauren said on the way home from physical therapy today?" Karin broke in. She gathered the corner of her pillow in her hand and pulled it up under her chin.

"No, what?"

"She said she couldn't go through with it—the transplant. She said if her recovery was dependent on someone else dying, she'd rather be crippled for the rest of her life."

"Why didn't you tell me?" I asked, rolling back to face Karin.

"I haven't had a chance to talk to you all day," she replied.

"What did you tell her?"

"I gave her the obvious, intellectual response; no one wants anyone to lose their life, but it happens every day. If there were anything we could do to stop it, or prevent it, we would...but there's not. If anything good can come from a tragedy, then wouldn't God want that?"

"Good answer," I whispered. "Did that help her?"

"She agreed, of course. Then we dropped it, thankfully, because I'm as upset as you and Lauren. I guess it's something we'll have to work through in our own minds."

"That's what I've been doing all day. I don't think I'm any closer to a resolution, though." I arched my back in an attempt to stretch away the onset of a major backache.

"Your back hurting again?" Karin asked.

"Yeah, maybe it's the bed," I responded. "I gotta get back to the gym. Maybe I'll start Monday morning."

"Why don't you get up on Monday and use the stationary bike in Andrea's room?" Karin suggested. "Do that for a few mornings and get limbered up before you go gangbusters at the gym."

"Good idea." I grabbed Karin's hand. "Now we better try to get some sleep, right?"

"Okay, Chumley," my pretty wife said. She kissed me on the cheek before rolling over. "Just remember, worry about nothing, pray about everything."

"You're the second person to say that tonight," I mumbled as I turned over again.

For the rest of the weekend, sleep came fitfully. Dr. Conner's words played in my head like a broken record:

A significant risk of infection because of her previous wound infections…So an appropriate donor would most likely be female, preferably young, of similar size and stature to Lauren…of similar size and stature to Lauren…of similar size and stature to Lauren.

Chapter Ten

Turn your eyes upon Jesus,
Look full in His wonderful face,
And the things of earth will grow strangely dim
In the light of His glory and grace.
—"Turn Your Eyes upon Jesus"
Helen H. Limmel, 1922

A PROFOUND AND extraordinary peace pervaded our house just before dawn on Monday morning. Cushioned and hushed in the carpet, my footsteps roused no one as I walked into Andrea's empty bedroom, closed the door, and seated myself on the exercise bike. I remember the only sound being that of the calm, reassuring whisper of air circulating through registers.

I propped a book on the handlebars of the cycle, then pushed the pedals, producing another soothing whisper as the wheel turned against the restraint of the nylon tension strap. The pale morning light was barely sufficient for reading, so I turned instead to the water, earth, and sky awakening before me through the windows on my right.

The world outside appeared as a palette of muted pastels surrounding the deep indigo of water, all softly illuminated by the impendent presence of a gentle, warming sun. As I watched, the faded pastels brightened in harmony with the slow rotation of the earth. In that moment, with all of nature perfectly balanced, an awesome sense of serenity, security, and overwhelming safety reigned.

And then, for a moment, the earth stood still.

I turned from the window, and He stood there before me. There was no fear, no surprise, for I knew Him instantly. His presence was as natural as the morning's first light tenderly glowing in the window.

Robed in white, He stretched both arms toward me and turned the palms of His hands as if to frame my face. At that moment, I knew that in all the universe there was no one more cherished, more protected, or more loved than I.

Don't look up.
Don't look down.
Don't look from side to side.
You keep your eyes only on Me.

Though not spoken, I understood His every word.
Then He was there no more.
And the earth resumed its rotation.

Chapter Eleven

Then will the eyes of the blind be opened and the ears of the deaf
unstopped. Then will the lame leap like a deer, and the mute
tongue shout for joy....

—Isiah 35:5-6

ALL STILL SLEPT when I left the house that Monday
morning. I raced to work. As soon as I sat down at my desk, I
called home.

"Hello?" Karin answered.

"Hey," I rushed to the point. "What are you doing today
at lunch?"

"Well," Karin began almost dreamily. She was obviously
savoring a few precious minutes of free time. "Lauren doesn't
have physical therapy today, so she and a friend are going to meet
some high school girls from Young Life at lunch. Since I don't
have to take Lauren to physical therapy, I'm going to catch up
with the laundry. Then I'm going to run over to Augusta and
check on some places for Andrea and Marc's reception. There's

not much time to spare, because September will be here before you know it, and—"

"I need to meet you for lunch," I said, cutting her off in mid-statement.

"Why, what's wrong?" Karin shifted into crisis response.

"No, no, I'm sorry. I didn't mean to scare you. There's nothing wrong. In fact, there's something right, really right. But I can't tell you over the phone. But it's important!"

"Gosh, Michael," Karin protested, "this is the only day that I've had to begin to think about Andrea's wedding. What's so important that you can't tell me over the phone?"

"Just trust me." I answered. "It's important. Meet me at Subway at 11:30, okay?"

"All right, but you're making me nervous."

"Just trust me," I said again, feeling sorry for jangling Karin's frayed nerves. "I'll see you at Subway."

A few hours later, Karin and I pulled into the shopping center parking lot simultaneously. We entered the restaurant and slipped into a nondescript booth by a window. It provided a view of the ordinary sidewalk and the front ends of ordinary automobiles, being driven by ordinary people, going about their ordinary business on an ordinary day.

Then I told my wife my extraordinary story.

"No one would ever believe me," I said when I'd finished.

"That doesn't matter. It happened, and I believe you," Karin said.

"That's because you know me," I answered. "But why me? No one could be more ordinary than me. I've never been anything but average; just your everyday guy. Why me?"

"Remember a few months ago when Lauren was so hurt?" Karin answered. "I said, 'Why you, Lauren?' Do you remember her reply? She said, 'Why *not* me, Mama?' So now I'm saying, 'Why *not* you, Michael?'"

We stared silently out the window while that sank in.

Then Karin continued. "What did Becky always say? 'Nothing happens unless the Lord can make good come of it,' right? Meaning, if He can't make something good come out of everything, even tragedy, He won't let it happen."

I nodded.

Karin smiled. "All through the anguish we've all felt over this transplant—even the guilt we feel because our child can't walk again unless someone else's child dies—He's telling you that we have to give it to Him, Michael. It's beyond our capacities to reconcile it. So don't even try."

Karin leaned back and turned her gaze to the sidewalk outside the window. I got up and ordered a couple of subs. When I returned several minutes later, I found Karin in the same position, still staring at the sidewalk.

The sound of the paper crackling as I unwrapped my sandwich brought her attention back to me.

"We let go," she said quietly.

"Let go of what?" I pushed her sub across the table.

"We let go of Him. We let go of Jesus. We came to a point where we couldn't make sense of things anymore—at least not from our human point of view. So because we couldn't understand and our faith was not yet strong enough, we cut off communications. We couldn't even talk to Him. We couldn't even pray."

I waited expectantly, knowing my wife had more to share.

"But Michael," she finally continued, wide-eyed. "*He* never let go of *us*. When you and I could no longer find the strength to hold on to Him, He held on to us. Don't you see? Now that we've found Him, He's not going to let us go. He won't. You, me, Lauren, all of us...we are, we really *are* in His grip!

"We just have to be patient and trust Him. He said to keep our focus on Him, so we'll just trust...and obey."

As if responding to a command, spring came forth with a rush—a natural, vast explosion of flowers and fragrances that renewed and transformed. And though there had been many seasons before and there would be many seasons to come, there would never again be such a glorious season as this one. The changes wrought by His Word, for us, were everlasting.

Surrendering the unanswerable questions to Christ, we wrapped ourselves in His infinite grace and waited.

One evening in May, Lauren sat in her wheelchair on the front porch while Robbie, Karin, and I rocked, watching fireflies spark under the trees across the street. Cicadas droned, and the scent of honeysuckle mingled with jasmine and magnolia hung sweet and heavy in the warm, damp air.

Graduation day at Clemson had come and gone. Lauren's classmates, including roommates Emily, Katie, and Leslie, had walked the stage at Littlejohn Coliseum, received their diplomas and begun new lives. Emily was bound for graduate school, Katie planned a wedding in July, and Leslie started a career in advertising in Greenville.

With another year before his graduation, Robbie was taking a couple of courses in summer school at Clemson while he worked at an on-campus job. Weekends generally found him at our house.

Karin, in long-distance consultation with Andrea, worked on the details of Andrea's September wedding. In anticipation of out-of-town company at the end of the summer, I worked in the yard a lot.

Lauren maintained her rigorous physical therapy regime, but progress had gradually slowed, reached a plateau, and stopped. Regular appointments with Dr. Hines brought no mention of how or when he planned to rebuild Lauren's leg. We no longer asked.

Instead of fretting, Lauren immersed herself in the ministry of Young Life.

Given the circumstances, we could have focused on what *should* have been. We could have grieved over what *could* have been. We could have worried over what *might* be still to come. Instead, we focused on what we were right then, on that front porch: a family touched by God and determined to be content in the moment. Not because we deserved to be (we didn't), and not because we needed to be (we did), but because we were blessed enough to have finally learned to call on Him. And He always answers.

As we rocked, the cicadas turned up their serenade. It was so loud that we barely heard the phone ringing. I ran inside to pick it up.

"Hi, Mike, this is Diane in Dr. Conner's office in Seattle. I wasn't sure I'd catch anyone at home. It's after five here on a Friday, so I know it's after eight out there."

"We're just sitting out on the porch," I said. "Does Dr. Conner need another x-ray or something?"

"As a matter of fact, he's going to need that and more," she replied. "We've found a donor for Lauren."

I pulled a barstool over and sat down.

"That's...f-fantastic," I stammered, almost in a state of disbelief. "But Diane, it's only been a couple of months. We were expecting many months, even a year or longer."

"You just never know, Mike," Diane replied. "These things are in God's hands, not ours. Dr. Conner has already explained the procedure, but let me take a minute and tell you what happens next."

"Do I need to take notes?" I stretched to grab a notepad and pencil off the calendar.

"No, we'll be sending you a letter. I just want to give you all a heads-up. As you know, a bone transplant is not like an organ transplant. You don't have to rush out here tonight. In fact, the bone will go through a series of tests and procedures to make sure it's viable and ready for transplantation. There's a chance we won't be able to use it. I don't think that will be the case, but you need to understand the possibility does exist.

"We need to go ahead, though, and tentatively schedule the surgery. Dr. Conner has vacation scheduled around the end of June and early July. We can't wait until after he returns, because the tissue will lose it's viability by then. How does June 26 sound?"

"We'll make it work," I replied.

"Good," she answered. "Lauren will need to be out here a few days before the surgery. Plan on her being in the hospital for a week to ten days after that."

"No anti-rejection drugs are necessary, right?" I said, confirming my earlier understanding.

"That's right. That's another big difference between this and an organ transplant. The body won't reject properly prepared and transplanted bone. In fact, we hope and expect that Lauren's bone will knit into the transplant.

"One more thing, Mike," Diane continued. "You'll need to contact Lauren's orthopedist down there and let him know that Dr. Conner will need his full cooperation when Lauren gets home. Tell him to expect a letter soon from Dr. Conner. It will give him the information he'll need and hopefully answer any questions he may have."

"Sure, Diane," I said, sounding more confident of the outcome of that meeting than I felt. "Thanks so much for all you've done and are doing. I can't tell you how much this means to not only Lauren, but also to our whole family. We'll bring you and Dr. Conner a big basket of peaches. That'll make it all worth while."

"Okay, Mike. We'll be expecting it. Give your family, and especially Lauren, my best."

I hung up and walked out to the front porch.

"I'm gonna quit being the one to answer the phone around here," I declared. "But never mind that. Who wants to celebrate the Fourth of July in Seattle?"

Committed to be a bridesmaid for her friend Lindsey in Charleston in late June and for Katie in Clemson in late July, the surgery couldn't have been scheduled at a better time as far as Lauren was concerned. And with a date set, Andrea and Karin could begin to firm up plans for Andrea's September wedding.

Although aware that we needed to contact Dr. Hines, several hectic days slipped by. But early one morning, I had just settled in for the day's chores at work when Karin called.

"Michael!"

I knew immediately something was amiss. "What's wrong?" My jaw clenched involuntarily.

"I just got a call from Dr. Hines. He was absolutely livid! I'm literally shaking!"

Karin had taken a lot lately, and she had invariably remained calm. If she was upset, it had to be bad.

"He got the letter from Dr. Conner in Seattle," she went on. "Michael, he called us 'backstabbers'! He said we had gone behind his back by not involving him in the search for someone to fix Lauren."

"That's baloney!" I shot back. "What'd you say?"

"I reminded him that we had asked him repeatedly to outline what Lauren's next step should be," Karin replied, "and he had refused to discuss it, telling us only that she wasn't ready. I said that the three of us disagreed with him and that we—Lauren, you, and I—felt Lauren was more than ready. And since we are the ones who are ultimately responsible for Lauren's recovery, we agreed that it was in Lauren's best interest, physically and emotionally, to determine the next steps in her treatment. Since he obviously chose not to be a part of that, we honored his choice but continued our path forward."

"Wow," I answered. "Great reply! So then what?"

"He calmed down a little. But get this…" Karin paused, and I held my breath. "He now says he wants to do the surgery."

"What?" I shouted into the phone. "He refuses to discuss it for weeks, but now he says he can do Lauren's surgery? He can do what Mayo, Shands, the Cleveland Clinic, and all the other people and places we've spent weeks researching, can't do? And he waits until *now* to tell us?"

"That's what he says," Karin answered. "He wants us to meet him at his office on Monday morning to discuss it."

"Oh, boy!" I replied. "That ought to be fun."

It wasn't.

The following Monday morning, Karin, Lauren, and I waited in a small examination room in Dr. Hines' office, braced for a meeting with Mr. Hyde, hoping Dr. Jekyll would show up instead.

A day or so earlier, Karin had phoned Dr. Conner in Seattle. She told him of her conversation with Dr. Hines and asked what he thought about Dr. Hines doing the surgery.

"He's a wild man," Dr. Conner had replied. "He has no idea what he'd be getting into. If he were qualified to perform an operation like this, I would know it."

It had been enough to remove any doubt about who should do the surgery. Yet, sitting in that bland little exam room, I felt like an errant school kid waiting for a paddling in the principal's office. I looked at Karin, sitting with her legs tucked tightly under her chair, ankles crossed, and the toe of one shoe tapping nervously.

With her crutches propped against the wall, Lauren sat stiff and upright on the exam table, anxiously twirling a lock of hair. One leg hung over the table's edge, while the braced leg extended across the table like the center of conversation it would soon be.

What a bunch of baloney! I thought. *It's been seven months since the accident, and my daughter, who has done nothing to hurt anyone, and my wife, who has suffered through every minute of our daughter's pain, are waiting for a tongue lashing...from a guy who is being paid handsomely to—supposedly—work for us! And we're just going to sit here and take it?*

The door opened. Without a word of greeting, Dr. Hines entered and sat down in the only remaining chair.

"I'll get right to the point," he began coldly. The endearing, easy-going, Southern charm was conspicuously absent. "Since I last spoke to you, Mrs. Tarrant, I received a phone call from Dr. Conner. I had already received a letter from him, which prompted me to call you last week. He asked me to provide follow-up care after he performs the allograft in Seattle.

"I don't know why you all found it necessary to go behind my back and seek another surgeon for the allograft."

Before any of us could protest, the doctor continued. "Lauren's allograft is not that unusual. I have performed dozens of allografts and am perfectly capable of performing this one. If for some reason you did not feel comfortable with me performing the surgery—as you obviously don't—then I could have recommended several colleagues right up the road at Emory. I would still recommend that approach."

He continued deliberately, without pausing for comments from us, and turned directly to Lauren.

"If you insist on traveling 3,000 miles to have Dr. Conner perform this operation, I will not see you when you return. And, frankly, I don't know anyone else who would, either. Asking me to provide follow-up care for a procedure that was done in the other corner of the country is totally unfair. Also, if you think you're just going to go out to Seattle and have this done, and that's the end of your visits, you're wrong. You're going to find yourself going back and forth to Seattle several times for the first few months, and then probably at least once a year after that. You're setting yourself up for a lot of inconvenience and expense."

Before Lauren could respond or Dr. Hines could continue, Karin broke in like a mother bear protecting her cub.

"I need to clarify something, Doctor, before you go on. As I said when you and I spoke on the phone last week, we did not go behind your back. We asked you repeatedly to tell us Lauren's next steps. You refused—yes, refused—to discuss it. There's more to Lauren's injury than just her leg. For her emotional well-being, she needed to know a path forward. We asked you for that, and you refused."

Realizing she had seized control of the meeting, Karin leaned forward and continued.

"If you thought we would stand by and do nothing until *you* decided you were ready to talk about it, then you don't know this family. Had you broached the subject at any time over the past several weeks, we'd have certainly told you about our search."

"Who besides Dr. Conner have you contacted?" Dr. Hines asked, wilted somewhat by Karin's retort.

"Mayo, Johns Hopkins, Cleveland Clinic, Shands, the Hospital for Special Surgeries in New York, among others," Karin replied.

"Who referred you to these places?" the doctor queried.

"I worked for Best Doctors a few years ago," Karin replied. "I contacted them and they provided a list of orthopedic surgeons who specialize in this type of surgery. Dr. Baxter in Baltimore also recommended that we speak with several of his colleagues, one of which is in Charlotte, who ultimately directed us to Dr. Conner in Seattle."

"I see," the doctor replied, the wind temporarily out of his sails.

"What about physical therapy?" Lauren asked, leaving the beleaguered curl she had been twirling alone momentarily. "Will I still be able to work with Anna? She's been much more than a therapist; she's become a friend."

"No," Hines answered, seemingly pleased at another opportunity to be difficult. "If you're not my patient, it won't be possible for you to use our facilities for physical therapy."

"So where do we go from here?" I asked in an effort to bring the ordeal to a close, all the while knowing full well where Lauren, Karin, and I would be going,

"I'd say Lauren has a decision to make." Dr. Hines looked directly at Karin and me.

"The decision's been made." At the sound of Lauren's voice, the doctor turned to his former patient.

"My surgery in Seattle is already scheduled, and I'm not going to change it." Lauren reached for her crutches. "I appreciate everything you've done for me. I'll miss you and all the staff here, especially Anna. But right now, I'm doing what I know is best for me. If you choose to no longer have me as a patient, then that's your choice, not mine."

With that, we left Dr. Hines' office for the last time. Crutching along determinedly, Lauren led the way out.

"We'll have to find another orthopedist and another physical therapist," she called to Karin and me as we walked behind our daughter. "But that's okay. We can do it. Just look what we've done so far. Philippians 4:13 says we can do all things through Christ who strengthens us. And we can do this!"

Twenty-four hours later, Dr. Paul Walton and the physical therapy department of Southern Orthopedics agreed to accept

Lauren's case when she returned from Seattle—with no strings attached.

On the eve of our leaving for Seattle, Karin and I walked down Dock Street in Charleston. We crossed the street at the cemetery, where island ladies sat under live oaks weaving baskets out of sweet grass, pine straw, and palm fronds. Then we entered the historic old St. Phillip's Church. The steeple above us, by legal decree the tallest structure in peninsular Charleston, had pointed the way to heaven for centuries, withstanding wars, earthquakes, hurricanes, and fires.

Taking seats in a boxed pew, we were enveloped in this glorious manifestation of man's attempt to characterize the timeless and incredible majesty, mystery, and omnipotence of God. The crucifix, in its eminence, drew my eyes, and my thoughts returned to the words so recently spoken: *"Don't look up, don't look down. Don't look from side to side. You keep your eyes only on Me."*

The awesomeness of that event remained beyond my comprehension. Would there ever be an answer to the question, *Why me, Lord? Why me?*

In the days since that morning, and especially since we learned that a donor for Lauren had been found, Karin and I had earnestly, even desperately, beseeched the inclusion of Lauren and the donor's family on every prayer list we could find. Still, with the uncertainty of the next several days now upon us, the greatest reassurance was in doing as He had commanded, "You keep your eyes only on Me."

Boo frolicked in the tall, green fescue lawn surrounding Andrea's apartment in Charlotte. It was Sunday, June 23, Andrea's birthday. The fine texture of the grass, so different from the stiff, broad-bladed St. Augustine grass in her own backyard, provided a special treat for our little white dog, who had been such a loyal companion for Lauren during the long, cold days of the past winter. Nurse Boo, as we'd come to call her, darted back and forth, checking out the scents of other dogs at her home for the next couple of weeks while we were away.

True to form, Boo ceased her cavorting and ran to Lauren when she saw tears streaming down her face. Lauren, Andrea, Karin, and I stood outside, watching Robbie's black Ford Ranger, gleaming in the noonday sunshine, swing around the corner and disappear from sight.

"Our plane doesn't leave for another five hours," Lauren cried. "It's the last chance I'll have to be with him for weeks, and there he goes, leaving to play golf with his dad. I wish I could be mad, but I'm just sad. The whole thing is even scarier without him, and I miss him already."

Andrea held her sobbing little sister, just as she had so many times over the past winter. A pleading look passed from me to Karin.

She responded with a quick, almost imperceptible, shake of her head.

"Come on, Larnie," she chirped. "Let's get Boo and go back inside where it's cool. You can't blame Robbie for spending some time with his dad. After all, he's hardly seen his parents all year. He could have spent only a couple of more hours with you at most, and I'm sure he was torn. But you spent all day yesterday with him in Charleston at Lindsey's wedding."

"Maybe he'll be waiting at the airport when we get there," Lauren brightened, wiping the tears from her cheeks. She began a careful ascent of the steep steps up to Andrea's apartment. "Maybe he has to go home and pack, and he'll be waiting for me on the plane."

"Chicken, I don't think that's going to happen," I said, hoping to spare her further disappointment.

But when Andrea dropped us at the airport later that afternoon, Karin and I noticed Lauren peering into the crowds as we made our way to the gate.

"He could be here," Lauren insisted. "He could have gotten here early, so we wouldn't see him until we got to the gate."

With no Robbie waiting at the gate, Lauren was still not without hope. "He'll be on the plane. I'm not giving up until the wheels are off the ground."

The moment the seatbelt sign was turned off, Lauren turned to Karin. "Mama, help me down the aisle to the restroom, okay? I need to take a tour of the plane."

With Karin steadying her, Lauren hobbled on her crutches up and down the narrow aisles of the jet, trying, almost comically, to appear nonchalant as she searched every seat for Robbie's face. Finally convinced that the love of her life was not aboard, she returned to her seat.

"I said I wouldn't give up hope until we were in flight," Lauren declared, "but unless he stowed away in the baggage compartments, Robbie's not on this plane. I know it was probably too much to hope for, but I just had a feeling that Robbie would be with me. But he's not, he's not going to be, and there's no use crying about it anymore."

It was well after midnight, eastern time, when we deplaned at SeaTac. Searching for the car rental agencies, we wound through the huge, confusing, and almost empty maze of corridors that comprised the airport. Pushing a wheelchair, juggling baskets of peaches, and pulling carry-on suitcases, we avoided escalators, because escalators, of course, don't accommodate wheelchairs. I finally realized we were going in circles hunting for elevators. I parked Lauren with Karin amidst the peaches and suitcases and set off on my own to scout a trail.

I turned back for a last look at my family just as a figure stepped out from behind a pillar and clasped his big hands over my unsuspecting daughter's eyes. She reached up to pull herself from the intruder's grip and gasped.

"I knew you'd come!" Lauren cried before she saw the face that belonged to the familiar hands. "I knew you'd come!"

Robbie stepped in front of her and wrapped his arms around both Lauren and the wheelchair.

"How'd you do it?" Lauren asked, this time wiping away tears of joy.

"Hey, yours wasn't the only plane from Charlotte to Seattle, you know," Robbie replied. "Dad and I drove right past you while Andrea was dropping you all off at the airport. I thought for sure we'd been found out."

"And you two," Lauren turned to Karin and me. "You knew it all along, didn't you?"

Amidst laughter and hugs we easily found our way out of the airport.

But as we walked out, I couldn't help wondering how in the world Robbie had managed to find us, when none of us knew where the heck we were!

The Monday morning sunshine illuminated a city of astonishing beauty, with emerald hills that would have been mountains in our part of the world, rain-forest flora, and trees of massive proportions. Water was everywhere, and always—

towering in the distance—stood magnificent Mount Rainier. The city itself rose sleek, modern, and tall from the shores of Puget Sound. It beckoned us to explore as much as we could.

We met briefly with the affable Dr. Conner and Diane. As promised, we presented them with our offering from the South. From then on, he referred to Lauren as his Georgia peach. We made repeated but futile efforts to instruct him that our proper geographic location was Carolina and not Georgia. No matter to him! The accent was the same.

For two days, we pretended we were vacationers. We took pictures from the top of the Space Needle and from the Bainbridge Island ferry. We rode the Duck through downtown and out onto Lake Washington. We ate at Pike Place Market and drove to a Pacific Ocean beach, where Robbie swam in water colder than we thought salt water could get. We saw where the Seahawks play, ate crab legs at the waterfront, and only occasionally brushed the butterflies from our stomachs when fleeting thoughts of why we were here crossed our minds.

Wednesday brought the return of the now-familiar, purgatorial waiting. Finally, after seven hours in surgery, an exhausted Dr. Conner met us in a conference area late that afternoon.

"I'm getting too old for this," he said. Still in scrubs, he turned and tossed x-rays on a viewer. "I'll be honest with you. It was more difficult than I had expected. The fit for the graft was tight, real tight."

He flipped on the backlighting and pointed to the illuminated pictures.

"That's a result of two things: first, the graft is a little larger than the original bone. The condyle is a good match, but because

Chapter Eleven

Lauren's been without any bone structure for some time, the area of missing bone has decreased in size. We had to reduce the size of the graft, several times, and still stretch to make it fit."

Karin slipped her hand in mine. Robbie stood quietly beside us while the doctor continued.

"Lauren did fine, but she lost a liter of blood. I ordered a transfusion while she's in recovery. As for pain management, she has an epidural. There's a chance the epidural won't work. If it doesn't, we'll know it within a couple of hours and we'll take a different route. If it does work, we'll be able to manage the pain really well, and we can leave it in for several days. That way, we can manage not only post-op pain, but we can get Lauren on the CPM, the Continual Passive Motion machine, sooner and make early progress in regaining mobility."

Earlier in the day, before the surgery, we had met briefly with Dr. Conner. He had looked fresh and energetic. His optimism about Lauren's chances of walking and resuming a nearly normal life had made this day of waiting and constant clock-watching bearable. But the past several hours had obviously sapped the man of not only his energy, but much of his optimism, too.

"What will she eventually be able to do?" He paused and looked directly at each of us before he answered his own question. "Her knee is really, really stiff. I don't know how much she'll get back. But I'm hopeful she'll get a ninety-degree bend."

Well, Lord, I thought as we weaved our way up stairs and through corridors to wait in Lauren's room for her return, *that's a lot more than she can do now. And like I first heard eight months ago, "No matter what, we've still got our daughter."*

The window of Lauren's small hospital room provided a panoramic view of Lake Union, with Seattle's impressive skyline and Puget Sound in the distance. As afternoon began to fade to evening, Karin, Robbie, and I passed the time waiting for Lauren to return from recovery. We silently watched the tiny dots on the water that were boats crisscrossing the lake.

"What the heck is taking so long?" Robbie finally asked, breaking our silent musings.

"It must be the transfusion," Karin answered, reassuring herself as much as Robbie and me. "You know how long it takes to administer a unit of blood. That's got to be it. I'm just relieved she's getting the transfusion right away. Dr. Conner said she'd lost a lot of blood."

We nodded agreement, sat down in the room's straight chairs, and shifted our gazes to the tiles on the floor. Finally, after another thirty minutes, we heard the wheels of a gurney rolling in the silent hallway.

The orderlies parked the hospital bed containing our battered daughter and left without a word. With shockingly pale, greenish skin, blue lips, and sunken eyes shut tightly in deeply bruised sockets, the sleeping girl bore little resemblance to the one who had cheerfully toured this emerald corner of the country for two days and had entered the hospital only hours earlier.

Lauren appeared too frail to touch, but to our relief, within minutes a nurse came in and got her settled and hooked up to the requisite myriad of wires and tubes. The nurse quickly finished and was gone. For the next couple of hours, the three of us took turns sitting beside the bed. Lauren's deep sleep indicated the epidural was doing its job. Meanwhile, the hospital remained profoundly, almost eerily, quiet. No nurses came in; no visitors walked the halls.

"Is something wrong?" Karin whispered to Robbie and me from her position beside Lauren's bed. "It's been a couple of hours since we saw anybody. It seems like someone should have been in every half-hour or so, at least, to check."

Just then, Lauren roused.

"Mama," she uttered in a barely audible croak. She struggled to open her eyes and hold her head up. "I think I'm going to be sick."

"Okay, Chicken," Karin whispered as she lay Lauren's head back. "I've got you."

Karin then turned to Robbie and me. "Quick! Can ya'll find the spit-up bowl and get me a cold washcloth?"

I slammed through the bathroom looking for linens, but there were none. Robbie tore through the cabinets and closets, but could find no utensils.

"Push the call button," I directed. "There's nothing here. We should have looked earlier."

"It's okay, it's okay," Karin said quietly. She leaned forward to push the call button while she stroked Lauren's forehead. "She's gone back to sleep. Crisis temporarily averted."

It was some time before a somewhat portly man, looking to be in his mid thirties, appeared with the missing items.

"My name is Roger," he announced in normal volume, seemingly without regard for the sleeping, nauseated patient. "I'll be your nurse on this shift, probably for the rest of this week. Lauren is your daughter, right?"

Karin and I nodded, then whispered introductions for ourselves and Robbie.

"Roger," Karin said softly, "I've been watching the read-out on the blood pressure monitor. It's been steadily dropping. Is that normal? No one's been here since Lauren got back from surgery, and I'm getting a little worried."

"Oh, no," he answered without glancing at the monitor. "No problem. The epidural sometimes causes a drop in blood pressure."

He seemed eager to chat and in no hurry to leave us, though the three of us were far too tense to carry on a conversation.

"So, you guys are from South Carolina, I understand," he said, changing the subject. "I guess you heard about Strom Thurmond then?"

Karin was focused on Lauren, and Robbie had turned back to the window, leaving me to continue the conversation. I was disinclined to do anything other than watch the LED readouts flashing by Lauren's bed.

"We heard the report of his death on CNN," I answered, still trying to keep my voice down. "He was really a great man; a real hero, especially to South Carolinians."

"I don't imagine he'd have been much of a hero here," Roger responded with a slight smirk. I found it particularly irksome, despite, or maybe exacerbated by, the current situation.

Karin, knowing I'd not let such a comment go unanswered under almost any circumstance, turned from Lauren and shot me a look of admonition. Ignoring my wife's pleading expression and against my better judgment, I responded.

"Is that right? And why would you say that?"

"It's just that we're a lot more liberal and tolerant here in Washington state. I'm sure you've seen evidence of it if you've spent any time here at all. We're very accepting of everyone. Most people here don't stereotype others or condemn them if they're different or a minority. Take me, for instance. There aren't that many men who are nurses, you know, but I don't catch any flak because of it. Of course, I'm married and straight, but there are lots of couples around here who aren't...straight, I mean. And that's okay with us."

"My brother's son is a nurse," I replied, struggling to maintain my voice at just above a whisper. "He's in the navy. He's a big guy, and I'd pity anybody who'd be foolish enough to insult his masculinity. So how many folks do you know from South Carolina?"

"Other than you people, I've never met anyone from South Carolina. I was born and raised here in Washington," Roger answered. "I haven't made it down South, not even to Florida."

"Well, Florida ain't really the South," I said with a wry grin. I noticed that Robbie, as well as my wife, had turned in my direction. Their looks implored me to end the conversation.

"Anyway," I said before turning back to the displays, "what some people call 'tolerance,' others just consider a lack of standards of behavior. Strom Thurmond wasn't perfect; none of us are. We've all made mistakes. But he had standards, and at the same time he loved the people of South Carolina as much as they loved him.

"It was good to meet you," I finished. "Thanks for bringing the stuff. Keep a check on us every now and then."

"Oh, sure," Roger said. Then he left, I imagined, to ponder my inbred intolerance. But my attention had already turned to the red numbers on the blood-pressure monitor.

"Karin," I said, dropping my voice to a whisper. "Those numbers are falling a lot, aren't they?"

"If this display is correct, then Lauren's blood pressure is eighty-five over thirty-two," Karin whispered back. "I'm going to push the call button and get somebody back in here. Something's not right."

She pressed the call button pinned to the bedclothes. Several minutes passed with no response.

"I'm going down the hall to find somebody," Robbie announced. "There's got to be a nurse around here somewhere," he muttered as he strode purposefully out of the room.

Just then, Lauren blinked open her eyes. "Mama, I'm going to be sick."

"Okay, Chicken, let me get the pan," Karin ordered, "Michael, get Lauren's head."

I leaned over the bed and slipped my arms around my little girl, cradling her head in my hand.

"Daddy," she murmured. She looked at me with a faraway smile, as if seeing me through a mist.

Then her eyes rolled backward and disappeared.

"Lauren!" I called. A feeling of helplessness washed over me like a thundering wave, threatening to knock me off my feet. "Lauren!"

"Lauren!" I cried again, desperate for a response that was not forthcoming. "Come back to me, Chicken Little!"

"Karin!" I yelled as she rushed out of the bathroom with a pan and a washcloth. "Lauren's unconscious!"

Karin slammed the big, red button marked EMERGENCY above the bed.

I gently shook Lauren's limp shoulders, but there was no response.

Whether due to Robbie's foray down the hall, or the emergency button, or a combination of both, the room was suddenly filled. Karin and I were brushed aside. Seconds later, Lauren was on oxygen, new IVs were hung, and—though vomiting—our daughter was revived.

When the emergency passed, a nurse whom we had not seen before stepped over to the three of us huddled together near the window.

"We're bringing up two units of blood," she said. "I'm confident she'll be okay. She's just lost a lot of blood, and it hasn't been replaced."

"What do you mean, it hasn't been replaced?" Karin responded. "What about the transfusion she received in recovery?"

"She wasn't given blood in recovery," the nurse replied, looking at the chart in her hands.

"Dr. Conner specifically told us she was being transfused while she was in recovery," Karin insisted.

"There was no transfusion," the woman answered. "Of that I am positive."

We each took two-hour shifts watching over Lauren for the rest of the night. About 3:00 AM I left my chair by the window to relieve Karin at her bedside watch.

"How you doin'?" I quietly asked my wife. The only light in the room was the muted television mounted on the opposite wall, ESPN replays of earlier baseball games. The dimness couldn't obscure the stress of the day and the sleepless night reflected on her face.

"I'm okay," she whispered back. How about you?"

"I'm okay now," I answered. "Did you think it would be this tough?"

"I don't know," she said. "I don't think so. I mean, it's been tough every time, but you repress unpleasant memories, you know? But I think some of this could have been avoided. It certainly didn't have to reach crisis proportions. His fault or not, I don't care if I ever see that Roger again."

"I know what you mean," I responded. "But you know what? For some reason, even though we're 3,000 miles away, I don't feel as far away from home as I did when we were in Baltimore, or even in Greenville, if you can believe that."

"Yeah, me neither," Karin looked at me, and I could see the surprise in her eyes as the television light played across her face.

"You've been talking to Him just like He's right here in this room, haven't you?" I whispered.

Karin nodded.

"Yeah, me too," I breathed.

We sat side by side in silence for a long time, holding onto each other's hand.

"You better go see if you can't stretch out a little better and doze off," I said finally, though reluctant to let go of Karin's hand. "It'll be Robbie's shift soon, and you won't have had any rest at all."

Karin nodded in the direction of the big guy cramped in the tiny chair by the window, valiantly attempting to sleep.

"Is that dedication or what?" she whispered. "He could be at home or back at Clemson. He could be getting daily updates on how Lauren's doing. Everyone would have admired his devotion, even at that. But instead, he's right here with her, with us, living this whole ordeal."

"I don't think he'd have had it any other way," I answered.

"He brings her a surprise every day," Karin added, smiling. "He goes out for a walk, shops around, and finds something to cheer her up with. Isn't that neat?"

"Yeah," I answered. "And you know what will be even neater? When Lauren can go for a walk with him."

We both smiled.

By 7:30 in the morning, the miraculous fluid of life had been completely administered, and Lauren was resting quietly.

None of us ever saw Roger again.

On the fourth day after surgery, physical therapists helped Lauren stand beside the bed for the first time, fitted her with a new brace, and placed her leg into a CPM. The CPM gently bent her knee to a preset angle. The epidural rendered the maneuver virtually painless.

While the days and nights were feverish and nauseating for Lauren, they were exhausting for Robbie, Karin, and me. We slept when we could, where we could. We even stole away to a physical therapy room when it wasn't being used, and fell asleep on a cold, hard, empty therapy table.

One evening Karin made a suggestion. "Why don't you guys go to the motel tonight and get a decent night's sleep? Lauren's resting a little better, and I can handle the night shift."

"Are you sure?" I asked, savoring the possibility of genuine slumber on an actual bed.

"Go!" Karin commanded. "Come back rested!"

Driving up I-5 toward the Ramada Inn, the anticipation of a hot shower, a comfy bed with clean, crisp sheets and fluffy pillows, and the uninterrupted peace of a quiet, dark, air-conditioned motel room was intoxicating. There would be no nurses coming in every couple of hours, no traffic in the halls. With Lauren under Karin's watchful eye, we could rest easy.

Robbie and I pulled into the parking lot, securing a space right below our third-floor room. The motel was of an older style, sturdily built of brick that had been painted white. Like most older motels, instead of an interior central hallway, each room opened onto a covered, outside corridor. Since Lauren had entered the hospital, the room had functioned solely as a place for Robbie, Karin, and I to visit on a daily basis to shower and change. Neither of the two queen beds had been slept in. They served instead as clothes hampers and a convenient place to pile and stack stuff. So upon entering the room, the first order of business was to move the suitcases and stacks of clothes that had accumulated over the past many days.

Though exhausted, I carefully moved and restacked Karin's and my stuff; Robbie did the same with his. After some time, every available chair, table, and dresser held neat stacks of clothing, each stack of a different ilk—my clean shirts, my dirty shirts, Karin's clean tops, Karin's dirty slacks. We'd place the stacks back on the beds in the morning, knowing which piles were ready to be worn or packed and which piles would need to be hauled down to the laundry room at the motel when time permitted.

Finally, with that chore done and showers completed, it was
lights out about midnight. A real bed had never felt so good. I
didn't plan on getting out of it until 9:30 or 10 o'clock the next
morning. The steady hum of the air conditioner sang me off to
a deep sleep in a matter of minutes.

What seemed like moments later, a horrendous buzzing sat
me upright in bed. The deafening noise eradicated my sleepy
bleariness, but without my glasses I could distinguish nothing
in the dark, blurry room except the little eight-inch, alarm-clock
radio on the nightstand between the beds. The device was a
Rubik's cube of sliding switches and push buttons, none of
which were illuminated. The only discernable feature was the
time display: 5:30 AM.

What fiend had set the alarm for such an hour then left it on
for the next unsuspecting, slumbering guest? The roar continued
unabated as I frantically slid switches and pushed buttons. In all
the universe, there had never been such a tiny box that produced
such a tremendous racket.

Robbie similarly bolted up in the next bed and shouted
over the clamor.

"Shut if off! Shut it off!"

"I can't," I hollered back. "I've pushed everything and it's
still going off! You try it!"

I threw the alarm clock across to Robbie, then crawled under
the night stand to unplug the shrieking device. I located the plug
in the dark and pulled it out of the socket, but still the ruckus
continued. Finally, I found the bedside lamp and switched it
on.

"I unplugged it," I shouted. "It must have a battery. Take
it out!"

Robbie frantically groped the box, trying to locate the battery
compartment. At last, a small plastic cover flew off across the
room. He held up two tiny AAA batteries and stared at them
in amazement. Still, the alarm wailed!

"Oh, my gosh!" I shouted. "We must be in a nightmare. We gotta wake up!"

"No!" Robbie yelled back. "It's not the alarm clock. It's the fire alarm. The place is on fire!"

At that moment, there came a pounding on the door. A man shouted, "Fire in the motel! Everybody get out! Evacuate! Evacuate!"

We bolted for the door and flung it wide open. Dawn had broken; a crowd had gathered in the parking lot directly below us. Women in bathrobes and curlers, men in pajamas and slippers stood looking up at the building we still occupied. The two of us stood in front of the gathering throng, our boxers billowing in the breeze. A quick glance up and down the corridor revealed neither flames nor smoke. We ran back into the room and slammed the door behind us.

The ear-splitting siren still shrieked throughout the building.

"We gotta get out of here!" I shouted at Robbie. "But if this place is really on fire, we're going to lose all of our stuff. We'll be left up here, 3,000 miles away from home, with nothing but our boxers."

"Let's take the chance and pack up as much stuff as we can and get it out of here!" Robbie shouted back. "If it gets really bad, we can always climb the balcony railings to get down."

Flinging the neat and tidy piles we had created the night before, we stuffed belongings into suitcases. Dirty socks and underwear smashed into neatly folded blouses. Shoes fell on clean shirts. Dry-cleaned trousers wrapped themselves around wet toothbrushes. We threw on anything that hadn't been slammed in suitcases and hauled everything out onto the corridor and down to the parking lot in less than four minutes.

Just as we hit the pavement, the wailing siren ceased. The crowd began milling back toward the motel. A barefoot guy stood next to me, dressed in a worn-out T-shirt and pajama bottoms decorated with pink flamingos.

"So it's over?" I asked.

"Yeah, I guess so," he said.

"Was there a real fire?"

"Oh, yeah," he answered. "See that scorched spot in the mulch around that plant there, on the edge of the parking lot?" He pointed to about a square foot of blackened pine bark.

"I guess someone threw a cigarette in there last night. It must have set the mulch smoldering." Then he and his flock of flamingos strode back toward the building.

It wasn't quite 6:00 AM when we got back to our room. The adrenaline rush made going back to bed out of the question, so we headed back to the hospital.

Karin stretched blearily as we walked into the room. "Wow! You guys are up bright and early. You must be really rested. Did you enjoy the peace and quiet?"

"Robbie and I talked about it on the way over here this morning." I answered. "We've kind of gotten used to the routine here at the hospital. It's a good feeling knowing we're close by if Lauren needs us. We think we'll bunk here from now on. We don't need that much peace and quiet anymore."

After sixteen days in Seattle and another 3,000 mile plane trip, we rolled Lauren up the backyard ramp late one evening—home again.

Outwardly, Lauren appeared the same young girl as when she had first come home after the accident almost eight months earlier: weakened and debilitated, tethered to painkillers and antibiotics, still disabled, and more exhausted than ever.

But inside, everything had changed. A physical framework upon which to base hope had been bestowed. It was a gift from a family whose faith, courage, and unselfishness overwhelmed inexpressible grief and let God's infinite grace shine through.

Each day, for the rest of our lives, our family will ask God to grant them His peace.

Chapter Twelve

I lift up my eyes to the hills—Where does my help come from?
My help comes from the Lord, the maker of Heaven and Earth.
He will not let your foot slip—he who watches over you will not slumber;
Indeed, he who watches over Israel will neither slumber nor sleep.
The Lord watches over you—the Lord is your shade at your right hand;
The sun will not harm you by day; nor the moon by night.
The Lord will keep you from all harm—he will watch over your life;
The Lord will watch over your coming and
going both now and forevermore.

—Psalm 121

"COME ON, LANCE," Lauren pleaded. "Just tie it back… please. It's September already. I've got a lot more work to do if I'm going to make it across that stage at Littlejohn Coliseum in December to get my diploma. The last thing I need right now is my physical therapist going soft on me. So tie it back, and let's get this over with!"

"You know how much I enjoy inflicting pain, Larnie," joked the tall, athletic-looking man. He stood beside a tanned, perspiring Lauren, who sat on a therapy table, dressed in black shorts and a Kappa Kappa Gamma T-shirt. "But you've just been through a pretty tough workout. Even I wouldn't enjoy seeing you suffer any more today!"

"Now *that* I don't believe," Lauren joked in return. She pulled a lock of hair from her pony tail and began to twist it around her fingers. Her cell phone rang. She retrieved the gadget from her pocket, flipped open the case, and glanced at the caller ID.

"It's just Daddy," she said, snapping the phone shut. She shoved it back in her pocket.

"Poor ol' Just Daddy!" Lance quipped, shaking his head. "I'm going to have to start calling him JD. The man probably just wants to make sure his beloved daughter made it from Clemson to Augusta this afternoon in one piece, and you ignore his call. Now had that been Robbie…"

"I'll call Daddy back in a minute," Lauren replied with a smile. "But first I want my leg tied back."

"So, how is the weekly trip from Clemson to Augusta going?" Lance asked, obviously trying to change the subject. "Not that you're busy or have anything better to do, right? You're only taking, what? Fifteen hours this semester?"

"I'm taking seventeen hours. At the same time, I'm finishing up nine hours of incompletes from fall 2002," Lauren answered with mock indignation. "I'm also going to physical therapy up there *every* afternoon for an hour and a half, going to Young Life's Quest one night a week, and meeting my Young Life kids in Anderson at 6:00 for breakfast a couple of mornings a week. I'm trying to stay caught up with Kappa stuff, and…"

Lauren took a breath. "There's this one other thing, just in case you've forgotten. I'm the maid of honor in my sister's wedding next weekend. That's on top of a 250-mile round trip down here to be hammered by you on a weekly basis. So, can you *please* just tie my leg back and let me out of here?"

Chapter Twelve

"How about I just ice it down, instead?" Lance offered.

"You can ice it after you tie it back," Lauren replied. "I've *got* to get to ninety degrees, right? You said so, Dr. Walton here in Augusta said so, and Dr. Conner said so. That's what I've been working on ever since I left Seattle. And that's why, on top of everything else, I spend hours with my leg in that CPM machine. Dr. Walton gave me pills if my leg gets too sore, so please, tie me back so I can go home!"

"Oh, all right," Lance finally agreed. His smile revealed his characteristic good nature. "But I'm not going to leave you tied for the full fifteen minutes."

Lauren had been a daily visitor to the new, state-of-the-art physical therapy and sports medicine facilities of Southern Orthopedics since her return from Seattle in mid-July. Immediately comfortable with Dr. Walton, the orthopedic surgeon who had agreed to follow her case when Dr. Hines wouldn't, Lauren quickly formed a special bond with Lance Ryder, the easy-going, highly-skilled director of physical therapy for Southern Orthopedics.

In late August, when Lauren packed crutches and wheelchair and returned to campus, Lance had arranged continuation of daily physical therapy in Clemson, but he authorized no one but himself to tie back her leg. The excruciatingly painful but extremely effective procedure involved Lauren lying flat on her back on the therapy table with a thirty-five-pound weight, cushioned by a pillow, on her thigh. With a latex band tied around her ankle, her injured leg was bent as far back as it would go and lashed to the table leg.

"I've seen grown men cry and beg to be let go," Lance said when he'd tied back Lauren's leg. "But you never make a sound, Lauren Tarrant, and you never ask to be let out before your time is up. How do you do it?"

"I'm never alone when I'm tied to the table," Lauren replied, watery-eyed and with clenched teeth.

A devout Christian, Lance nodded in understanding.

I smiled at Karin. She sat beside me on the pew in the front row of the chapel of Trinity on the Hill Methodist Church, set behind the long-leaf pines and crepe myrtles shading Monte Sano Avenue in Augusta. Twenty magnificent, old, stained-glass windows, each depicting an event in the life of Christ, deflected the last rays of the late summer sun that still blazed outside, creating a reverent glow for those within the cooler sanctuary.

The wedding party and Andrea's family members sat scattered across the chapel, intermingled with Marc's family. The Coloradans fanned themselves from their encounter with the unaccustomed Southern heat.

I glanced at my watch: 6:45 PM, Friday, September 12, 2003.

"Okay, ya'll," Liz, the wedding director, called from the front of the church, clapping her hands lightly to regain the throng's attention.

"Everyone did really well on that walk through. I think tomorrow night is going to be absolutely beautiful. But right now I need the bride down front with me. Andrea, where are you, dahlin'? Oh, there you are. Come right down front here with me, please."

Wearing a somewhat puzzled look, our older daughter walked to the front of the chapel and stood next to Liz, who put her arm around Andrea's waist.

"You look so pretty in your white dress and pink flowers. I hope Marc knows what a lucky man he is."

Karin and I, seated up front, overheard Liz's whisper to Andrea, who beamed at the compliment.

"I want to make sure we have the music timed just right for the bridesmaids and maid of honor to walk in to," Liz announced in full volume so everyone could hear. "So Andrea, I want you to watch as they walk down the aisle. I'm going to ask the organist to start playing now."

With the first notes of Canon in D, Young Heidi, smiling broadly, slowly walked down the aisle and took her assigned place near the altar. As she turned to face the congregation, Ruthie, Andrea's best friend, entered and began her slow steps to the front of the chapel, then turned just as Young Heidi had done moments before.

The music continued. There was a longer pause as Lauren, in a blue sundress that revealed the full length, black-metal brace on her right leg, adjusted her crutches and started down the aisle, trying valiantly to proceed with the melody as Heidi and Ruthie had done.

Half a dozen steps, and she stopped.

She pulled the left crutch from under her arm and propped it against the pew on her right. Carefully placing the remaining crutch next to the first, Lauren stood, alone and unaided, in the center of the aisle.

There was an audible gasp above the notes of *Canon in D.*

Then, as Andrea watched in amazement, her little sister took a step.

Haltingly, as though deliberately in time with the music, she took another step. Then another, and another...until at last she walked into the arms of her now sobbing big sister.

"I did this for you, Andrea," Lauren whispered through their tears. "You stood up for me when I couldn't stand up for myself. And now I will stand up for you."

The congregation rose to their feet, and amid applause and cheers, our two girls stood locked in an embrace they had waited nearly a year to share.

Within weeks of those first few, hard-won steps, Lauren often moved without crutches around the off-campus apartment she shared with three other girls. The hilly Clemson terrain, on the other hand, continued to mandate the use of crutches or a wheelchair. But the structure that provided the greatest challenge—not only for Lauren but for the entire Clemson family, was also the most important, at least for the fall semester: Death Valley!

By the beginning of November, the 2003 season looked lackluster at best. Lauren out performed the football team, getting around the stadium without her wheelchair, largely due to piggyback rides furnished by Robbie.

After Clemson suffered a humiliating loss to Wake Forest on November 1, the chances of Lauren walking unaided across the stage to pick up her diploma looked far better than the Tigers ending up with a winning season, much less a bid to a bowl game.

But the previous twelve months had taught our family nothing if not that there is always hope. The next Saturday, Karin and I, along with our newlywed daughter and son-in-law, traveled to Death Valley and watched in amazement as Clemson ripped up Florida State, twenty-six to ten!

That marked the beginning of a winning streak for the Tigers, as well as continued good fortune for Lauren. Clemson mortified the always hapless Duke team and then, in a grand finale, handed the University of South Carolina a devastating sixty-three to seventeen loss.

By the end of November, Clemson had a lock on a major bowl game. Lauren had personally presented her senior thesis to the president of the university, an analysis of the campus through the unique perspective of a student both with and without a disability.

One week before Christmas, only a little more than six months behind schedule, but with a lifetime's worth of perspective, Lauren walked, unaided, diploma in hand, across the stage of Littlejohn Coliseum.

As Karin and I heaved several trash bags full of holiday clutter through the kitchen on the way to the garbage, the Christmas music that had played on the stereo practically non-stop for weeks, suddenly ceased, followed quickly by Celine Dion in her most sultry voice.

"At last," the CD crooned, "my love has come along…my lonely days are over…and life is like a song."

We stopped pulling our bags to watch as a long, shapely leg slithered around the open door between the kitchen and dining room. While Celine sang on, a feminine hand appeared next, then an arm, then the whole girl. Lauren slinked her way into the kitchen, where she coyly displayed the new, smaller brace on her right leg.

"How do you like the new Don Joy?" she breathed, her back to us, her head tilted over her shoulder and eyelids half closed. "Don't you think diamonds will go well with this navy?"

Karin and I looked at each other, then laughed with Lauren until tears rolled down our faces.

"Seriously, don't ya'll like this navy blue?" Lauren asked when we'd regained composure. "If I gotta wear this thing for the rest of my life, I might as well like it. I think it looks rather nice." Then, joking again, "After all, navy goes with everything. And soon, I'll be wearing a diamond, you know."

"I was certain Robbie would give you one for Christmas," Karin said with consternation.

"Not me," Lauren replied. "I knew it wouldn't be at Christmas. It's going to be while we're up in North Georgia with his parents, either before or right after the Peach Bowl."

"If that happens, you'll be engaged before you start working for Lance over at Southern Orthopedics," I guessed.

"What a difference a year makes," Karin said, smiling at the happy girl before her. "Last year right after Christmas, you were...we *all* were...well, let's not go back there. Now, here you are, a Clemson graduate, starting work next week for Southern Orthopedics. You can work for Lance in the mornings and have physical therapy every afternoon. It's perfect."

"I always saw myself going to work for an advertising agency in some big town like Greenville or Charleston," Lauren said as she plopped on a barstool and grabbed a Christmas cookie. "I couldn't imagine being content staying in Aiken. But I've learned a lot in the past year or so. One thing is: there's no place like home!"

She chomped on the cookie and added with a mischievous smile, "And another thing is, diamonds really are a girl's best friend!"

With thousands of stunned Volunteer fans packing the Georgia Dome, Clemson clobbered Tennessee twenty-seven to fourteen in the Peach Bowl. But Lauren came home and started her new job at Southern Orthopedics without an engagement ring.

"Valentine's Day," Karin and I predicted. "He's waiting until Valentine's Day. It's on a Saturday this year. You're going to Clemson for the weekend. It's the perfect setup!"

But when Lauren returned home, there was still no ring.

"I have always despised Valentine's Day," Lauren fumed when returned home. "And this year has done nothing to change the way I feel. That Robbie McKenzie!"

That Robbie McKenzie had plans—plans he had shared with Karin and me. So when Lauren mentioned that Robbie wanted to take her to Pretty Place to see the sunrise on a Saturday morning in early March, we feigned ignorance.

"Where's Pretty Place?" Karin asked.

"It's near Caesar's Head," Lauren replied. "It's a YMCA camp, I think. It's beautiful. There's an outdoor chapel built on the side of a mountain. The entire state of South Carolina seems to fan out before you. You feel like you can see all the way from the mountains to the ocean."

"Sounds pretty romantic if you ask me," Karin had said, holding up two crossed fingers.

The engagement announcement that followed that weekend pictured Lauren and Robbie together at sunrise on a mountaintop. Though it couldn't be seen in the picture, the ring on Lauren's left hand was adorned with three diamonds: the diamond on the left represented Lauren; the diamond on the right represented Robbie; and the diamond in the center—the center of their new family—represented Jesus Christ.

They were all there in that Augusta church on that Saturday afternoon in July: all the people who loved Lauren and would come to love Robbie and all the people who loved Robbie and would come to love Lauren.

Betty Freedman, who had adopted our family as her own when we were in Baltimore, was there.

Lance Ryder, who taught Lauren to walk again, was there.

The entire McKenzie clan, from Michigan to Florida, was there.

And though they couldn't have known it, a family from Washington state, whom none of us had ever met, was there in our prayers.

The church bells chimed the hour.

The doors at the back of the church swung open. The kilted bagpiper began to bring up the drones then stepped down the aisle. The lessons of the last two years condensed into the hymn his instrument proudly proclaimed:

> Amazing Grace, how sweet the sound
> That saved a wretch like me.
> I once was lost, but now am found.
> Was blind, but now I see.

He reached the front of the sanctuary and turned. The magnificent pipe organ joined the bagpipe's continuing proclamation. The congregation stood.

With Lauren on my arm, we walked to the young man waiting for her at the front of the church.

> Through many dangers, toils, and snares,
> I have already come.
> 'Tis grace has brought me safe thus far,
> And grace will lead me home.

> "The Lord has promised good to me,
> His Word my hope secures.
> He will my shield and portion be,
> As long as life endures.

Chapter Twelve

The music stopped. I placed Lauren's delicate hand into the hand of the only other man I would ever trust to love and care for our daughter. Then I took a seat by my glowing wife.

In the twinkling of an eye, Robbie and Lauren were joined together by God and rushed toward the summer evening sunshine glowing through the open doors.

The pair stopped when they reached the threshold. Hand in hand, they looked at each other and smiled. And then, lifted by the power of our Lord's infinite love and grace, the new husband and his wife kicked their feet up and, with a leap, bounded across the threshold and into the brand-new life shining before them.

And just at that moment, for a split second, with the two of them suspended in mid-air, the earth stood still.

Epilogue

Therefore go and make disciples of all nations, baptizing them in the name of the Father and of the Son and of the Holy Spirit, teaching them to obey everything I have commanded you. And surely I am with you always, to the very end of the age. Amen.
— Matthew 28: 19-20

AS THE ROAD took us from one sea island to another, the muscles in my back and shoulders began to relax at the sight and smell of the salt marsh enveloping the causeway connecting St. Helena Island to the Harbor Island bridge.

"Karin," I said to my wife beside me in the front seat, "look over across the Sound at Edisto. Have you ever seen the water tower and the houses so clearly? What a beautiful Saturday for February! Crystal-clear skies and temperatures in the 70s. You couldn't ask for a better winter's day at the beach."

Across tiny Harbor Island, over the Johnson's Creek bridge, and we were on Hunting Island and in another world. We turned onto the one-lane road and wound through the green maritime forest of palms and live oaks, then over ancient dunes held intact by the roots of pines and saw palmettos. We crossed lagoons where turtles sunned themselves on logs and alligators remained ever vigilant, watching us pass as they basked in the winter sun.

We parked, pulled the cooler from the trunk, and hurried out onto the deserted beach. Zipping our jackets to ward off the stiff ocean breeze, we kicked off our shoes and scuffed our feet as we walked in the sun-warmed sand.

"I love this place!" Karin shouted into the breeze. "I absolutely love it! I am more at home here than anywhere else in the world. I never get tired of it, no matter what the season. I wish I had a house right there." She pointed to a crescent-shaped break in the forest, an open semi-circle shaded by towering palms with fronds tinged brown from the relentless salt spray.

I smiled at my wife, dancing and spinning in the sand, just like she'd done on this very beach when we'd first met. We had both been barely out of our teens. I wouldn't have thought it possible then, but she was even more beautiful today.

"Why do I love it so much, Michael?"

I had to think about that.

"Because it's the first thing that connected you and me," I finally answered. "This ocean is what connected a girl in England with a boy in South Carolina. If not for all that water and our mutual love for it, we might never have found each other."

"Well," Karin said, "Like Becky always said, 'Ain't nothing don't happen unless the Lord can make good come of it.' He must have had a good reason to bring us together across all this water."

"Speaking of Becky," I said, "She made the best tuna-fish salad ever."

"Are you getting hungry?" Karin asked, looking at me suspiciously.

"Well, yeah," I admitted. We sat on the sand and Karin handed me a sandwich.

"I remember being about six," I reminisced as I ate. "Daddy would come home for lunch and Becky would have fixed tuna fish. She'd serve it on a big, ripe tomato and a leaf of lettuce, with sweet tea and a lemon wedge! After we'd eaten, she'd sit down at the kitchen table by herself and say the blessing. I remember how worshipfully she'd fold her hands. She had pretty hands, with brown fingers and pink fingernails, trimmed so neatly. Funny, isn't it, the things you remember, and the things you learn when you don't even know you're learning."

"I've learned a lot in the last two and a half years," Karin said as she nibbled a cracker.

"Yeah, me too. You go first," I said. "What all have you learned?"

"Oh, lots of stuff," Karin started. "Like never, *ever* leave someone you care for who's seriously sick or hurt, alone in the hospital. And I never realized how important blood transfusions are. From now on, *you're* going to give blood every time you can."

"Yeah," I agreed, and then it sank in. "Hey, wait a minute!"

"Speaking of medical stuff," Karin went on, ignoring my interruption, "I have a heightened respect for what doctors, nurses, and everyone in health care, do every day. But I also realize that you can't be intimidated, either. For all their education and dedication, doctors are just people like anyone else. They've got their egos, their opinions, their ambitions, and some even have their own self-serving motives. You can't be afraid to speak up when you disagree or if you feel something's just not right. After all, you're buying a service, though a very important and complex one. The bottom line is, you're paying for it. You have every right, no...the *responsibility* to make sure you're getting the best care possible. If that means you have to be more assertive than you're comfortable with, well, you just have to pray yourself up a shield, remember that God's got your back, and step into the fray."

"It didn't take you long to learn that, did it?" I quipped. "Remember the nurse who walked into Lauren's room and didn't wash her hands? I sure do, and I'll bet she does, too!"

"Another thing I've learned," Karin went on, turning her gaze to the ocean, "you can't make choices for your children, as much as you'd like to. At some point, you've got to let go and let them make their own choices, even if you think it may not be the best choice."

"You're thinking about Lauren going to work for Young Life now, aren't you?" I asked.

"Among other things," Karin replied. "I love the fact that Lauren works for Lance at Southern Orthopedics. She loves Lance; we all do. I know he looks out for her, keeps her from overdoing it. Who knows what she'll get for a boss next time. Plus, she's right there for physical therapy every day. I just worry that she'll not be able to keep up her PT. "

"Worry about nothing, pray about everything," I chimed in.

"I think Young Life is her calling," Karin continued. "That's why you have to let her make her own choices. If her life's work is to bring people to Jesus, like she says it is, then what better way to do that than through Young Life? Just think! If there had been no Young Life, Lauren might not have had the friends to support her through her accident, which was every bit as important as the medical procedures. She may never have met Robbie—and there could never be anyone for Lauren but Robbie."

We stood up. I put my arm around my wife's waist and we walked. The little waves at the edge of the beach sometimes splashed the chilly water onto our bare feet. But we were unaware of the cold, each of us awash in our own thoughts.

Before we knew it, we'd walked half the length of the island.

Karin broke the silence. "I think I know why bad things happen to good people. Well, at least partly."

I stopped. "You do?"

"Yeah," she answered. "The Bible is full of promises, you know. But God never promised that life on Earth was a smooth ride for anyone, not even for His children. It's the travels through the valleys that make you a strong person who realizes where your strength comes from. That's where you really build your relationship, in your one-on-one relationship with God."

"Some might say it's easy for us to say that now," I answered. "They might even say this whole episode in the life of our family ends like a fairy tale. Lauren can walk, she's married the love of her life, and she's about to start a career helping kids find themselves and Jesus. It's almost like a movie, you know?"

"Lauren might take exception with you on that fairy-tale thing," Karin said. "She'll have physical therapy for a long, long time, and it's pretty painful. She walks with the help of a brace, and who knows what's down the road for her, long range. But I know what you're saying. She...well, *all* of us...are so blessed. God has almost made it easy for us. But sometimes I think of how terribly this whole thing could have ended. Then I think of all the families who have to endure unspeakable tragedies and unhappy endings. What then?"

Again, Becky's words popped into my mind.

"'The Lawd don't let nothin' happen that He cain't make good come of it,'" I answered. "We're not all-knowing, but God is. As horrible as something might be for us here on Earth, we know God will ultimately use it for good. We can't always know what that good is, but we can trust that we serve a gracious and truthful God. If He says he'll use something for good, even though it's beyond our finite understanding, we know He will."

I looked up at the white clouds streaking across the deep blue sky. "I think I've learned to look beyond the immediate, and just anticipate the reward for getting through the trials."

"What do mean?" Karin stopped and unwrapped my arm from her waist.

"Sometime recently, during this whole ordeal, I don't remember exactly when or where—or even who—but someone said to me that the Bible says to be joyful when you encounter trials. It's in James, I think. I didn't give it much thought at the time. To be honest, I thought they had to be kidding or nuts. Who in their right mind wants to suffer? But I think I understand a little better now. I don't think it is God's intention that we get pleasure from suffering. I mean, we're not supposed to be masochists. But we can find joy by anticipating the results that God has in store for us."

"Like what?"

"Well, for one thing, you and I have learned perseverance. We looked to God to give us the strength and the wisdom to get through road block after road block. Each time, He gave us strength and wisdom. Now I really understand what daily, sufficient grace means. And when you know you can count on daily sufficient grace from God, well, there's nothing this world can throw at you that you can't get through. God's grace is how you handle the bad that life flings your way. If you don't understand that God's grace is there for you, well, the bad stuff in life is gonna destroy you."

There was one more thing I had to say.

"If none of this had happened, I wouldn't have the friend in Jesus that I now have."

Karin nodded. "And I would never have understood that once God has me in His grip, He will never let go, not even if I do," she said. "What an incredible, priceless understanding!"

We looked out over the waves and the seemingly endless expanse of water beyond. There was so much that we understood now that we had never understood before.

Still, there was so much more we had to learn. And there was one thing in particular I didn't understand, something that had been foremost in my mind for nearly two years. It was a question for which I desperately wanted an answer, but in its asking, I would have to allow another person a glimpse into my soul.

Summoning all of my courage I turned to Karin. There would never be another time.

"I know it's been a couple of years," I began, "but still, the question nags at me for an answer...the right answer."

"What's the question?" Karin's eyes searched my face.

I hesitated for a moment, digging deep within myself.

"Why did He appear to *me*, Karin?" I asked. "Why did Jesus come face to face with me that Monday morning?"

"Oh, Michael, don't you know yet?" Karin asked, her eyes fixed on mine.

I tried to swallow the lump that had suddenly appeared in my throat. I wanted to answer, but I could only shake my head.

So Karin tenderly took my face in her hands and whispered the answer for me.

"He didn't come face to face with just you on that morning. He appeared to everyone...because you'll tell the story, Michael. You will tell the story."

CPSIA information can be obtained at www.ICGtesting.com
Printed in the USA
LVOW060511281011

252412LV00004B/1/P